TOTTEL'S *SONGES AND SONETTES* IN CONTEXT

Material Readings in Early Modern Culture

This series provides a forum for studies that consider the material forms of texts as part of an investigation into early modern culture. The editors invite proposals of a multi- or interdisciplinary nature, and particularly welcome proposals that combine archival research with an attention to the theoretical models that might illuminate the reading, writing, and making of texts, as well as projects that take innovative approaches to the study of material texts, both in terms the kinds of primary materials under investigation, and in terms of methodologies. What are the questions that have yet to be asked about writing in its various possible embodied forms? Are there varieties of materiality that are critically neglected? How does form mediate and negotiate content? In what ways do the physical features of texts inform how they are read, interpreted and situated?

Consideration will be given to both monographs and collections of essays. The range of topics covered in this series includes, but is not limited to: History of the book, publishing, the book trade, printing, typography (layout, type, typeface, blank/white space, paratextual apparatus); technologies of the written word: ink, paper, watermarks, pens, presses; surprising or neglected material forms of writing; print culture; manuscript studies; social space, context, location of writing; social signs, cues, codes imbued within the material forms of texts; ownership and the social practices of reading: marginalia, libraries, environments of reading and reception; codicology, palaeography and critical bibliography; production, transmission, distribution and circulation; archiving and the archaeology of knowledge; orality and oral culture; the material text as object or thing.

Tottel's *Songes and Sonettes* in Context

Edited by
STEPHEN HAMRICK
Minnesota State University–Moorhead, USA

ASHGATE

Published by
Ashgate Publishing Limited
Wey Court East
Union Road
Farnham
Surrey, GU9 7PT
England

Ashgate Publishing Company
110 Cherry Street
Suite 3-1
Burlington, VT 05401-3818
USA

www.ashgate.com

British Library Cataloguing in Publication Data
Tottel's *Songes and Sonettes* in context. – (Material readings in early modern culture)
1. Tottel, Richard, d. 1594. Songes and sonettes. 2. Tottel, Richard, d. 1594 – Appreciation.
I. Series II. Hamrick, Stephen.
821.2-dc23

The Library of Congress has cataloged the printed edition as follows:
Tottel's *Songes and Sonettes* in Context / edited by Stephen Hamrick.
    pages cm.—(Material Readings in Early Modern Culture)
    Includes bibliographical references and index.
    ISBN 978-1-4094-6465-5 (hardcover:alk. paper)—ISBN 978-1-4094-6466-2 (ebook)—ISBN 978-1-4094-6467-9 (epub)
    1. Tottel, Richard, d. 1594. Tottel's miscellany. 2. Tottel, Richard, d. 1594—Criticism and interpretation. 3. English poetry—Early modern, 1500–1700. I. Hamrick, Stephen, editor of compilation.
    PR1205.T638 2013
    821'.208—dc23
                                                                        2012041062
ISBN 9781409464655 (hbk)
ISBN 9781409464662 (ebk)
ISBN 9781409464679 (epub)

Printed and bound in Great Britain
by MPG PRINTGROUP

For Kara and Elisabet

Contents

Notes on Contributors

Catherine Bates is Professor and Head of Department, English and Comparative Literary Studies, Warwick University. Her publications include studies of Renaissance courtship, Shakespeare, and gender. Her current project is *Masculinity and the Hunt: Wyatt to Spenser*, due to be published in 2013.

Alex Davis is Lecturer in English at the University of St. Andrews. He is the author of *Chivalry and Romance in the English Renaissance* (2003) and *Renaissance Historical Fiction* (2011).

Stephen Hamrick is Associate Professor, Department of English, Minnesota State University, Moorhead. His publications include studies on *Songes and Sonettes*, George Gascoigne, and Queen Elizabeth. His current publications include *The Catholic Imaginary and the Cults of Elizabeth, 1558–1582* (2009).

Peter C. Herman is Professor, Department of English and Comparative Literature, San Diego State University. His publications include studies on Sidney, royal poetry, and antipoetic sentiment. His current publications include *Royal Poetrie: Monarchic Verse and the Political Imaginary of Early Modern England* (2010) and *The New Milton Criticism*, co-edited with Elizabeth Sauer.

Amanda Holton is Visiting Fellow, Faculty of Humanities, University of Southampton. Her publications include studies of the sonnet and of Chaucer's sources and poetics. Her recent publications include editing *Tottel's Miscellany: Songs and Sonnets of Henry Howard, Earl of Surrey, Sir Thomas Wyatt and Others* (2011) with Tom MacFaul.

Seth Lerer is Distinguished Professor of Literature and Dean of Arts and Humanities, University of California San Diego. His publications include studies on philology, courtly letters, and Anglo-Saxon language and literature. His current publications include *The Wind in the Willows: An Annotated Edition* (2009) with Kenneth Grahame.

Tom MacFaul is Fellow and Departmental Lecturer in English at Merton College, University of Oxford. He is the author of three books: *Male Friendship in Shakespeare and his Contemporaries* (2007), *Poetry and Paternity in Renaissance England: Sidney, Spenser, Shakespeare, Donne and Jonson* (2010), and *Problem Fathers in Shakespeare and Renaissance* Drama (2012), and has co-edited *Tottel's Miscellany* (2011) with Amanda Holton.

Paul A. Marquis is Professor and Chair of the Department of English, St. Francis Xavier University. His publications include articles on Sidney, Spenser, Isabella Whitney, and Tottel's *Songes and Sonettes*. He is also editor of *Richard Tottel's* Songes and Sonettes: *The Elizabethan Version* (2007).

Acknowledgements

A project such as this requires many participants and I remain indebted to them all. I first thank the contributors for their excellent work and unwavering commitment to the collection. Thanks to the anonymous reader for the highly useful feedback. I thank Erika Gaffney, comissioning editor, for her astute guidance. As always, I thank Kara for her patience and love.

Introduction:
Songes and Sonettes Reconsidered

Stephen Hamrick

Printer Richard Tottel's *Songes and Sonettes* (1557) remains the most influential poetic collection printed in the sixteenth century. Copied by a monarch, set to music, sung, carried overseas, studied, appropriated, rejected, edited by consumers, transfered to manuscript, and gifted by Shakespeare, this multi-author verse anthology of 280 poems transformed sixteenth-century English language and culture.[1] Immediately and immensely popular, the first two editions of the text emerged from the press in 1557 only a staggering two months apart. With at least 11 printings before the end of Elizabeth I's reign, Tottel's collection greatly influenced the poetic publications that followed, including individual and multi-author miscellanies.[2] Many of these later collections, moreover, lifted poems directly from *Songes and Sonettes*, further indicating the significant and early appeal of the landmark anthology. In addition to popularizing a new kind of English verse, the text, as the following chapters will demonstrate, engaged politics, friendship, religion, sexuality, gender, morality, and commerce in complex and, at times, contradictory ways.

Despite the collection's immense popular appeal, scholars continue to marginalize the text and fail to understand its complexities. As its earliest readers and the essays assembled in this volume attest, however, the impact of "Tottel's Miscellany," as it has been known since the nineteenth century, extends across early modern culture. W.A. Sessions, in fact, aptly dubs the text "the turning-point in English Petrarchism," marking a moment at which artistic, erotic, and political discourses converged and dramatically changed the roles of verse in England.[3]

Substantial developments in our understanding of sixteenth-century history, literature, and religion, as well as the recent publication of two editions of *Songes*

---

[1]   Throughout the introduction, *Songes and Sonettes* refers to the second edition of the text; *Richard Tottel's Songes and Sonettes: The Elizabethan Version*, ed. Paul A. Marquis (Tempe, 2007). See also *Tottel's Miscellany: Songs and Sonnets of Henry Howard, Earl of Surrey, Sir Thomas Wyatt and Others*, ed. Amanda Holton and Tom Macfaul (London, 2011).

[2]   *Tottle's Miscellany, 1557–1587*, ed. Hyder Rollins (2 vols, Cambridge, 1965), vol. 2, pp. 107–124. See also, Wendy Wall, *The Imprint of Gender: Authorship and Publication in the English Renaissance* (Ithaca, 1993), pp. 24–5. On the editions, see Marquis, *Richard Tottel's*, pp. xv–xvi. See also J. Christopher Warner, "'Sonnets en Anglois': A Hitherto Unknown Edition of Tottel's Miscellany (1559)", *Notes and Queries*, 58.2 (2011):204–6.

[3]   W.A. Sessions, *Henry Howard, The Poet Earl of Surrey* (Oxford, 1999), p. 188.

and Sonettes, edited by Paul Marquis in 2007 and Amanda Holton and Tom MacFaul in 2011, clearly indicate the need to reassess Tottel's ground-breaking text. Embracing a broad range of critical and historical perspectives, the eight essays within this volume offer the first sustained analysis of the many ways that consumers read and understood *Songes and Sonettes* as an anthology over the course of the early modern period.

Influenced unduly by C.S. Lewis and Harold Mason's negative evaluations of *Songes and Sonettes*, however, scholars have long ignored or misunderstood the collection. In discussing sixteenth-century literature, Lewis writes, "*drab* is not used as a dyslogistic term. It marks a period in which, for good or ill, poetry has little richness either of sound or images. The good work is neat and temperate, the bad flat and dry. There is more bad than good. Tottel's *Miscellany*, 'Sternhold and Hopkins', and *The Mirror for Magistrates* are typical Drab Age works."[4] As such, Lewis reductively places early Tudor poetry within an evolutionary literary history: the collection remains both "unpromising" and simply preparatory for what would follow. "At its best," he continues, "it has a severity, a neatness, a precision, which bring it much closer to the work of the Augustans than to Sidney, Spenser, and Shakespeare."[5] As scholars continue to find, Lewis's concept of a "post-Tottel wasteland" of bad verse followed by a "Golden Age" of poetry severely distorts our understanding of Tudor culture, including Tottel's groundbreaking collection.

Lewis's denigration of *Songes* as "drab"parallels Mason's dismissive critical burial of the text. Mason devalued the "significance of the collection," writing "that it marked a downward turn to sterility, and, though the first in time of the series of anthologies that became such a feature of the second half of the century, it is in fact the grave of Early Tudor poetry."[6] Such a narrow evolutionary literary aesthetic or hermeneutic unwisely removes Tottel's from its actual material history, including the history of the book, political history, the history of gender, economic history, and others—to name but a few of the discourses in which *Songes and Sonettes* participates.[7]

Seemingly obsessed with individual poems and/or poets included in the text—and not the text as a whole—previous criticism has disjointed, decontextualized, and cannibalized *Songes and Sonettes*. Further constructing an evolutionary literary history that decenters the anthology, scholars have examined individual poems in relation to continental precedents and have provided some generalized bibliographical and editorial analysis of the work. Literary historians, moreover, have almost exclusively examined how *individual* poems provide readers with

[4]   C.S. Lewis, *English Literature in the Sixteenth Century Excluding Drama* (London, 1954), p. 64.

[5]   Ibid., pp. 239–40.

[6]   Harold Mason, *Humanism and Poetry in The Early Tudor Period* (London, 1959), p. 253.

[7]   Elizabeth Bellamy, "The Sixteenth Century," in Frank Magill (ed.), *Critical Survey of Poetry. Revised Edition* (8 vols.; Pasadena, 1992), vol. 8, p. 3808.

didactic models of courtly performance, self-advertisement, and place seeking, thereby disregarding the anthological context created by Tottel.[8]

Simultaneously defined as the first embodiment of "modern" English verse and as the distortion of that verse, *Songes and Sonnets* receives some grudging acknowledgment even as scholars dismiss it. As the original editor of the text added titles to the poems and regularized the meter of much of the verse, scholars have derided Tottel for distorting the 'original' poems rather than understanding it as an integrated anthology. In jettisoning the containing context of *Songes and Sonettes*, however, critical readers themselves, ironically, have distorted the text. Paul Marquis establishes in Chapter 1, however, that such "reshaping" creates a substantive interpretive context. As such, a collection of contextual essays on *Songes and Sonettes*, considered as an anthology, provides a much needed corrective.

Even those scholars who address *Songes and Sonettes* and note its immense popularity devote little sustained critical attention to the text. Critics who ignore *Songes and Sonettes*, proceed so, in large part, because it failed to establish the sonnet as the Renaissance form *par excellence*, which, according to their readings, finds it apex in the sonnets of Philip Sidney, Edmund Spenser, William Shakespeare, and, to a lesser degree, John Donne and Mary Wroth. A disconnect between such critical perceptions and early modern poetic practice emerges, however, in the fact that the term "sonnet" remained vague throughout the period.[9]

Although the prolific and influential writer George Gascoigne defines the sonnet as a 14-line poem with a concluding couplet in 1575, he also admits that "some thinke that all Poemes (being short) may be called Sonets." Further undermining modern and reductive formalist readings of early modern poetry, writers experimented widely with the form, altering length, rhyme scheme, and subject matter.[10] Less than twenty percent of the poems included in *Songes and Sonettes*, moreover, fulfill Gascoigne's definition; Tottel's second edition of 1557—(Q2)—contains 54 sonnets out of the 280 poems.[11] If the modern focus on the sonnet, as well as deference to Lewis and Mason's denigration of *Songes and Sonettes*, marginalizes Tottel's unfairly, the collection's popularity tells a different story.

---

[8]   For a bibliography of Tottel's see Paul Marquis, "Recent Studies in Richard Tottel's *Songes and Sonettes*," *English Literary Renaissance*, 28 (1998): 299–313. and Stephen Hamrick, "*Tottel's Miscellany* and the English Reformation," *Criticism*, 44.4 (2002): 329–61.

[9]   For example, Clement Robinson's *A Handful of Pleasant Delights: Containing Sundry New Sonnets* (London, 1584), contained no sonnets as defined in the modern period. See William Parker, "The Sonnets in *Tottel's Miscellany*," *PMLA*, 54.3 (1939): 672.

[10]   See, for example, Sunil Sarker, *Shakespeare's Sonnets* (New Delhi, 2006), Chapters 2–4. George Gascoigne, 'Certayne Notes of Instruction', in G. Smith (ed.), *Elizabethan Critical Essays* (2 vols., Oxford, 1904).

[11]   Parker, 'Sonnets in *Tottel's*', 669–77.

Scholars have usefully contextualized *Songes and Sonettes* within early modern book culture, tracing its role in altering the place, popularity, and circulation of verse within culture. Wendy Wall, for example, traces the roles played by Tottel's collection at the moment in which both manuscript and print culture operated and interacted. As she writes, Tottel's "tells us that the 'idea of the book' and the 'book commodity' were entities being negotiated and fashioned both through their material format and through the rhetoric that writers and publishers used to identify the social place of writing."[12] As Hyder Rollins records, moreover, readers of *Songes and Sonettes* actively engaged the text, emending, changing, and editing their purchased copies extensively—literally writing on and/or erasing the printed texts; multiple hands and multiple copies within different editions of the popular text suggest that this practice enjoyed some appeal. The practice of physically editing the printed copies of *Songes and Sonettes* supports Wall's claim that "not only the foregrounding of the poetry's occasional status but also the work's very heterogeneous format aligns it with manuscript texts; for manuscript forms are deemed to be 'open' in that they inspire the reader to reassemble literary material rather than to admire its cohesion within a totality."[13] *Songes and Sonettes* demonstrably retained its material form as an anthology—even as readers physically altered and edited the collection—and the text's "cohesion within a totality" arguably contributed to its popularity and growing cultural authority.

Arthur Marotti further establishes the centrality of *Songes and Sonettes* in redefining discourses of authority, focusing specifically on the institutionalization and transfer of lyric from manuscript circulation into print. He also establishes that the landmark anthology influenced the publication of multiple popular anthologies in the next two decades.[14] By adding titles to each of the poems in the collection, asserts Marotti, Tottel created a distinctly literary document and culture. Cutting the poems out of their original and immediate contexts, Tottel initiated "a recontextualizing process ... in which the works lost their vivid particularity of meaning and began to speak a language whose general and abstract terms were a hybrid of poetic conventionality and culture-specific code words."[15] Some critical work in the twentieth and twenty-first centuries has sought to chart the abstract terms and codes deployed within Tottel's collection. This work has illuminated both individual poems and distinct codes, yet readers also encountered *Songes and Sonettes* as an interconnected package or totality, i.e., a collection, which indicates the need to analyze the text as an anthology of connected poems, cultural themes, and structures.

---

[12]   Wall, *Imprint of Gender*, p. 29.

[13]   Rollins, *Tottel's Miscellany*, vol. 2, pp. 36, 100–101; see also Arthur Marotti, *Manuscript, Print, and the English Renaissance Lyric* (Cornell, 1995), pp. 144–5.

[14]   Marotti, *Manuscript, Print*, p. 212.

[15]   Ibid., pp. 218–19. Contrast this with Wall, *Imprint of Gender*, p. 25. See also, Elizabeth Heale, *Wyatt, Surrey and Early Tudor Poetry* (London, 1998).

Literary historians both overlook the complexity and fail to account for the popularity of Tottel's as a collection because, all too often, such an anthological context goes unheeded in the face of other overarching critical concerns. Steven May, for example, struggles to account for the success of *Songes and Sonettes* because, he asserts, it found little in common with Tudor courtly verse. Focusing on such a courtly context, May overlooks his own long-standing claim that the courtier poets were a "privileged few"; he counts 32.[16] As trendsetters, 32 courtier poets (and their followers) created some demand for *Songes and Sonettes*, yet such a small group surely failed to create the need for the two editions printed inside of two months in the summer of 1557. While briefly entertaining other possibilities, May then rejects them, stating "but, in fact, we have no idea who bought these inaugural editions of the Miscellany or why."[17] With the Tudor courts as his interpretive *axis mundi*, May necessarily overlooks significant elements that help explain the popularity of *Songes and Sonettes*. As the chapters in this collection indicate, the popularity of Tottel's anthology stems, in part, from its utility in amorous, religious, political, and other contexts.

To some considerable degree, the popularity of *Songes and Sonettes* stemmed from its ability to provide a coded language of political critique useable by a broad range of readers. Reconstructing the complex political, linguistic, and poetic discourses that constitute Tudor culture, scholars have established that Wyatt, Surrey, Tottel, and other humanists redefined the social and cultural roles of the English language for political and economic reasons. As the increasingly autocratic Tudor dynasty used language to redefine authority as originating primarily or only in the monarch rather than in the English church, in the Papacy, or in an independent aristocracy, Wyatt, Surrey, and others responded by redefining the concepts of "honor" and the "poet" in order to create alternative sources of cultural and moral authority.[18] Writers and publishers based these alternate forms of authority in a shared linguistic excellence and in a humanist desire to reform society. Recognizing the place of *Songes and Sonettes* within such an oppositional discourse helps account for its popularity with some readers.

Modern scholars have also ignored and/or misunderstood the popularity of *Songes and Sonettes* because, using the aforementioned evolutionary model of literary history and/or a bias towards elite writers, they have focused on writers

---

[16] Steven May, *The Elizabethan Courtier Poets* (Asheville, 1999), pp. 4, 19.

[17] Steven May, "Popularizing Courtly Poetry: *Tottel's Miscellany* and its Progeny," in Mike Pincombe and Cathy Shrank (eds.), *Oxford Handbook of Tudor Literature 1485–1603* (Oxford, 2009), pp. 419–20.

[18] See Davis' discussion in Chapter 3 , pp. 69–70. On poetry and the reign of Henry VIII, see Greg Walker, *Writing Under Tyranny: English Literature and the Henrician Reformation* (Oxford, 2005); Sessions, *Henry Howard*, chs. 8–10; W.A. Sessions, "Surrey's Wyatt: Autumn 1542 and the New Poet," in Peter Herman (ed.), *Rethinking the Henrician Era: Essays on Early Tudor Texts and Contexts* (Urbana, 1994), pp. 168–92; and Tom Betteridge, *Literature and Politics in the English Reformation* (Manchester, 2004), pp. 44–86.

rather than consumers, i.e., readers, of the anthology. Although Tottel begins his prefatorial "To the reder" discussing the writing of poetry, he ends with a discussion of reading. Permanently altering popular understanding of English verse, Tottel addresses potential naysayers, writing,

> If perhappes some mislike the statelynesse of the style removed from the rude skil of common *eares*: I aske helpe of the learned to defende theyr lerned frendes, the authors of this woorke: and I exhort the unlearned, *by reading* to be more skilful, and to purge that swinelike grossenesse that maketh the sweete majerome not to smel to their delight. [My emphasis]

Rather than primarily writing, Tottel's encourages consumers to learn to appreciate *reading* and *hearing* the kind of English poetry he offers, as his reference to "the rud skil of comon eares" indicates. Again, Tottel focuses on consumers, exhorting them "*by reading*" to appreciate the new poetry he offers (my emphasis). "Smel" moreover serves as a metaphor of reception or consumption, not of production, which vehicle, again, focuses attention on reading and hearing. His exhortation, moreover, to "bee more skilful" refers to the aesthetic "skil of [their] comon eares," because he only uses the term "skill" in his prefatory comments in regards to "eares." In essence, previous scholarship has primarily focused on *Songes and Sonettes* through a writerly hermeneutic rather than, as Tottel stresses, through the experience of readers.

Reading aloud, in fact, remained the dominant popular practice in the early modern period, which, again, defines "skil of comon eares" as the material practice of reading and not as a metaphor for writing poetry.[19] Although historians rightly analyze the practices of reading and writing in tandem, Tottel's letter focuses repeatedly on consumption of the written or spoken word; most consumers, moreover, would more easily read or hear than write poetry. In focusing on the stylistic and metrical differences between Tottel's and later poetry, scholars have largely ignored non-writing readers, certainly the largest group of consumers that purchased *Songes and Sonettes*.

Such critical misdirection notwithstanding, Tottel's paratextual efforts provide a historically resilient discursive context in which readers, writers, editors, and others engaged the anthology. Debating the editor's identity, analyzing the lack of courtly analogues, and asserting a lack of imitators, nevertheless, all avoid

---

[19]   On silent reading, see Andrew Cambers, *Godly Reading: Print, Manuscript and Puritanism in England, 1580–1720* (Cambridge, 2011); Elspeth Jajdelska, *Silent Reading and the Birth of the Narrator* (Toronto, 2007); Guglielmo Cavallo and Roger Chartier (eds.), *A History of Reading in the West*, trans. Lydia Cochrane (Amherst, 2003); Paul Saenger, *Space Between Words: The Origins of Silent Reading* (Palo Alto, 2000); and David Cressy, *Literary and the Social Order: Reading and Writing in Tudor and Stuart England* (Cambridge, 1980).

explaining why Tottel's achieved such rapid and widespread popularity.[20] In providing readers with a redolent lexicon of religious, political, and erotic terms and tropes, therein enabling them to address a broad range of period conflicts and concerns, *Songes and Sonettes* established the type of anthology popular with readers throughout the period.

In "Printing History and Editorial Design in the Elizabethan Version of Tottel's *Songes and Sonettes*," Paul Marquis begins the collection by demonstrating that the text indubitably functions as a complex anthology. Revising our understanding of Tottel's, normally dubbed a "miscellany," Marquis establishes that "what Tottel published in 1557, however, were anthologies, selections of the choicest verses available to him at the time, arranged and sequenced in a particular order." Although the term "miscellany" will, perhaps, continue to inhibit understanding of Tottel's achievement, Marquis' essay analyzes the great care that Tottel used in editing Q2—the second edition published in 1557—making it an integrated, complexly organized, and structured anthology far more accessible to the reader than its predecessor. Marquis's attention to the text's editing, moreover, leads him to conclude that Tottel remained a religious moderate rather than a Catholic or Protestant partisan. Expanding upon Marotti's understanding of manuscripts as "sites of contested ideologies," Marquis establishes that such a contest can also be read "in the dialogic interplay of verses in *Songes and Sonettes*" and, potentially, in other verse anthologies.

In addition to providing such a comprehensive analysis of the text's own editorial practice, Marquis also places Q2 within the contexts of classical, continental, and domestic traditions of editing in which authors and editors arranged poetry "not as random aggregations of unrelated verse but as carefully designed and orchestrated arrangements of private and public sentiments." Tottel thus responds well to the dominant "culture of coherence," which sought to understand the complex whole of a given text and its "dialogic interplay of verses." Since Q2 served as the copy text for every following edition of *Songes and Sonettes*, Q2's editorial arrangement provided readers with a resilient formal context that demonstrably shaped interpretation of that text. Reconstructing the "formal integrity of the anthology," Marquis brings a much-needed corrective to the critical practice of divorcing poems, themes, and authors from their place within the anthology.

In Chapter 2, "Profit and Pleasure? The Real Economy of *Songes and Sonettes*," Catherine Bates compares Tottel's prefatory "To the reder"—and its rhetoric of readerly "profit"—to the often abrasive economic imagery used consistently throughout the anthology. Adapting Pierre Bourdieu's findings concerning gift exchange, Bates offers a much-needed revision of critical practices that have simply read Tottel's preface at face value. Rather than a sure key to courtly preferment, *Songes and Sonettes* represents "a testament to the pitfalls of a capitalist economy." Instead of "the prospect of money in the bank or cash in

---

[20]   The identity of the editor of *Songes and Sonettes* remains uncertain. See Holton and Macfaul, *Tottel's Miscellany*, p. xxi.

hand," Tottel's anthology, measured against its ambitious prefatorial promises of profit, offers a commodity "arguably a whole lot more valuable: an elementary lesson in market economics."

In addition to economic loss, Tottel's text also diminishes the erotic profit ostensibly offered by the text. Tottel's anthology, in Bates's compelling reading, eviscerates such concepts of love and reward. Creating meaning through the linking, juxtaposition, and recollection of economic attitudes, ideas, and themes, *Songes and Sonettes* functions as an anthology that, for Bates, nevertheless fails to deliver its promised profit.

In Chapter 3, Alex Davis examines the use of the "matter of Troy" in *Songes and Sonettes*, demonstrating the fashion in which the anthology deploys this complex classical allusion as a connective theme and/or trope. Throughout the text, images and references to Troy, as Davis demonstrates, fashion a complex political discourse "marked by a puzzling rhetorical excess … that has constant recourse to images of loss, betrayal and death; of dynastic ruin, and of a city on fire." Such symbolic "excess" provides readers with a "roadmap that can guide" them "through the various interests of the collection and the kinds of cultural work it performs." Like Marquis and other contributors, Davis establishes that the placement of a poem within the collection created contextual meanings that effected distinct "cultural work." Of particular interest, Davis finds that "Troy establishes a line of connection between zones of history (distant and proximate, real and imagined) that we might otherwise seek to keep conceptually distinct." Davis thus foregrounds the fact that Tottel's *Songes and Sonettes*—within and across poems—draws upon and engages important and disparate historical discourses to create holistic meaning.

Writing in Chapter 4, "Chaucer's Presence in *Songes and Sonettes*," that Tottel's anthology "interacts with Chaucer's work in a conscious and purposeful way," Amanda Holton demonstrates that the collection uses Chaucer's poetry to fashion a complex anthology that, nevertheless, dethrones Chaucer as the premiere English poet and, as a central part of that process, defames women and the female voice. Precisely because of the cultural dominance of Chaucer in the sixteenth century, the fact that Tottel included only one of his poems in *Songes and Sonettes* merits close analysis.

Tracing the complex ways in which the anthology will both "recall and resist" Chaucer, Holton provides a comprehensive and convincing analysis of the many ways that Chaucer's characteristic concerns, language use, and verse forms structure both erotic love and the characterization of female voices in *Songes and Sonettes*. "The kind of interest Chaucer shows in women and their suffering in love," writes Holton, "is effaced from the *Miscellany*." Language associated by Chaucer with "suffering vulnerable female lovers and predatory deceitful men" is "repeatedly usurped to describe female duplicity and male suffering and victimhood." Whether in the representations of the Petrarchan beloved or in the use of classical images of women, Tottel's verse comprehensively disregards Chaucer's skepticism concerning men and masculine dominance within erotic discourse. As Holton indicates, although the one Chaucer poem in the collection appears anonymously, Chaucer's presence remains clear to readers throughout the collection. In editorial placement of contrasting poems, as well as in the treatment of traditional love tokens and amorous objects, the collection nevertheless relies heavily upon Chaucerian style and concerns while simultaneously working to reject or, at least, minimize them in favor of Wyatt and/or Surrey. In this, Holton advances our understanding of *Songes and Sonnets* within early modern gender discourse, engaging and extensively advancing the type of scholarship forwarded by Elizabeth Heale and others.

In a *tour de force* of historical recontextualization, Peter C. Herman provides a powerful reassessment of the religio-political contexts created in and by *Songes and Sonettes.* Seeking to uncover the "implicit religious and nationalist politics of this collection," Chapter 5, "*Songes and Sonettes*, 1557," works to establish "what the *Songes and Sonettes* may have meant at the time of its original publication in the summer of 1557 rather than viewing this text in the light of its subsequent meanings." Further participating in a revisionist reading of English Reformation literatures (with such writers as Tom Betteridge and Greg Walker), Herman argues, the text originally read as a pro-Catholic and anti-Henry VIII publication.

Even though "Richard Tottel seems to have been motivated by profits," Herman argues—in contrast to Marquis in Chapter 1—that he also published *Songes and Sonettes* in order to create a "distinctly English, distinctly Catholic culture intended to answer the Protestant nationalism arising in response to Mary I's attempt to bring England back into the Catholic fold." In examining the publication of pro-Catholic texts in the period, Herman argues that "Tottel's linguistic nationalism and his aesthetic vision form part of the more general project to forge a new English literary culture, one that is distinctly Catholic." Rather than corruptions of the poetry, Herman suggests that Tottel's editorial emendations allow him to distance his text from the Protestant plain style favored by English Protestant reformers. In centralizing the executed Henry Howard, earl of Surrey, moreover, Tottel also fashions Surrey as a true Henrician and Catholic martyr in order to powerfully contrast the "false martyrs" popularized by Protestant hagiographers like John Foxe. Herman's reading of Tottel as pro-Catholic provides a useful counterpart to Marquis's assertion that Tottel remained a religious moderate, hopefully evoking further discussion on the place of *Songes and Sonettes* in reformation cultures.

Focusing primarily upon the dramatist's sonnets, Tom MacFaul argues in Chapter 6, "*Songes and Sonettes* and Shakespeare's Poetry," that the Stratford playwright maintained a distinct reliance upon *Songes and Sonettes* throughout his career. Rather than serving as a graveyard of obsolete poetic forms, Tottel's anthology deeply informs Shakespeare's work in multiple ways. MacFaul argues, in fact, that Shakespeare "engages in a very various dialogue with the moral and erotic verse of the collection, creating complicated patterns of feeling out of the apparently simpler stances of early Tudor verse. In particular, he uses material from the Miscellany to focus his thoughts about poetic memory and immortalization."

For MacFaul, Shakespeare's respect for *Songes and Sonettes* results from treating it as a valued sourcebook of ideas and meditations. Building upon the achievements of his forebears, "he treats Tottel's collection as an echo-chamber and source for variations, rather as jazz musician might use a song-book of standards." Favoring technical and ideational details and modes found in the anthology, Shakespeare fails to deploy its themes. As MacFaul writes, "a complex nostalgia, then, marks Shakespeare's use of the *Miscellany*. The fragile immortality that printed verse can provide informs his attitude to selfhood and its potential to make connections with the world." Far from an old and outdated text, *Songes and Sonettes* served Shakespeare well and, as MacFaul writes, "Shakespeare never lost touch with an older form of verse and its attitudes."

Chapter 7, Seth Lerer's "Cultivation and Inhumation: Some Thoughts on the Cultural Impact of Tottel's *Songes and Sonettes*," reads the text as an anthology structured by the contemporary and interconnected imagery of horticulture and decay, which also served a broad range of writers and genres throughout the period. For Lerer, "images of growth and death, of cultivation and inhumation, and of the textuality of desire, interlace throughout the volume's poems." As he indicates, it is precisely in Tottel's period that writers transferred horticultural concepts of "culture" to social and personal discourses. Lerer's highly original focus on such intertwined imagery reconstructs the fashion in which Tottel effectively yokes contemporary concerns over life, death, and renewal to the new modes of printing, editing, and reading texts. "To consider the book's cultural impact," writes Lerer, "is to consider how it traces a trajectory along the axes of death and didacticism."

For Lerer, *Songes and Sonettes* serves as a "guide to the perplexed" that, even as it offers new forms of poetry, inhumes an "earlier generation of literary performance," which then serves as a highly popular kind of discursive compost for cultural growth and personal development. Tottel achieved such popularity, in part, he argues, precisely because of its didactic value. "The volume's contents and its claims were posited and read ... as much a manual of cultivation as any handbook of good manners or guide to disciplinary instruction." Through the anthological arrangement of poems in Q2, Lerer demonstrates, Tottel fashions a "tale of textual recovery and publication told as a narrative of personal cultivation." Such "cultivation" readily aligns with Bates's understanding that the text functions as a didactic tool, regardless of any profit offered.

Chapter 8, "'Their Gods in Verses': *Songes and Sonettes*, 1557–1674," provides a reception history of the anthology in its first century. Although scholars have repeatedly noted the publication of multiple editions of Tottel's anthology, in this chapter Hamrick argues that they have largely failed to consider the longevity of Tottel's text in their interpretations. Read and purchased alongside other so-called "Golden Age" texts, Tottel cannot simply be relegated to one moment in the sixteenth century. As the chapter demonstrates, much of the text's popularity over the span of the century resides in its applicability to different needs. Critical comments on *Songes and Sonettes* written in the first century after its initial publication identify such utility, yet they remain largely unstudied. To begin to understand Tottel's great popularity, Hamrick provides a history of its reception in the period 1557–1674.

As has already been demonstrated, the following chapters eschew monolithic interpretations and, instead, incorporate different and often contrary positions on *Songes and Sonettes*. Marquis's assertion that Tottel remained a religious moderate rather than partisan, for example, contrasts to Herman's reading of the anthology as pro-Catholic. Rather than privileging any one interpretation of the anthology *per se*, *Tottel's Songes and Sonettes in Context* preserves a broad range of critical reactions to the text not unlike the range of responses offered by the text's first readers. The chapters, nevertheless, each share a concern to balance close reading of texts with appropriate historical reconstruction.

If the predominant focus within *Tottel's Songes and Sonettes in Context* remains somewhat traditionally upon Wyatt and Surrey (whose poetry constitutes about half of Tottel's anthology), the findings presented here confirm that, in addition to being the two most popular (and taught) poets of the collection, they remain the most complex. Such analysis, moreover, will surely lead others to reconsider the remaining poems and poets from new perspectives. Arguably, however, the inclusion of chapters that focus on Tottel's influence upon Shakespeare and upon earlier, mid-century writers, expands our critical perspective greatly.

Reflecting the dominant theme of the anthology, the majority of contributors approach *Songes and Sonettes* as primarily a collection of amorous or erotic tales, but do so without simply reducing the text to a one-dimensional focus. Even as, for example, Bates examines erotic discourse, she focuses consistently on the (negative) economic lessons offered by the text. Marquis's bibliographical analysis, Herman's historical contextualization, Lerer's cultural focus, and Hamrick's reception history each approach the text recognizing that early modern erotic discourse functions, at times, as far more than a repository of conventional moral didacticism or a simple record of passion.

Chapter 1
Printing History and Editorial Design in the Elizabethan Version of Tottel's *Songes and Sonettes*

Paul A. Marquis

Some verse anthologies in the English Renaissance were popular but most were not; those that were, were often reprinted; those that were not, were seldom reprinted more than once. Before they were reprinted, popular anthologies were revised, or *enlarged*, as the *Short Title Catalogue* says; poems were added, some omitted, and sequences were generally rearranged according to author, verse form, and *topoi*. Enlargements expanded the focus of self-reflective personae lamenting the agonies of love to include verses linked figuratively and analogically to contemporary issues. The popular anthology acquired status not only because it spoke to the age in which it was produced, but because it transcended its own temporal particularity to address larger human concerns. The revised version of Richard Tottel's *Songes and Sonettes* (1557) is the prototype of this English genre. It is the first surviving example of a verse anthology in English whose vocal resonance is emulated by later editors, authors, and publishers, at least until Donne's *Songes and Sonets* (1633). Whatever we think of Tottel's work in the context of Marian England, however, his position on reformed protestants, his curious nostalgia for Henry VIII's England, his distaste for the Edwardian Somersets, and his nonpartisan nationalism can better be understood if we address the primary question of how to read his anthology of 280 poems.

The popularity of Tottel's compilation is evident. It was reprinted twice in 1557, once between 1557 and 1559, twice in 1559, twice in 1565, and once each in 1567, 1574, 1585, and 1587. George Puttenham alludes to it in *The Arte of English Poesie* (1589), praising it as a source for lyrics worthy of emulation by Elizabethan poets.[1] Slender, in Shakespeare's *Merry Wives of Windsor* (1597–1598)*,* regards it affectionately as a primer of love poems (1.2.165–6). Its reputation as both a source book of poetic forms and a primer for the language of love indicates the range of its appeal. There is more than a slim chance, however, that both Puttenham and Slender were not referring to the first edition of Tottel's *Songes and Sonettes* but a reprinting of the second edition which had been enlarged and redesigned during the summer of 1557. Q1 was published on 5 June 1557; Q2, *Anr. Ed., w. omissions and additions*, as the *STC* indicates, was published on 31 July 1557.

---

[1]   George Puttenham, *The Art of English Poesy: A Critical Edition*, eds. Frank Whigham and Wayne A. Rebhorn (Ithaca, 2007), pp. 161–360.

A careful analysis of Q2 reveals a more sustained editorial attention than what is present in Q1 and in any other edition after Q3. By the time Tottel died in 1593, *Songes and Sonettes* had gone through 11 printings. Until recently, the text available to modern readers has been Hyder E. Rollins's two-volume edition of *Tottel's Miscellany 1557–1587*, published in 1928–1929, reprinted in 1965, and the Scolar (1966) and Menston (1970) editions, both facsimiles of Q1. Rollins identifies the work as a "miscellany" and that is what he compiles: appended to his copy text of Q1 are the poems included in Q2 out of the order they were provided in that edition, accompanied by a second volume which includes a bibliographical description of the contents of each reprint until 1586, including lists of variants. What Tottel published in 1557, however, were anthologies, selections of the choicest verses available to him at the time, arranged and sequenced in a particular order. Q2 is distinctly different from Q1, and perhaps more anthologic, one might say, because even more organized than Q1; hundreds of substantive changes in diction and prosody are included in the eight weeks separating the two versions: 30 poems by Grimald are omitted; 39 new poems added to the Uncertain Auctours section; and an entirely new arrangement given to the lyrics in Q2 as a whole. As all subsequent editions in the sixteenth century follow the arrangement of Q2, this is the version of *Songes and Sonettes* known to most Elizabethans.[2] That Tottel would redesign Q1 is understandable, given the impression left by that version and his penchant for producing coherent texts evidenced in his other publications. He would have understood that a more carefully impressed text, ordered and arranged in a significant manner, would influence the success of Q2.

Tottel's interest in textual design is evident throughout his career. In fact, his success as a printer of law books was facilitated by his ability to produce work of high quality in a market burdened by degrees of competence and neglect, especially in the printing of law books. Before Tottel acquired his monopoly in 1553, students and lawyers had to contend with books poorly printed and inadequately translated, if at all, from Latin and French, where legal statutes and precedents were barely comprehensible. Tottel produced clear translations and lucid explanations of legal issues which were appreciated by a growing clientele. Along with his close ties to reputable London lawyers and judges, these improvements helped secure his monopoly to print texts of common law for seven years.[3] Similarly, when Mary Tudor ascended the throne, and reformist printers were exiled, imprisoned, or silenced, Tottel stepped in to fill the gap, redesigning and reprinting books that had been published earlier by reformist printers, such as Lydgate's translation of

---

[2]   A more recent edition based on Tottel's 31 July 1557 text has been published by the Arizona Center for Medieval and Renaissance Studies, *Richard Tottel's Songes and Sonettes: The Elizabethan Version*, ed. Paul A. Marquis (Tempe, 2007); also, *Tottel's Miscellany*, eds. Amanda Holton and Tom McFaul (London, 2011).

[3]   Christopher A. Knott, "Richard Tottel," in James K. Bracken and Joel Silver (eds.), *Dictionary of Literary Biography*, vol. 170, *The British Literary Book Trade 1475–1700* (London, 1996), pp. 308–9.

Boccaccio's *The Fall of Princes* (1555, 1556) and Hawes's *The Pastime of Pleasure* (1555). His keen awareness of the fickle state of religion and politics also led him to print Smith's *A Bouclier of the Catholic Fayth* (1554)*,* dedicated to Mary I, and the *Works* of Sir Thomas More (1557). As a man of business, Tottel's response to the religious extremes of radical Protestants and conservative Catholics was more moderate than partisan. By 1557 he was one of the most important printers in London, employing four apprentices and likely possessing three presses. That year he published nine law books, as well as Thomas Tusser's *A Hundreth Good Points of Husbandry*; at least two editions of *Songes and Sonettes*; books 2 and 4 of Surrey's translation of Virgil's *Aeneid*; Thomas More's *Works*, in 1458 folio leaves; as well as Rastell's *Correccion of all the Statutes*, in 550 folio leaves. In 1557, Richard Tottel was on top of his game as a printer and publisher of culturally significant texts. He could afford to redesign Q1 soon after its release, especially if he thought, as I argue, that Q2 could be much more impressive, not only prosodically, but politically and ethically as well.

How the poems in *Songes and Sonettes* came into Tottel's possession remains a mystery, but given the range of possible manuscript sources, even the simplest scenario is complex. Derived from as many as 29 manuscripts, the variety of possible sources attests to the extraordinary cultural reach of Tottel's project. The selection of available verses would have involved what Sir Philip Sidney calls an "idea or forconceit" of the anthology as a whole.[4] Tottel's motives were as much educative and altruistic, spurred by a sense of nationalism, rather than merely by self-interest or monetary gain. The preface "To the reder" emphasizes his desire to produce a text that would "exhort the unlearned, by reding to learne to bee more skilful," and his wish to publish verses that had been "heretofore envied" or kept hidden by "the ungentle horders up of such treasure." He hoped that the "several graces in sundry good Englishe writers" would "purge … swinelike grossenesse" and ignorance from the common reader and enhance the "profit and pleasure" of the English tongue. His commitment to publish a book that would improve language skills and contribute to national pride is carried out with Promethean zeal: even as he scorns the hoarders and ridicules the "unlearned," the anthology is popular at the book stalls. The ethical basis of Tottel's project is clear, as he identifies an injustice inflicted on the less fortunate who had been deprived of a crucial educative tool by those reluctant to share the obvious advantages of reading verse.

As he acquires manuscript copies of the poems, the editor sets about strengthening their prosodic line, with especial attention given to the works of Surrey and Wyatt. Verses were arranged according to author, lyric genre, iambic stress, line length, and *topoi*.[5] Most were new to the reader: only 7 of the 280

---

[4]   Sir Philip Sidney, "An Apology for Poetry," in Katherine Duncan-Jones (ed.), *Sir Philip Sidney* (Oxford and New York, 1991), p. 216.

[5]   For more information on the following discussion regarding manuscript sources, see Marquis, *Songes and Sonettes,* pp. xxvi–xxxiv.

poems in Q2 had been in print before 1557.[6] In the Surrey section, versions of 27 poems are found in four manuscripts, not one of which is a direct source.[7] Tottel obviously valued Surrey's "honorable stile," as he calls it in his preface, identifying his name on the title page and devoting the first section to works that might otherwise have been lost to posterity. Surrey's translation of Book 4 of the *Aeneid* appeared in 1554, though Tottel chose to print it along with Book 2 in a separate volume published 21 June 1557 (*STC* 24798). A similar concern with composition and design is apparent in his presentation of Wyatt's work. Of the 154 poems attributed to Wyatt in the sixteenth century, only 96 are included in Tottel's compilation,[8] selected from manuscripts and commonplace-books.[9] As with Surrey's poems, the editor avoids those already printed. Thus, Wyatt's paraphrase of the seven Penitential Psalms published in *Certain Psalms* (1549) is not included. His secular poems are printed, however, including translations of Petrarch's sonnets and canzone, experiments with the rondeaux of Jean Marot, the strambotti, ballades, and epigrams of Serafino d'Aquilano, and the epistolary satires of Luigi Alamanni.

Of the 134 poems by Uncertain Auctours in Q2, 40 have possible sources in verse manuscripts.[10] The Arundel Harington MS has versions of 21 poems, while other manuscripts possess a range from 1 to 5 poems. There is little to go on in terms of authorship. It may be that Tottel was not concerned about the "*other*" poets; as long as he possessed the poems, he was free to publish them.[11] Even when authorship was known, Tottel was not interested in providing details, as in Q2's poem 207 which had been printed with variations in earlier editions of

---

[6]   Surrey's poems 31, 33, and 35, in Q2, were printed before 1557. Wyatt's poems 70, 84, and 91, in Q2, appeared in the first edition of *The Court of Venus*, circa 1538, Peter Beal, ed. *Index of English Literary Manuscripts, vol. I: 1450-1625, Part 2: Douglas-Wyatt* (London and New York, 1980), pp. 596, 606–7. Poem 207 was printed in Chaucer's poems, Pynson (1526), and Thynne (1532, 1542, and 1545). See A.S.G. Edwards, "Manuscripts of the Verse of Henry Howard, Earl of Surrey," *Huntington Library Quarterly*, 167.2 (2004): pp. 283–93.

[7]   See F.M. Padelford, "The Manuscript Poems by Henry Howard, Earl of Surrey," *Anglia*, 29 (1906): 273–337; and William A. Ringler, Jr., *Bibliography and Index of English Verse in Manuscript 1501–1558* (London, 1992).

[8]   See *Sir Thomas Wyatt: The Complete Poems*, ed. Ronald A. Rebholz (New Haven, 1981). See also Jason Powell's forthcoming edition of *The Complete Works of Sir Thomas Wyatt, the elder* (Oxford, 2012).

[9]   For further information on Wyatt's manuscript sources, see Beal, *Index of English,* vol. 1, part 2, pp. 589–626.

[10]   For further information on the possible manuscript sources for poems by Uncertain Auctours, see Steven May, *Elizabethan Poetry: A Bibliography and First Line of English Verse, 1559–1603*. 3 vols. (London, 2004); Ringler, *Bibliography and Index.*

[11]   As Adrian Johns, *The Nature of the Book: Print and Knowledge in the Making* (Chicago and London, 1998), p. 228, points out, "publication without express authorial consent seems to have been an acknowledged reality."

Chaucer by Pynson and Thynne. Finally, the sources for Nicholas Grimald's poems are presently unlocated, though John Bale lists 31 works by Grimald in *Index Britanniae Scriptorum*. Two of these works could have contained poems found in Q1. *Congratulatorium carmen* contains 150 poems celebrating the release of Somerset from prison, and though one may assume that not all were on the subject of Somerset, certainly those in Tottel's Q1 (but omitted in Q2) addressed to the Mistresses Seymour, the daughters of Somerset, could have been from this text. Bale also lists Grimald's *Carmina et Epigrammata*, from which some of the poems in the Tottel editions may have had their source. Since *Index Britanniae* was published in 1556, Bale does not list the 40 poems published in Q1, but there is a good chance that most were selected from these lost texts. The point here is that Tottel was carrying out his intentions as announced in the preface to the anthology. In an attempt to prove that English verse could rival that of Latin and Italian, he improved the iambic lines in many unpublished poems and arranged them in such a way as to enhance the educative import of the text as a whole.

Reading Verse Anthologies

Tottel had more poems to choose from than he included in *Songes and Sonettes*. Why he published certain poems and not others is a "mystery" that might be explained by how these poems fit into the overall design of the text.[12] The form of the printed book lends itself to sequential design; one page follows another, allowing formal and rhetorical links to synthesize each poem and provide a context in its relation to poems that precede and succeed it. This formal arrangement is at least as old as the classical period when the purpose of verse anthologies was both educative and aesthetic. As vehicles for cultural commentary, the Latin compilations of Catullus, Propertius, Tibullus, Statius, and Martial, whose works were studied in English grammar schools as part of the humanist revival in the early sixteenth century, are echoed in Tudor verse anthologies.[13] Elaine Fantham argues that in the classical period anthologies were read as commentaries on the changing historical and cultural landscape of the Roman community. Words were the "chief political weapon" in lyric compilations and as such, hidden layers of meaning are discovered in close readings. "Infinite varieties of arrangements" emerge between "individual poems separated from each other" that draw upon "the pleasures of comparison and contrast, expectations and surprise."[14]

---

[12]   See Steven May, "Popularizing Courtly Poetry: *Tottel's Miscellany* and its Progeny," in Mike Pincombe and Cathy Shrank (eds.), *Oxford Handbook of Tudor Literature 1485–1603* (Oxford, 2009), pp. 419–420.

[13]   See Jacob Blevins, *Catullan Consciousness and the Early Modern Lyric in England: From Wyatt to Donne* (Burlington, 2004), pp. 1–17.

[14]   Elaine Fantham, *Roman Literary Culture: From Cicero to Apuleius* (Baltimore, 1996), pp. 22, 65–6.

The emphasis on close reading as a hermeneutic strategy for understanding anthologies is also found in the work of Italian humanists who were influenced by classical authors in the construction of texts and whose commentaries explore the particular demands of the genre. Angelo Poliziano (1454–1494) insists that those wishing to understand his *Miscellanea* (1474) must read it closely, for its diversity of topics is based on a policy of "*fastidii expultrix*," a loathing to expel or reject anything topical.[15] The virtues of this new genre, Poliziano contends, lie in its structural logic, the illumination of which must be provided by critical commentary. A classical example of this form is found in the intricate designs of Statius' *Sylvae* (1480–1481) for which Poliziano provides a commentary based on meticulous attention to textual detail, which is, he argues, the only way readers will understand the complexity of the man, his verse anthology, and the culture from which it arises and to which it speaks.[16] Similarly, Julius Scaliger (1484–1558) observes that Martial's compilation of *Epigrams* achieves coherence in its use of *topoi* on language, politics, and culture, which are structured asymmetrically as part of an aesthetic that accommodates allusive commentary on disparate events in private and public life.[17] What Tudor authors and editors learn from Italian commentaries on classical anthologies is that the complexity of poetic arrangement defines the way anthologies should be read.

By the mid sixteenth century, the anthologic genre in Europe is well established.[18] Theodore Beza's *Poemata* (1548), a compilation of lyric genres, including sylvae, elegies, epitaphs, and epigrammata, is the likely source for most of Grimald's revised translations of poems which provides closure to Tottel's Q2. At least two members of the French *Pléiade*, Pierre Ronsard and Joachim du Bellay, published collections of lyrics in the early 1550s. In England, evidence of the genre is found in the verse clusters, prosodic variety, and allusive political references in fragmented versions of *The Court of Venus* (1547–1564).[19] As elsewhere, even in affiliated subgenres, collected editions acquire distinct cultural and political voices. Sir Thomas More's *Epigrammata* (1518), an anthology of epigrams in the fashion of Erasmus's *Adages* (1500), praises Henry VIII's decisive rule and advises him on the art of kingship. But the tone of the epigrams becomes more critical as More assumes the position of royal advisor in 1518 and finds

---

[15]   L. Ruberto, "Studi sul Poliziano filologo," *Rivista di filologia e diistruzione classica*, 12 (1884): 235–7, cited in Anthony Grafton, *Defenders of the Text: The Traditions of Scholarship in an Age of Science, 1450–1800* (Cambridge, 1991), p. 260.

[16]   Grafton, *Defenders of the Text*, pp. 33–6.

[17]   James Hutton, *The Greek Anthology in Italy* (Ithaca, 1935), pp. 64–5. See also Anne Baynes Coiro, *Robert Herrick's "Hersperides" and the Epigram Book Tradition* (Baltimore, 1988), p. 56.

[18]   See Elizabeth Pomeroy, *Elizabethan Miscellanies: Their Development and Conventions* (Berkeley, 1973), p.125, note 5.

[19]   *The Court of Venus*, ed. Russell Fraser (Durham, 1955), pp. 1–46; and also Russell Fraser, "Political Prophecy in *The Pilgrim's Tale*," *South Atlantic Quarterly*, 56 (1957): 67–78.

Henry's rule arbitrary and inconsistent.[20] Similarly, John Heywood's anthology of *Proverbs*, first published in 1546, but revised and enlarged throughout his career, reflects his position as court jester for Henry VIII, Edward VI, and Mary Tudor, skirting the thin line between humor and political activism, which finally drives him into exile when his Catholicism grows too dangerous for Elizabeth's court.

The initiative to organize and arrange hundreds of lyric fragments into complex patterns is evident as a schematic principle in the habits of Tudor authors and compilers. Anne Moss reveals that even in sixteenth-century commonplace-books, fragments of lyric poems, excerpts from prose tracts, and spiritual treatises orchestrate lyric voices to decry the vagaries of politics, religion, and culture, the effect of which exemplifies the individual's struggle between virtue and vice. These books, she suggests, "presuppose a universe of knowledge and moral activity in which everything is loosely connected by association of ideas, by similarity and difference."[21] Arthur Marotti points out the ubiquitous influence of collecting and gathering in scribal manuscripts and canonical printed anthologies in works by Sidney, Jonson, Herbert, and Donne. He argues that manuscripts, rather than printed miscellanies and anthologies, provide a clear sense of the sociocultural functioning of commonplace-books as they are unaffected by commercial commodification which complicates the latter and obscures the more authentic voices in manuscripts.[22] Nevertheless, both manuscripts and print collections are revealing; H.R. Woudhuysen argues that "their fate" is designed at the hands of printers and publishers.[23] This design, Harold Love suggests, reflects the "separate act of will" of compilers who aspire "to continue the life of the text."[24]

The culture of coherence prevalent in sixteenth-century English literature, in its classical antecedents and European counterparts, allows us to consider poetic anthologies not as random aggregations of unrelated verse but as carefully designed and orchestrated arrangements of private and public sentiments. If commonplace-books can be sites of contested ideologies of politics, religion, ethics, and aesthetics, what can be said about the dialogic interplay of verses in *Songes and Sonettes* evident in a close reading of its formal design? While Marotti finds in manuscripts the authentic versions of the sociocultural anxieties of authors and editors, I argue that they are also present in the printing and reprinting of anthologies such as Tottel's. Indeed, Tottel's revised anthology interrogates "the cultural attributes of change," a characteristic of the literature in the English Renaissance.[25] Enlarged and rearranged editions reflect the pressures of the age and the courageous aspirations

---

[20]   Coiro, *Robert Herrick's "Hesperides"*, pp. 65–77.

[21]   Anne Moss, *Printed Commonplace-Books and the Structuring of Renaissance Thought* (Oxford, 1996), pp. 122–23.

[22]   *Manuscript, Print, and the English Renaissance Lyric* (Ithaca, 1995), pp. 222–3.

[23]   *Sir Philip Sidney and the Circulation of Manuscripts* (Oxford, 1996), p. 224.

[24]   *Scribal Publication in Seventeenth-Century England* (Oxford, 1993), p. 45.

[25]   See John Guy, *The Reign of Elizabeth I: Court and Culture in the Last Decade* (London, 1995), p. 15.

of the publishers to exploit the potential of a market for "profit and pleasure." As popular aesthetic artifacts, these texts embody moments of oracular intensity that can be assessed as one might assess a musical score for its contrapuntal phrasing, as poems engage with the concerns of other personae and provide profound and relevant responses to personal and public concerns. Revised and expanded anthologies such as Tottel's disclose not only the fragile and dangerous climate of the times, but the ethos of authors, editors, and readers willing to accommodate and support the production of such culturally significant work.

As one progresses through *Songes and Sonettes* from the first to the last poem, the formal integrity of the anthology is manifest. The *excusatio* is employed as a rhetorical device when personae explain, justify, and excuse their attempts to inscribe in verse attitudes towards human affairs. The lyrics are self-contained and independent expressions of *prosopopoeia*, in which personified voices are described in various emotional states, and arranged in the sequence according to the principle of *variatio*, which lends fluidity to the sequence and provides narrative coherence. Variety also enables individual poems a separate and self-contained existence, even while they answer or anticipate the queries and opinions of personae in other poems, thus introducing readers, as Ann Moss states, to "the pleasures of comparison and contrast, expectations and surprise."[26] The astute reader finds meaning in the way poems are thematically and structurally linked, in how they acquire complexity as *topoi* are identified and addressed from different perspectives by personae whose voices resonate aesthetically in an historical, political, and ethical context.[27] One can understand the confidence with which the second edition of *Songes and Sonettes* was edited and redesigned. Tudor readers would have delighted in the larger patterns of arrangement and pondered the educative thrust of the editorial changes in Q2. They would have appreciated how the Janus-like relationship of each poem to other poems involves personae assessing their place in human affairs by folding into themselves the drama of the world and providing momentary coherence to the anxiety of disaffection and alienation inflicted upon them by personal rejection and sociopolitical oppression.[28] The polyphonic effect of the interlaced vocal exchange in anthologies anticipates the presence of many of the same poems in Elizabethan song books. The prosodic lines of the verses are easily assimilated into popular melodies circulating in ballads, motets, and madrigals, which help to produce the poems' resonant meanings and ensure the popularity of the work.[29]

---

[26]   Moss, *Printed Commonplace-Books*, p. 122.

[27]   See Germaine Warkintin, "'Love's sweetest part, variety': Petrarch and the Curious Frame of the Renaissance Sonnet Sequence," *Renaissance & Reformation*, 11 (1975): p. 18.

[28]   Paul Allen Miller, *Lyric Texts and Lyric Consciousness: The Birth of Genre from Archaic Greece to Augustan Rome* (London and New York, 1994), p. 4.

[29]   Ros King, *The Works of Richard Edwards: Politics, Poetry and Performance in Sixteenth Century England* (Manchester and New York, 2001); and "'Seeing the rhythm': An Interpretation of Sixteenth-Century Punctuation and Metrical Practice', in J. Bray,

5 June 1557: Tottel's Q1

Before commenting on the revisions in Q2, a more in-depth look at Q1 will reveal the problems that needed to be addressed. The 271 poems initially published by Tottel were grouped authorially: Surrey's poems (1–36); then Wyatt's (37–127); Grimald's (128–167); and the Uncertain Auctours (168–261). Two final clusters by Surrey (262–265) and Wyatt (266–271) bring the compilation to an end. Though running titles are found throughout the text, pointing is inconsistent. *Songes* on the verso pages, for example, is not always followed by *and Sonettes* on the recto pages. Points appear or not following the headings, and in a few cases the headings are reversed. These anomalies may be the result of compositorial idiosyncrasies and poor inking, which complicates the assessment of the outer and inner formes of the skeletons based on the running titles. Nevertheless, it is clear that Q1 does not possess the formal coherence one would see if the sequence of skeletons were related to the sequence of authors. Running-titles of the authorial sections by Surrey and the Uncertain Auctours, for example, conclude on recto leaves, while poems by Wyatt, and again by Surrey near the end of the text, commence at the top of verso leaves. The printer saves paper and avoids unnecessary expense by using white spaces that would otherwise have been empty verso leaves. A more conventional and aesthetic presentation would begin authorial sections on recto leaves and conclude on verso leaves. Inconsistencies also occur in the catchwords that are placed at the bottom right of the page to guide the compositor to the first word of the next line on the succeeding page. At least half of the discrepancies between catchwords and text occur at the point of transition between the outer and inner formes of leaves.

Tottel appears to have all but completed the production of Q1, with its authorial arrangement of verses by Surrey, Wyatt, Grimald, and Uncertain Auctours, when he acquired several other verses by Surrey and Wyatt. His preface to Q1 suggests that he conceived of a second edition early in the project. Q2 would allow him to correct the running titles and catchwords, rearrange the authorial sections, add and omit some poems, and entirely revise the sequential order of poems, in other words, to enhance the aesthetic qualities of the text. A moderate print run for Q1 made sense. Wendy Wall speculates that the average run in England in the mid-sixteenth century "consisted of only 300 to 400 copies."[30] Much would depend, though, on the kind of work published. Secular works could range from 100 to 1000 copies, with sacred works and commissions from propagandists sometimes reaching as high as 1500 copies. If the venture proved unsuccessful, fewer rather than more copies in Q1 would be easier to absorb financially; alternatively, if the

M. Handley, and A. Henry (eds.), *Marking the Text: The Presentation of Meaning on the Literary Page* (Aldershot, 2000), pp. 235–52.

[30] Wendy Wall, "Authorship and the Material Conditions of Writing," in Arthur F. Kinney (ed.), *The Cambridge Companion to English Literature 1500–1600* (Cambridge and New York, 2000), p. 72.

public showed an interest, "more hereafter" could be provided expeditiously, as he implies in his preface.

In the numerous manuscript sources from which the poems in *Songes and Sonettes* may have been derived, there are few headings to the poems. But in Q1, the poems are provided headings and grouped in the first three authorial sections according to lyric genre, prosodic measure, line length, and *topoi*, which range from the private concerns of the poet-lover to public exhortations on the role of virtuous action in the human community. A tally reveals that variants of the word *love* are found in the headings of 143 poems. In the first half of the poems by Surrey and Wyatt (1–127), *love* appears predominantly before being replaced by morally educative topics. In the Grimald section, *love* is thoroughly outnumbered by meditations on classical principles of virtue and almost equally matched in the Uncertain Auctours section by concerns relating to the transience of human experience. Poems addressing the subject of love employ Petrarchan conventions and generally take the form of songs, ballads, sonnets, and canzone; poems on public and political issues take the form of epigrams, epitaphs, elegies, and satires.

In Q1 the Surrey section commences with a display of lyric virtuosity. His first poem, a terza rima in 55 lines, provides an *excusatio*, a justification for writing in which the persona hopes that his "carefull song" will "print in [her] hart some parcell of [his] tene [i.e., grief]" (1.51–2).[31] This is followed by a sonnet in two rhymes; a song in eight quatrains of alternate rhymes which describes the *innamoramento*, the moment of falling in love; and two poems in poulter's measure of nearly 50 lines each. A sonnet cluster follows (6–14), arranged according to rhyme scheme largely in the English and Italian forms. Elegy 15 introduces political and historical motifs that are developed in the latter part of the Surrey section. Poems 16 to 26 are composed in a variety of different forms, interwoven with Petrarchan *topoi*, including feminine personae in poems 17 and 19 that complain *of the absence of her lover upon the sea*, as their headings suggest. In poulter's measure, the persona in poem 18 is described as a victim of an *injust mistaking of his writyng*, one who has failed in his *excusatio* by not acquiring the "unjoynted" style of a lover (18.20). Disaffection with the whole of womankind in poem 22 is followed by the *commitao* in poem 23 where the persona *forsaketh* love. The final third of Surrey's poems are educative. Translations of epigrams by Martial and Horace advance the classical virtues of moderation and self-discipline, which would help avoid suffering caused by disappointment in love. Wyatt's virtue is admired and praised as an exemplum of personal control, and the final four poems provide a consort in varying genres in which the reader is encouraged to embrace a life of virtuous action. The heading of Surrey's final sonnet 36 recalls the Petrarchan context, but

---

[31]   "It is a small wonder," writes William Sessions, in *Henry Howard, Earl of Surrey* (Boston, 1986), p. 81, "that this poem is the first in *Tottel's Miscellany*" for it provides a "musical distillation of forms, themes, and motifs that reveals Surrey's debt to Dante, Chaucer, and Wyatt, and presents a powerful model of love poetry for the English Renaissance."

the speaker actually leaves unspecified the *fansie* that has always been an enemy to his "ease" (36.2). Be it amorous, political, or moral, all he has hoped for in life, evident in the preceding poems, remains unattainable.

The Wyatt section is designed in a similar manner, showcasing the poet's virtuosity in lyric form as the narrative trajectory evolves from private to public concerns. An arrangement of 15 sonnets is followed by small clusters of epigrams, ballads, songs, sonnets, canzone, and rondeaux, establishing a pattern the iterations of which occur until poem 93. Sonnets 94 to 103, in the Italian form of octaves and sestets, are followed by a cluster of 10 lyrics of various kinds (104–13), 10 epigrams (114–23), 3 verse epistles (124–6), and an unfinished song (127). Through much of the section, the caustic and witty tone of the epigrams responds to the amorous flourishes by the speakers in sonnets, ballads, and songs. The final cluster of epigrams, however, marks the end of Petrarchan sentiment and the shift in the personae to issues of cultural and political importance.

Wyatt's poems cohere around two Petrarchan cycles of experience, the *innamoramento*, the moment of falling in love in poems 40 to 87, and the *commiato*, the farewell to love in poems 89 to 99, before the emergence of politically and morally educative poems. In a conventional *excusatio*, love's ambivalent influence on the writing process "hinders" the persona so that where once there was "style," there is now only "a gap" (60.15–16); he cannot find the words to persuade her to return his love. But Cupid claims that his words are more effective than the noise he once produced because there are fewer of them. Meaning is enhanced in the context of the "gap," the space and silence in which words are spoken. A transformation has occurred that has changed him from a "clatteryng knight" who "selleth wordes" (64.76), to a poet with a "frame" (64.81), structured and coherent in expression so that his words acquire wings that "might upflie/To honor, and fame … higher/Than mortall thinges" (64.128–30).

The *excusatio* aims not merely to seduce the lady, but to construct verses to profit readers and immortalize the poet. The Petrarchan narrative is employed further in the final section in the many references to the word *love* in the headings, though the verses themselves are largely political.[32] In the final epigrams, love is abandoned, words have lost their meaning, and a withdrawal from the world is advised and enacted. The courtiers life is "fettred with cheines of gold" (119.7), which the personae reject in the following verse satires where Jhon Poins is advised to embrace the life of moderation, the "quiet life" (124.74), where one can seek one's "selfe to finde/The thing" that has been "sought so long" (124.97–8). In the court one must learn to "cloke the truth" and "prayse [courtiers] without desert" (125.20), but in the country there is peace and quiet in "kent and christendome:/ Among the Muses, where [he] read[s] and ryme[s]" (125.100–101). The

---

[32] Epigrams 71 to 74, whose headings refer to *love*, do not in fact mention "love." These poems, along with poems 101, 102, and 108, are concerned with political opportunism, Rebholz, *Sir Thomas Wyatt*, pp. 374, 366, 381; also see *Collected Poems of Sir Thomas Wyatt*, eds. Kenneth Muir and Patricia Thompson (Liverpool, 1969), p. 435.

unfinished *Song of Jopas* provides a suitable closure to the Wyatt section in that its cosmological account of aberrations among planets is analogous to the varied experiences of the personae in the social and political environment of the Tudor court as described in the preceding poems.

The Grimald section (128–67) also reveals the virtuosic talents of the author in the lyric form: three love songs (128–30); two companion pieces on marriage (131–2); a cluster of encomia, epigrams, riddles, and sonnets (133–8); a long section of occasional poems (139–47); another cluster of encomia and epigrams (150–55); a final group of epitaphs and elegies (156–66), and a concluding epigram (167). Didactic poems far outnumber love poems here. A portrait of the poet's *true love* (128.01), as the heading indicates, commences this cluster, though the idealization is challenged by poems 131 and 132, in which contrary opinions on the state of marriage are provided. Dialogue is abandoned in favor of praise for the muses, the sources of inspiration for various styles of writing and performance (133), while the epigrams that follow examine the classical principles that "work well" in the representation of "noble vertues" (134.1.12). Grimald's personal acquaintances are praised in poems 139 to 147 as they exemplify the virtue of moderation triumphing over impassioned desire. The poet accepts his moral obligation to provide images that allure "hevenly herts" (148.1–3), which follow in poems 154 and 155 where the imbalance between court and commons is corrected in a world beyond time, where friendship never fails (154.38) in "the blissful plott of garden" (155.2), which recalls Eden. The personae in the epitaphs and elegies in poems 156 to 164 lament the loss of exemplars of virtue largely from the pre-Marian past which recall friendship and community among Grimald's acquaintances for whom he is nostalgic.[33] The long narrative poems in blank verse that follow (165–66) portray the courageous resolve of two martyred figures, while the final epigram celebrates the immortality of Cicero and the immutability of art.

The strong contrapuntal motifs tragically resolved in the final verses of the Grimald section of Q1 are followed by the expansive Uncertain Auctours section (168–261), poems loosely arranged according to lyric genres, stanzaic structure, prosodic measure, and *topoi*. The plight of the Petrarchan lover is seen in the larger context of morally didactic poems, including elegies and epitaphs, encomia, negative exempla, poems on *contemptus mundi*, and on the mean estate. The familiar display of major lyric genres commencing this section includes an elegy, a moral epigram, a ballad, and a tale, which provides the *innamoramento* and *excusatio*, where we are told that the poems are meant to "perce [the] hert" of the beloved (168.68). But this sadistic and self-indulgent goal is placed in the larger context of the exempla of virtue in poem 169, and the *meane estate* in epigram 170, as the heading announces. The speaker of Pygmalion's tale, however, advocates

---

[33]   In Q1, 40 percent of Grimald's poems have as their subject historical figures, acquaintances of the poet, including Damascene Audley of the great Staffordshire family, by whom Grimald was befriended in his pre-Marian days as preacher, and the Seymour sisters, Jane, Margaret, Katherine, and Elizabeth, the daughters of Edward Seymour, the Duke of Somerset, Protectorate of Edward VI, until his fall.

the pursuit of fame by exploring how "fansie" can be infused in form (172.10), a theme explored in the poems that follow. In the encomia of poem 186, the beloved *White* has beauty and virtue, and like Pygmalion's statue, a mythical power to illuminate the world (186.4), but because she is alive, she can restore those who gaze on her (186.10). The aesthetic motif is thus followed by other examples of virtue, in the elegy on Sir James Wilford (189), the philosophy of moderation espoused in the *meane estate* (191, 194) and the *contemptus mundi* in poems 196 and 197. The question whether the lover can exorcise his "wanton will" (204.18) by writing alone is answered in the *commiato* of poem 212 when he bids farewell to love because his "hand and pen are not in plight,/As they have bene of yore" (212.15–16).

This is a long goodbye, however, for the concluding poems in this section involve the futile gestures of lovers in the latter stages of disintegration. Secular love is exclusive: "I carde for her so much alone,/That other God I carde for none" (226.39–40), even while the world itself is unsympathetic to love. One can be as constant as Troilus (237), but, as the translation of Chaucer's "Truthe" attests: "here is no home, here is but wildernesse" (238.18). Disparity between the ideal and the actual leads to a heated exchange between the sexes (241–8). Vice in women is disclosed (245–8), although corruption seems merely a part of the entropy of the natural world, the "canker" that leads to decay and dissolution. "Every thing that nature wrought,/Within itself his hurt doth beare" (249.8, 13–14). In such a world, "no frendship can be founde," (253.19). Even though beauty leads to enthrallment and death (259), the persona is resolute in his commitment to his beloved who is "sure excedyng all the rest," one "that God could not amende" (260.7, 27).

There is no sense of resolution in either the form or *topoi* of Q1. All that remains are the two small clusters of poems by Surrey and Wyatt. That poems 262 to 265 and 266 to 271 have little relation to the earlier sequence suggests that the editor came into their possession after the earlier sections by Surrey and Wyatt had been printed. In contrast to the preceding narrative trajectories, which evolve from self-interested Petrarchan concerns to didactic and morally educative perspectives, the Uncertain Auctours section in Q1 ends disparately. There is no suggestion here that love can be transformed by virtuous action in the community, as in Surrey's poems; or that it will be rejected and replaced by spiritual retreat, as in Wyatt; or that it naturally leads to self-sacrifice and martyrdom, as in Grimald. Q1 ends fragmented by several clusters of poems obviously out of place. A second edition of *Songes and Sonettes* would correct the formal problems stemming from the printing process and redesign the sequence to replace its apparently miscellaneous qualities with a more prominent anthologic impression.

31 July 1557: Tottel's Q2

At what point was it clear to Tottel that publishing Grimald's poems in praise of the sisters Somerset might not be well received, given that Princess Mary had been threatened and abused by Edward Somerset, Lord Protectorate, in an attempt to dissuade her from celebrating the Roman mass in Latin? The afterthought might have been enough to excise 30 poems by Grimald in Q2 and substitute his initials for his name at the beginning of the remaining 10 poems. Understandably, the two short sections of poems by Surrey and Wyatt were moved to their respective clusters in the first half of the compilation. But when 39 new poems by Uncertain Auctours were added and the entire section moved to the penultimate position in the text, and Grimald's translations of Beza were moved to the final section in the anthology, the gesture ensured that strong closure would be provided to the entire collection.

Q2 contains 280 poems divided into four sections: 1 to 41 by Surrey; 42 to 137 by Wyatt; 138 to 270 by Uncertain Auctours; and 271 to 280 by Grimald. Running-titles of *Songes* occur on verso leaves generally, while *and Sonettes* is found on recto leaves, with or without pointing. Identification of the skeletons based on the running titles and abbreviated folio numbers, with or without points, and catchwords, is possible, though, as in Q1, inconsistent pointing could be caused by the idiosyncrasies of the compositors which include inadequate inking in the printing process. Nevertheless, eight separate skeletons can be identified, with four used fairly consistently, and four others less frequently. Two presses were used with the second press machining 8 out of the remaining 24 sheets. The text was likely divided into page units before composition began in a process called "casting off." which would have provided a textual sequence from one skeleton to another. One must be impressed at the attention to detail in the redesign of the verse sequences. The printing process of Q2 was more deliberate than that of Q1, for editors and compositors had the first edition with which to compare. The result is that Q2 is more accessible than Q1. For example, 26 variant signatures in Q1 are reduced to 9 in Q2. Fifty mispointed running-titles in Q1 are reduced to 22 in Q2. In Q1, there are 108 leaves and 6 variant catchwords, while Q2 has 120 leaves and 7 variant catchwords. Given the large number of variants that were introduced to Q2, including the rearrangement of lyrics, the vigilance and professionalism of Tottel's editorial staff must be recognized.[34] That he wished to facilitate the reader of Q2 is evident when he includes pagination and appends a *Table* of opening phrases of the first lines of each poem in alphabetical order, followed by the folio page on which the poem commences.

If Tottel had not been in some way concerned with the anthology as a unified text, he would have simply replicated Q1, attaching the small clusters of poems by Surrey and Wyatt to their respective authorial sections, leaving all of Grimald's 40 poems in Q2, and appending the 39 new poems by Uncertain Auctours to their section. Instead, he altered the sequence of poems as found in Q1 in 54 places through a process of selective incorporation where each poem was inserted into

---

[34] Gerald O'Gorman, ed., *Ciceroes thre bokes of duties*, trans. Nicolas Grimald (London, 1990), p. 18, suggests that Tottel's compositors were "trained to respond to the exacting requirements of law texts," and so "by temperament and experience were faithful" to literary texts.

a complex of other poems to which it contributed and from which it acquired significance. He also introduced over 400 emendations to words and phrases in Q2. By moving the Uncertain Auctours section from the final position in the text to the penultimate position and concluding with Grimald's 10 poems, Tottel ensures that Grimald's work has a culminating influence on the compilation as a whole.

The two small clusters of poems by Surrey and Wyatt at the end of Q1are integrated in Q2 where they make more formal and thematic sense. Surrey's poems enhance the feeling of desperation among the personae and support the claim that Wyatt, as a poet and man of virtue, is worthy of emulation. Particular poems are emended to reveal an editorial attention focused on tonal and prosodic "corrections," which suggests that the editor was generally satisfied with the sequential design of the Surrey section.[35] He may have been less satisfied with the state of particular poems in Q1, since an analysis of substantive changes, involving words and their meanings, reveals an attention to what specific poems say. Several kinds of substantive emendations are found: the transposition of type involving the exchange of letters in a word or words on the page; the substitution of entire words in the diction of Q2 over that of Q1; and the revision of prosodic scansion that alters the vowels or consonants of the verse. The nature of substantive emendations is that they are not caused accidentally, though they could result from a blend of the compositor's and or the editor's idiosyncratic impressions and stylistic preferences. Careful attention to the differences between Q2 and Q1 reveals the importance of emendations to individual poems and to the text as a whole.

Surrey's poems contain seven transpositional variants where the addition or omission of vowels or consonants emends the meaning of the word: at Q2.5.34, for example, "Unwittingly" replaces "Unwillingly." The difference between acting unknowingly and acting under duress changes the persona's predicament entirely. In some instances, the editor attempts to "correct" misleading ambiguity: at.5.11, "heare" replaces "here." Diction is altered in several ways involving variants that substitute archaic words for modern words, or vice versa: at 1.5, "sins" replaces "since," a substitution that occurs 14 times in the entire anthology. As one would expect, however, Q2's editor is more apt to modernize an archaic form of a word than not: at 5.39, "I" replaces "ye." Words are also substituted in Q2 that have perhaps at best an analogical link with those they replace in Q1: at 13.12, "corner" replaces "cornet." There are approximately 20 emendations of this kind to Surrey's diction in Q1. Finally, the editor of Q2 also emends prosodic phrasing: in Surrey's 8.8, "With a kings child, who tasteth ghostly food" replaces "With kinges child, where she tasteth costly food." In Q2, 11 prosodic changes in phrasing occur in the Surrey section.

The cluster of six poems by Wyatt attached to the end of Q1 is inserted after poem 117 in Q2 where links are established to the large group of Wyatt's epigrams that precede the final verse epistles. They expand the image of suffering brought on

---

[35] The term "correction" does not mean right over wrong; it simply refers to the change that the compositor or editor made thinking he was correcting the text.

by sensual love and encourage further engagement with virtuous action, thereby contributing to the emerging narrative trajectory in the compilation as a whole. Among other changes, 7 variants are caused by changes in vowels or consonants: at 91.28, "Plaining" replaces "Playning"; 9 variants are due to alterations in grammar: at 107.2, "with" replaces "which"; 16 instances of modernisms: at 73.1, "heard" replaces "herd"; 8 instances of archaisms: at 95.43, "swarved" replaces "swerved"; 32 instances of entirely altered diction: at 68.89, "honour" replaces "nurture"; and 24 changes in the prosodic line: at 108.63, "so toucheth me within" replaces "that toucheth me so within."

Most of the reshaping of Q2 occurs in the Uncertain Auctours's section, followed by Grimald's translations of poems by Beza. With 39 new poems added to the penultimate section, there is even more of an opportunity for resonance in the *topoi* among the speakers. Added to the existing 94 poems from Q1, the additions provide a total of 134, or almost half of the poems in Q2. From a generic perspective, they include songs, laments, encomia, complaints, epigrams, sonnets, epitaphs, and epistles. *Topoi* favor Petrarchan conventions, with more than half involving a lover wanting, having, or recalling that he once had his beloved. The remaining poems provide morally educative alternatives to the repetitive cycle of love and despair. A careful reading of the revised sequential design of Uncertain Auctours discloses the importance of *variatio*. Following Wyatt's *Song of Jopas*, Tottel prints the first 10 poems in the Uncertain Auctours section of Q1 without interruption, 138 to 147, which elaborates the *excusatio* where the personae debate the aesthetics of compositions in writing and sculpting, and the kind of "subject" or model that ensures fame and immortality in a world of social corruption and physical decay.

Another cluster of 23 poems from Q1 follows in Q2, 148–70, in which Petrarchan motifs are matched and exceeded by epigrams on the "mean estate," epitaphs on virtuous men and women, and poems of *contemptus mundi*. Poem 234 from Q1 then answers Q2's 170, before another 39 poems from Q1 follow in Q2 in which the personae ponder a number of complex issues, including the desire for sexual and spiritual fulfillment, its relation to truth, constancy, virtue, infidelity, mutability, and death (172–210). The parallel between Q2 and Q1 in the following nine poems involves a vigorous debate between the sexes, including accusations of slander and seduction, followed by a positive *exemplum* for women, two meditations on natural decay and communal discord, and a lover's complaint (211–19). Finally, Q2's 220 and 221 correspond to poems 259 and 260 from Q1; in the former, the lover draws an analogy between himself and Procryn, whose desire to know her beloved concludes in her slaughter, while in the latter, the beloved rises like a "Phenix" (221.1) in a blazoned body.

Seventeen new poems are then inserted into Q2, 222–38, in an arrangement of songs, epitaphs, epistles, and sonnets, whose *topoi* recall preceding patterns in which love is followed by moral and didactic exhortation. The political complaint of poem 229 links the pursuit of sensual pleasure at the root of the fall of Troy, with that which now occupies the lover, to the recent disturbances in England's commonwealth.[36] When joy is found in these poems, sorrow soon follows, and thus we are provided several *contemptus mundi* poems with political and religious contexts.[37] In poem 234, as the heading states, *Totus mundus in maligno positus*, "the whole world is set on mischief" (*1 John* 5:18,Vulgate). In poem 233.14, where hope provides fruit, now "hope is nye gone" (234.2), nothing is certain; the ship of state sails on aimlessly; natural order is subverted: "Trouth is folly: and might is right" (234.30–32). From a religious perspective, "Mens harts are burnde with sundry sectes/and to echeman his way is best" (234.55–6). The metaphor of burning "sects" refers to the passions of opposing religious factions and Queen Mary's attempt to turn England back to the Church of Rome after the Church of England was established by her father, Henry VIII, and advanced by her half-brother, Edward VI. In the summer of 1557, the phrase would also remind readers of the martyrs who burned at the stake under Mary's policy of religious intolerance, which, as far as the poet is concerned, the Lord needs to "tamend" (234.62).[38] If the human community tends towards "mischief," how can one survive with integrity? The answers are provided in the epigrams that follow in which readers are encouraged to act always with the end of life in mind, and to trust those whose friendship has been "tried," that is, proven in action (235.1–6). As the heading of poem 236 suggests, *Wisdome* speaks *few wordes* and *work[s] much quiet.*

Poems 237 to 248, mostly repositioned from Q1 to form companion pieces with new poems, accelerate and intensify the dialogic exchange among the personae on topics of infidelity and greed. The increasingly misogynistic tone is disrupted by epitaphs that praise courage and virtue, in Master Henry Williams, for example, a soldier in the court of Edward VI. The six poems that follow illustrate unresolved differences between the sexes. Poems 249 to 254, new to Q2, encapsulate the preceding discordant *topoi* with a staccato-like version of a Petrarchan affair. An *innamoramento* (250), followed by a *commiato* (252), before epigrams of moral advice on the "mean estate" (253, and the importance of the virtue of friendship (254), provide an alternative to the apparently futile prospects of the lovers. The next two poems (Q1's 82 and 242), resume the debate on infidelity. Q2's poems 257 to 270, the last new poems by the Uncertain Auctours, are composed of songs,

---

[36] Hyder Rollins, *Tottle's Miscellany, 1557–1587* (2 vols., Cambridge, 1965), vol. 2, p. 322, suggests that the poem refers to the younger Wyatt's challenge to the throne in response to Mary's intended marriage to Philip II. Likely written shortly after the younger Wyatt's execution in April 1544, the parallels in poem 229 drawn between the excesses of Troy and the English court would be obvious by 1557. "Such was the time," the poet argues, "Troy trembled not so careles were the men…/Like to our time, wherin hath broken out,/The hidden harme" (229.31–2, 37–8).

[37] In Rawl. Poet MS. 32, Gabriel Harvey claims that poem 234 was composed by Sir John Cheke, a well-known proponent of Protestantism.

[38] *Songes and Sonettes* was published amid the Marian Counter-Reformation, when English dissenters were tortured and burned in the streets where booksellers sold their wares. Rollins, *Tottel's Miscellany*, vol. 2, p. 3, observes: "To the accompaniment of fire and martyr's shrieks the epoch-making book … made its appearance."

ballads, and laments in a variety of trimeter, tetrameter, and poulter's measure. The *topoi* commence with a portrayal of the contemptible nature of human existence, as the heading suggests, *the vanitie of mans lyfe* (257). The conflict between desire inspired by beauty and the transience of life soon drives the poet to despair. When he gazes on her "excellence divine," he despises "all earthly things" (260.7–10), and though he craves death, "yet [he] cannot dye" (261.3). A last will and testament is provided in poem 262 by an emotionally exhausted speaker, while poem 263 begins, "Adieu desert, how art thou spent?" He has failed to move his beloved to mercy, though he has spent his best years, "the flowryng time" (263.20), lamenting his plight. The final poems oscillate thematically between disdain and praise for the beloved.

The new design of poems in Q2, then, intensifies the unresolved relationships between the lovers and the world. The excesses of passion are amplified and opposed in the newly formed "companion poems," which disclose the problems encountered by personae enthralled by beauty and obsessed by desire, whose frustrations lead in the extreme to either misogyny or deification. Antidotes to the endless cycle of suffering are provided in the morally educative poems that remind us that lovers aim too high, that this world "is set on mischief" (234), and that we do well to live moderately and with discipline, by recalling those in the past whose virtues are worth emulating. The positive *exempla* provide a nostalgic strain that acts as a counterpoint to despair. While the rearrangement of poems by Uncertain Auctours affects the reader's response to the whole compilation, editorial alterations in particular poems support the significance of the larger textual design. In this section, there are approximately 38 variants involving the omission or addition of letters that emend the meaning of words in Q1; 36 poems with emendations unrelated to the words for which they are substituted; 35 poems whose "corrections" involve grammatical emendations; 34 poems the variants of which involve the exchange or inversion of letters; 26 instances in which the prosodic phrasing is emended; 16 poems where modernizations occur; and 6 poems where archaisms are inserted. All these changes indicate how closely poems were read.

The most effective gestures towards closure in the anthology is found in the Grimald section where 40 poems in Q1 are reduced to 10 in Q2 and placed at the end of the entire sequence, thereby extending the educative reach of the text. The selection and arrangement of these poems, mostly translations from Theodore Beza's *Poemata Juvenilia* (1548), address the major concerns expressed earlier in the compilation. The subject of physical love is all but dismissed when the editor of Q2 omits five poems from the beginning of the Grimald section in Q1. He commences with Grimald's catalogue of the muses, in which the mythical sources of inspiration for poets are invoked (271). The epigram that follows clarifies the choices available to the poet and the reader, according to the philosophy of Musonius: "Working well" allows one to endure suffering lightly and to achieve glory and noble virtue (272.1–4); "working wrong" by seeking pleasure brings one "fowl defame" (272.5–8). But what kind of work is virtuous? The next three poems provide various responses to this question, though one's life is finally defined through the classical virtue *Of frendship* (277), as the heading indicates, which, if realized, stabilizes the relationship between the individual and his or her community: it is a "heavenly gift" (277.1) like grace, given to "eche house, eche towne, ech realm" where "stedfast love" flourishes (277.19).

If Tottel's editor had concluded Q2 with poem 277, the reader would have been left with positive *exempla* as models for action in the mid-Tudor world; however, he did not. Instead, he follows with two translations of Beza in which friendship is betrayed for political ends. These poems recall the numerous *contemptus mundi* poems earlier in Q2 in which the poet laments the transience of this world, and the political poems that lament the "signes of our decay, which tong dares not expresse, … which never were before this time, no not this thousand yeres," but which are now apparent (218.22–4). The slaughter of Zoroaster and Cicero depicts those moments in history when "frenship fails" (277.38)**.** The former's execution is linked by the connective 'therefore', connecting poem 279 to the political assassination of Cicero. In the final poem of the entire anthology, however, poem 280 reaffirms the importance of virtue and the role of the poet in relation to the community. Poetry matters, we are told, because in it, Cicero "lives, and styll alyve shall bee" (280.4). He lives in his letters, his theories of rhetoric, and paradoxically, in his attempts to civilize the community that eventually executed him.

The final poems in Q2 gather the preceding concerns of the personae. In the Surrey section, the poet praises Wyatt as an exemplar of virtue and criticizes the barbarism of the age, while Wyatt's poems that follow expose the political treachery in the court and follow the poet in a quiet pastoral life. The voices of the Marian poets in the Uncertain Auctours provide an uncertain view of the place of virtue in the world. Some comfort is found, however, in the numerous encomia of virtuous men and women whose lives are celebrated and praised in this section. Largely from the courts of Henry VIII and Edward VI, these figures remind us of what virtue is and how it should be practiced: Master Devorox, Lord Ferres's son; Sir James Wilforde; Thomas Audley; Philip van Wilder; Lady Anne Wentworth; Sir Anthony Deny; the Countess of Pembroke; Henry Williams; and Mistress White. These poems are complemented by encomia for the gift of "good will"; the joy that accompanies generosity; the temperament of the "mean estate"; the style of Petrarch and the virtue of Laura; the liberating nature of truth; the comfort of a faithful wife; the wisdom of silence; and the importance of friendship.

One could argue, then, that the prominence of these poems in the Uncertain Authors section of Q2 provides a series of portraits with an educative potential to inspire readers to virtuous action. As moral *exempla*, these lyrics accumulate in effect to provide a standard against which all examples of self-interested action are measured. Grimald's final translations of Beza explore the complex nature of virtuous action, its importance to the survival of the human community, and its relationship to martyrdom and immortality. By focusing exclusively on Beza's translations, readers would be reminded of his active participation in the Reformation; as John N. King points out, "as Calvin's chaplain and the continuator of Marot's French Psalter, Beza was a sanctioned neo-classical model for the Protestant poet."[39] The final poems in Q2 urge the reader to admire and appreciate the courageous resolve of classical figures that chose the honorable path of martyrdom over a life of subjection to the forces of oppression.

Grimald's translations remind us of the difficulties involved in attempting to revive the voices of those figures who attempted to contribute to the construction of an improved human community. In spite of the endeavor in the early sixteenth century to inculcate classical ideals in the young through the study of Latin authors, mid-Tudor culture was no less vicious. Surrey was executed in 1547 on questionable charges of treason, and Grimald would have been burned at the stake had he not turned apostate in 1553. The poets are immortalized by the violence inflicted on them and transformed into prophets and cultural critics of the society they had hoped to sustain.

To conclude that Q2 is a pro-Marian text is difficult, especially if statements in the 39 new poems by the Uncertain Auctours, which could be read as political criticism of the Marian regime, are considered. In particular, in poem 229, we hear that the "hidden harme" has "broken out" in "our time" (229.37–8), and in poem 234, "the whole world is set on mischief," "measure and mean" are absent, "trouth is folly," and "mens harts are burnde with sundry sectes" (234.30–32, 55–6). These statements, combined with the claim by the persona in poem 218 that in this age "such troubles still apperes,/Which never were before this time, no not this in thousand yeres" (23–5), suggest that at least some of the poems by the Uncertain Auctours are critical of Mary's reign. But Tottel was a political survivor. His ability to maintain his lucrative monopoly as a printer of law books during the regimes of Edward VI, Mary Tudor, and Elizabeth I meant that he was not likely to forfeit his flourishing career in 1557 by publishing an anthology of poems that could be censored, or for which he would be prosecuted and sent to prison, if not worse. Tottel's book sold in 1557, and continued selling through the Elizabethan period in part because its poems reflected a variety of private and public perspectives on the individual and the community in the mid-Tudor world.

31 July 1557: The Third Quarto and Beyond

A discussion of the printing history and editorial design of *Songes and Sonettes* is not complete without consideration of what led to the publication of Q3, the colophon of which also lists 31 July 1557 as its date of publication. How does that date relate to the text of poems that precedes it?[40] From an analysis of entries in

---

[39] *English Reformation Literature: The Tudor Origins of the Protestant Tradition* (Princeton, 1995), p. 243.

[40] W.W. Greg, "Tottel's Miscellany," *Library*, 5.18 (1904): 113–33, 120–23, suggests that Q2 and Q3 are either "two successive editions, one a close reprint of the other, or else a work set up in duplicate." One might ask, however, how Q3 could be a "duplicate" of Q2 when so many readings in Q2 are discarded in Q3 in favor of the old readings of Q1?

the *STC*, it is clear that Tottel's standard practice was to reprint books, especially calendars of English common law, yearbooks, statutes, and books of tenures using the colophons of titles printed earlier. For example, at least two books by Tottel, the colophons of which claim 1557 as the date of publication, were printed in later years.[41] This practice continued throughout Tottel's career, for, as the listings in the *STC* reveal, 44 texts were reprinted using colophons from earlier editions, 20 of which were published initially in 1556.[42] These books of various sizes were essential reading for legal practitioners. By retaining the original date of the colophon in later reprints of law books, Tottel likely assumed he was insuring his copyright and providing a sense of authenticity for his reader. One can argue, then, that when Tottel wished to reprint *Songes and Sonettes* after 31 July 1557, and before 1559, a revised Q2 was given to his compositor to reprint, and that following what he took to be the house style in the matter of the colophon, the compositor carefully set the date that was before him.

Yet, attention was also given to the stature of Q3 as a literary monument. In contrast to the first few leaves in Q2, which provide the title page and the preface *To the reder* crowded to the left and right margin, with only a slight funneling in the last few lines of the text, Q3's type is recast to compose pages that are centered and more graphically shaped. The prefatory remarks *To the reader* on A_1^v pivots on the word "delight" at the bottom of the page. Compared to the largely elongated rectangular shape of the address in Q1 and Q2, the editorial design of the opening leaves of Q3 is strong and impressive. The change in format in Q3 projects the book as a monument of literary significance in its own right.[43] An analysis of

---

Rollins, *Tottel's Miscellany*, vol. 2, pp. 13, 19, was closer to the mark when he observed that if the editions are "successive," then, the colophon of Q3 "may possibly be only a mechanical reproduction of the colophon" of Q2 (*Tottel's Miscellany*, vol. 2. pp. 13, 19).

[41]   I have Dr. Peter Blayney to thank for calling to my attention Tottel's practice of reprinting the dates of earlier colophons in later editions. The two texts are *STC* 9809 and *STC* 9863, both printed first in 1557 and again in 1566.

[42]   These 44 texts are interspersed between *STC* numbers 9582 to 9967, the entries of which record the publication of yearbooks, and *STC* 15737 and 15774, where a record of translations of French law books by Sir Thomas Littleton, published by Tottel and various other printers, is recorded. These entries by no means exhaust Tottel's record in the *STC*. For a complete list, see Alfred Pollard and G. R. Redgrave (eds.), *A Short-Title Catalogue of Books Printed in England, Scotland, & Ireland and of English Books Printed abroad, 1475–1640* (3 vols., London, 1976–1991), vol. 3, Katherine F. Pantzer (ed.), index 1: "Printers and Publishers," under Richard Tottell (169–70), where no fewer than 719 entries are recorded in his name. As the editors of the *STC* acknowledge, "The date of some of Tottell's editions is often repeated in subsequent ones or is entirely erroneous. Although an attempt to establish the true dates has been made with the yearbooks (*STC* numbers between 9551 and 9967), multiple editions of the same date under other headings have not been re-examined" (p. 169).

[43]   Wendy Wall, *The Imprint of Gender: Authorship and Publication in the English Renaissance* (Ithaca, 1993), p. 151, has argued that the presentation of title pages and prefaces authorizes the legitimacy of the contents of books and "helps create and monumentalize the literary reputation" of the work.

the substantive variants of Q3 may also reveal a deeper purpose underlying the revisions. In Q3, Surrey's poems 7, 8, and 13, are revised significantly. In every instance, Q2's reading is replaced by Q1's. Sonnet 7 is altered in nine places, sonnet 8 in five, and sonnet 13 in eight. These poems receive more attention in Q3 than any others in the collection. Versions of the poems are also found in the Arundel Harington MS, but no attempt is made in Q3 to return the poems to the readings in that manuscript. Why would the editor emend the revisions in Q2 to correspond to the readings in Q1? If we accept Sessions' claim that "ghostly food" in poem 8 is a synecdoche for the Holy Eucharist which recalls Mary Tudor's religious education and instruction in the Roman Church, one might argue that Q3's reversion to "costly food" eliminates the subtle allusion to the Catholicism of both Mary and Henry Howard, the Earl of Surrey, the author of the poem. [44] Was Q3 edited in the early years of Elizabeth's reign, during a time when it was thought wise to eliminate such allusions? A marshalling of evidence in the revisions to Q3 might provide a sound basis for dating that text as Elizabethan.

Nevertheless, most of the revisions in Q3 seem motivated by matters of diction and prosody. The task, vigorously embraced by the editor of Q2, to ensure that Tottel's verses conform to iambic scansion, is continued in Q3. What the editor rejects, for the most part, are those instances in the revisions in Q2 that exceed the measure of the iambic line. Changes involve the transposition, substitution, inversion, addition, or omission of letters to construct words with different meanings. Revisions are also grammatical, where the editor of Q3 corrects what he considers the mistakes of Q2. Changes also involve capitalizing nouns to enhance their importance, or placing them in small caps to diminish their importance. Plural nouns are also replaced by the singular form to improve the sense of the line. At times, spacing between letters is altered to produce or eliminate compounds. Alterations also occur in Q3 where words or phrases are replaced to correct what were to the editor unsound emendations in Q2. These changes, along with others, suggest that in certain instances Q3's editor has a fastidious allegiance to Q1, recalling the scansion of the lines and resorting to the editorial authority of that text over Q2.

But instances also occur where Q3 abandons readings in Q2 and Q1 to provide its own, in all but a few cases improving the text. For example, there are 14 instances where Q3 rejects the archaic diction of Q2 and Q1. These modernizations diminish historical ambivalence in words and lead to a more accessible text for the "unlearned" reader for whom Tottel publishes his book. There are 15 instances in Q3 where the thematic thrust of the lyric voices in the verses is sharpened to reveal the attentive, though idiosyncratic, reading of Q3's editor. In some cases, it is merely a matter of correcting grammar, but elsewhere the editor strives for consistency in the thematic action of the verse. The result is often a verbal clarity that is missing in Q2 and Q1; for example, in 20.30, "sunne" replaces "sonne"; in 167.42, "Nor aging" replaces "No raging"; and in 213.15, "pase" replaces

---

[44]   W.A. Sessions, *Henry Howard, The Poet Earl of Surrey* (Oxford, 1999), pp.192–3.

"prease." He also revises the 39 new poems added to Q2 by altering grammar and diction which changes the prosodic line and tone. But Q3 continues the general initiative in Q2 towards impersonalization. In the few instances when Q2 opts for a more personal reference, Q3 reverts to the impersonal reading of Q1. For example, in 14.9, Q3 reinstates Q1's "Ladie" to replace Q2's "Garret," a reference to the family name of Elizabeth Fitzgerald, Surrey's idealized subject in 1542, the year he likely penned the sonnet.[45] Further, Q2 emphasizes the acrostic in poem 169, with the first letters of each line followed by a space spelling vertically the letters in the name "Edward Somerset," until the last line emphasizes the final letter by setting it apart spatially from the word to which it belongs ("bes T") at the end of the line. The editor of Q3, however, omits the emphasis by eliminating the spacing and allows the name to retreat back into the poem, erasing its significance to all but the keenest reader.

Evidence suggests, then, that the variants in Q3 do not radically alter the text of Q2. Indeed, the editor clearly accepts the most significant changes, the revised arrangement of authors, the exclusion of Grimald's 30 poems, the inclusion of 39 new poems by the Uncertain Auctours, and the shuffling of poems from one position to another, especially in the Uncertain Auctours section. Nevertheless, Q3 differs from Q2 substantively in approximately 140 instances: Surrey's poems receive 37 substantive variants; Wyatt's poems, 17; the Uncertain Auctours, 79, with one-third of the changes occurring in the 39 new poems; while the remaining 10 poems by Grimald have 7 substantive variants. Fewer than one-third of the total substantive changes in Q3 revert to Q1. Thus, though Q3's editor respects the readings of Q1, he is motivated less by a need to restore that text than by a desire to continue the initiative, evident from the beginning of the project, to provide consistent tone to individual poems and a uniform iambic measure to the verses as a whole to create a text more accessible to the reader. After Q3, *Songes and Sonettes* received inconsistent editorial attention. In Q4 and Q5, both dated 1559, errors, misprints, poor inking, and variant catchwords are more prominent than in earlier editions. By Q8, 1574, the wording in many of the poems in *Songes and Sonettes* is significantly different from that of Q2, leading Rollins to conclude that the Elizabethan reader "must frequently have had difficulty in understanding what the poets really meant."[46]

Perhaps Tottel's interest shifted away from *Songes and Sonettes* because the book had fulfilled its purpose in securing the public's interest. Q2 had become a cultural phenomenon with a life of its own. The influence of Surrey's "honorable stile," embodied in verses in which he champions the works of Wyatt, and Wyatt's own weighty and "depewitted" lament for the end of civility in the Tudor court, is exemplified in the verses of the anonymous Marian poets, and in Grimald's

---

[45] By 1552, through several successful marriages, Elizabeth Fitzgerald had become the enormously wealthy Countess of Lincoln, a figure the editor of Q3 might well have chosen not to identify after 1557.

[46] *Tottel's Miscellany*, vol. 2, p. 36.

translations of Beza. These verses show that the English language was equal to the technical and verbal accomplishments of Latin and Italian: how "our tong is able in that kinde to do as praise worthelye as the rest," as Tottel's preface asserts. Q2's revisions provide a narrative in which the various political and cultural anxieties are resolved in the images of martyrdom, where the self is annihilated for the sake of the community. If Tottel's intentions were to improve the speaking habits of the common reader, to demonstrate the value of the poetic anthology as a literary genre for the reader's "profit and delight," and to underline the importance of the poet as a social commentator, he must have been pleased that his book initiated a flourish of activity by authors, editors, and printers who compiled, arranged and published anthologies in the later Elizabethan period. While only several works rivaled Tottel's in popularity at the bookstalls, including Richard Edwards's *Paradise of Dainty Devices* (1576, 1578, 1580, 1585, and 1590), Francis Davison's *A Poetical Rhapsody* (1602, 1608, 1611, and 1621), and later John Donne's *Songs and Sonets* (1632, 1635, 1639, 1649, 1650, 1654, and 1669), many poetic compilations were published, including those by Googe, Turbervile, Kendal, Proctor, Gillford, Howell, and Robinson, before the cluster of anthologies near the turn of the century by Jaggard, Bodenham, Allot, and Chester. Each of these works deserves our attention for how it contributes to the development of English prosody in the anthologic genre as a whole. Moreover, since popular anthologies became source books for composers and editors of song books, such as those by Watson, Byrd, Morley, and Dowland, who valued variety in verse forms and prosody, further attention should be devoted to the emendations of poems as they were transcribed into songs accompanied by musical notation and melody. There might be found an explanation for why some anthologies enjoyed repeated popularity while others did not.

Chapter 2
Profit and Pleasure?
The Real Economy of Tottel's
Songes and Sonettes

Catherine Bates

By the end of the sixteenth century Tottel's *Miscellany* had achieved a market dominance that—however hopeful he may have been for its success at the time—its printer probably never imagined when he first launched the volume in the summer of 1557. When, some 40 years on, Shakespeare makes Abraham Slender confide in the audience that, in order to woo the lovely Anne Page, he "had rather than forty shillings I had my Book of Songs and Sonnets here," it was on the assumption that the title could command the kind of instant brand recognition that would be the envy of any commercial publishing house today.[1] By that stage, Tottel— who had died not long before—had seen the volume he published as *Songes and sonettes, written by the ryght honorable Lorde Henry Haward late Earle of Surrey, and others* through nine editions and eleven printings, the enterprise that he had originally undertaken at considerable commercial risk having proved, in the event, a highly profitable venture.[2] By that time it had directly or indirectly inspired the plethora of miscellanies, sonnet sequences, and anthologies (both group- and single-authored) that, from the 1560s to the 1590s, arguably changed the face and direction of English lyric, if not the English poetic tradition as a whole, for good. It is generally assumed that Slender is referring to the volume we now know as Tottel's *Miscellany* here, but even if he were gesturing more vaguely toward one of its many derivatives, this would not detract from the commercial buoyancy of the product that Tottel had so successfully branded back in 1557, its place in the

---

[1]   *The Merry Wives of Windsor*, I.i.198-99; all references to Shakespeare are to *The Riverside Shakespeare*, ed. G. Blakemore Evans (Boston, 1997). That the success of his volume probably came as a surprise to Tottel is noted by Hyder E. Rollins, ed., *Tottel's Miscellany 1557–1587* (2 vols, Cambridge, 1965–66), ii.4; and Steven May, "Popularizing Courtly Poetry: Tottel's *Miscellany* and its Progeny," in Mike Pincombe and Cathy Shrank (eds.) *The Oxford Handbook of Tudor Literature, 1485–1603* (Oxford, 2009), p. 418.

[2]   Tottel died in 1594; *The Merry Wives of Windsor* has been dated as early as April 1597 (although, as Stephen Hamrick notes later in this volume, the reference to the "Songs and Sonnets" appears only in the 1623 Folio and not in the First Quarto of 1602). As May notes, Tottel undertook the project at his own risk and ended up making a "handsome profit," "Popularizing Courtly Poetry," p. 427.

market all the more secure for the flood of imitations and spin-offs to which it gave rise and which, until the 1580s, it regularly outsold.

What probably started out as a speculative venture on Tottel's part, therefore, may be said to have paid good dividends, and not only for the printer. Tottel's volume was a success primarily because it sold—or at least marketed—success. Like the period's many courtesy books and conduct manuals, it promoted itself as a passport to gentility, a means by which a man might rise above the middling classes and kick the ladder away. Indeed, Tottel's volume could be taken as the manual of manuals since its contents would come to supply the main body of examples in Puttenham's *Arte of Englishe Poesie*, a text in which the poems of the "courtly makers" there championed would quite explicitly be turned to the making of courtiers.[3] Armed with his handy "Book of Songs and Sonnets", the would-be gentleman could speak as to the manner born, impress others with his apparently learned eloquence, win women to his love, marry into money, and generally improve his standing in society, just as, in Shakespeare's play, Slender's fellows refer to his need to win the heiress, Anne—to "affection the oman," to "carry your good will to the maid," to "carry … your desires towards her" (I.i.227, 231, 236–7)—the book of poems he badly needs being precisely what would bring about this desired outcome.

Such traffic in women keeps the wheels of patriarchal society turning, and if this self-serving operation is largely what Shakespeare's play sends up in the failure and farce that follow, it is nonetheless finally affirmed by the gentleman Fenton's success in carrying off the prize at the end. The courtship of women served the interests of men and if texts like Tottel's *Miscellany* were seen, at least potentially, as a means to that end, they held out the possibility—however imaginary in practice—of a substantial accrual on a man's initial investment. Over and above the modest outlay the reader may have paid at the bookseller's stall, he could look to a spectacular return on his money, rather as—in his hour of need and with a rhetorical hyperbole he might well have learned from its pages—Slender exclaims that he would willingly exchange 40 shillings for the precious volume he lacks. Given the social and economic advantage he hopes it will net him, the book is worth, to him, 40 times its retail price: a gratifying accumulation of goods, a handsome profit, effectively a form of interest payment, the kind of "usury" that, as Lorna Hutson has suggested, oiled the wheels of sixteenth-century patriarchal society and set its circulations happily in motion.[4]

---

[3]   George Puttenham, *The Arte of English Poesie*, ed. G. D. Willcock and Alice Walker (Cambridge, 1936), p. 60. Published in 1586, the year before the *Miscellany*'s final edition, Puttenham's volume might be seen to take up the baton and continue the process of marketing social mobility that Tottel had begun.

[4]   Lorna Hutson, *The Usurer's Daughter: Male Friendship and Fictions of Women in Sixteenth-Century England* (London, 1994); this aspect of Tottel's *Miscellany* is also discussed at length by Wendy Wall, *The Imprint of Gender: Authorship and Publication in the English Renaissance* (Ithaca, 1993). Other critics have noted the social and economic advantage that readers could expect to buy for the price of the book: for example, Arthur F.

Tottel may not have expected his volume to be such a success but he marketed it as if he did, and the promotional preface with which he advertised it to the reader must be one of the few of that genre whose hype would actually be borne out. In a series of highly balanced constructions, Tottel promises the reader an economy of incremental increase:

> That to haue wel written in verse, yea & in small parcelles, deserueth great praise, the workes of diuers Latines, Italians, and other, doe proue sufficiently. That our tong is able in that kynde to do as praisewortthely as ye rest, the honorable stile of the noble earle of Surrey, and the weightinesse of the depewitted sir Thomas Wyat the elders verse, with seuerall graces in sondry good Englishe writers, doe show abundantly.[5]

The product that the printer here peddles is thus only deceptively "small" because it leads to a "great" yield: the incalculable intellectual capital marked by cultural approval and praise. Moreover, if this (in itself very healthy) return proves quite "sufficient" to the continental investor, then a specifically national product (this being presented as equal to—as praiseworthy as—the other) will, by comparison, yield the patriotic investor a still more "abundant" return (namely, the gratifying spectacle of such cultural capital accruing to the national Muse). At each turn of the salesman's argument, small leads to large, large to larger, and that to more still if the "moe hereafter" that Tottel promises a couple of sentences later is to be believed: a multiplication of assets that is presented as positively exponential.[6] According to such a pitch, purchasing the volume would, as a piece of venture capital, be a very good investment indeed. Its contents might be "small" but they were precious and, like jewels, valued precisely for their dense, lapidary, and jewel-like qualities.[7] To be able to write "in small parcelles"—that is, in short lyrics, the *Songes and sonettes* of the title page—was particularly to be admired because, as Samuel Daniel would affirm some time later, it was considerably more difficult—"Al excellencies being sold vs at the hard price of labour, it followes, where we bestow most thereof, we buy the best successe"—and, in the case of

Marotti, *Manuscript, Print, and the English Renaissance Lyric* (Ithaca, 1995), p. 295; and Seth Lerer, *Courtly Letters in the Age of Henry VIII: Literary Culture and the Arts of Deceit* (Cambridge, 1997), pp. 165, 202.

[5]   Rollins, i.2.

[6]   Referring to further poems he hoped to secure and print in future: either (Rollins speculates, ibid, ii.128), those by Wyatt and Surrey that he acquired after writing the preface and would append to the end of the volume, or the new poems by "uncertain authors" that he would subsequently include in the second edition, or, speculatively, other content to appear in other volumes still to come; at all events, tantalizing the prospective buyer with the prospect of new products to come. Tottel's Preface is discussed by many of the contributors to this volume, including Herman, Lerer, and Hamrick.

[7]   See, for example, Patricia Fumerton, "'Secret' Arts: Elizabethan Miniatures and Sonnets," in Stephen Greenblatt (ed.), *Representing the English Renaissance* (Berkeley, 1988), pp. 93–133.

sonnets especially, it was "most delightfull to see much excellently ordred in a small roome."[8] It was Tottel's title page that first imported the word "sonnet" into the English language (a genuine contribution to "our tong"), and whether this foreign term was still, at this stage, taken as a diminutive form to mean any short poem or lyric (from the Italian *sonetto*, "small sound") or whether it was understood to refer specifically to the 14 decasyllabic poem with a given rhyme scheme that, once naturalized into the language, the word would come to mean over the next century (the *OED* reserves judgment on this); either way the point of Tottel's preface is to emphasize that small is beautiful.[9]

Tottel's description of the poems he gathers together in his anthology as "parcelles" is appropriate, moreover, because in the usage of the time the word could—as in the phrase, "part and parcel"—mean both a gathered collection of smaller units or the component part of a larger whole (with all the logic of the "supplement" that this implies). As a number of critics have noted, the word also intriguingly combines the courtly with the tradesman-like as the coterie exchange and circulation of manuscript poems comes to be presented as the movement of small parcels or packages (*OED*, parcel, sense 10) that could be ordered, delivered, sent, intercepted, opened, exchanged, and returned: much, indeed, as the writing of the period would routinely emphasize the material quality of such lyrics, representing them as items that could be slipped between the strings of a lute, thrust into a lady's pocket, smuggled in an orange, used as a card for winding silk, and so forth.[10] One might also note, furthermore, that a parcel could, in addition, mean "a small portion, item, installment, of a sum of money; a small sum" (*OED*, sense 4), suggesting that, as Tottel uses the term, the "small parcelles" he is selling are equivalent to the small outlay he is asking for them on the part of the reader—one that will yield them both substantial dividends—adding further to the argument that court and trade come together in his volume, and that the noncommercial system of coterie circulation his volume purports to be selling will have very real commercial benefits for anyone who buys into his scheme. In much the same way, the printer's claim that his public-spirited dissemination of good practice is designed for the general good—"It resteth nowe (gentle reder) that thou thinke it not euill doon, to publish, to the honor of the Englishe tong, and for profit of the studious of Englishe eloquence, those workes"—serves as a gracefully patriotic veil behind which lies very direct appeal to the reader's immediate, concrete, and

---

[8]   Samuel Daniel, *A Defence of Ryme* (1603), in *Poems and A Defence of Ryme*, ed. Arthur Colby Sprague (Chicago, 1930), p. 138.

[9]   *OED* sonnet *n*, senses 2 and 1 respectively. *OED* notes that the first citation in Tottel "perhaps includes sense 2. In many instances between 1580 and 1650 it is not clear which sense is intended, as the looser use of the word would appear to have been very common." All references to the *Oxford English Dictionary* are to http://www.oed.com/

[10]   *OED* parcel *n*, sense 10: a package consisting of something wrapped up, usually in paper, and often sealed for sending by post, messenger, or courier. Tottel's "parcelles" are discussed by Wall, *Imprint of Gender*, pp. 25, 28, 29, 50, and 69; and by Lerer in *Courtly Letters*, p. 202, and in Chapter 7, pp. 152–3.

personal benefit: "thine own profit and pleasure."[11] For the down price of a mere shilling, then, this small, pocket-sized quarto volume presents itself as a very attractive deal, offering its reader a share in a capitalist economy that offers, as if by compound interest, to turn the "small" into the "great," the "sufficient" into the "abundant," and the general "profit" of the nation into the private "profit" of the individual.

Caveat Lector

There are, however, inherent problems with Tottel's pitch and, as with any hard sell, the wary buyer might well consider its claims too good to be true. In the first place, the system of private capital the printer is effectively trading sits oddly with the product he is actually selling: namely, entry into a courtly class which defined its quality, superiority, and desirability precisely by distancing itself from any such grubbily mercantile practices, and by continuing to operate (or at least being perceived to operate) a supposedly "feudal", precapitalistic system of grace, favour, and patronage. As a number of critics have pointed out, this contradiction surfaces in Tottel's characterization of the authors whose works he is bringing out into the public domain as "the vngentle horders vp of such treasure" (his patriotic release of these goods into the market being, indeed, his main justification for publishing the book).[12] Hoarding was anathema to the courtly class, which distinguished itself from the mercantile precisely by cultivating the appearance of liberality, open-handedness, and conspicuous consumption (should the reader need reminding of this, Tottel's volume itself contained numerous poems that inveighed against the practice: "For horde hath hate," in Chaucer's authoritative phrase).[13] It was, of

---

[11] Rollins, i.2. Many of the contributors to this volume also comment on the avowedly nationalistic and patriotic nature of Tottel's project: see Marquis, pp. 15–17, Davis, p. 18, Herman, pp. 119–21, and Hamrick, pp. 165–6.

[12] See, for example, Wall, *Imprint of Gender*, p. 26; and Marotti, *Manuscript, Print*, p. 215.

[13] From Chaucer's well-known and widely circulated poem, "Flee fro[m] the prese" (238/207.3). Tottel entitles the poem "To leade a vertuous and honest life," although it generally went by the better-known title of "Truth." See also poem 114/124 entitled "Against hourders of money," and in which "an horde … Of golde" is exchanged for death (4–5); similar examples can be found in poems 183/152, 221/191, 251/218, and 270/122. Where poems from the *Miscellany* are cited, the first reference cites the number of the poem in Rollins's edition, which relates to the first edition of the *Miscellany*, and the second cites the number of the poem in *Richard Tottel's Songes and Sonettes: The Elizabethan Version*, ed. Paul A. Marquis (Tempe, 2007), which relates to the second and subsequent editions. Line numbers that follow relate to the lineation of the poem in question (and not Rollins's lineation, which is paginated). The text quoted is that in the first edition, although variants in Q2 are noted if substantive. In the case of poems that only appear in the second and subsequent editions, I have indicated this with Q2, followed by the number of the poem in Marquis.

course, also a key part of that courtly affectation—a carefully cultivated courtly *sprezzatura*—to make light of one's poems and to dismiss them as mere jottings dashed off in a moment and carelessly discarded, trifles, toys, worthless items of no value in themselves. To hoard is indeed an "vngentle" practice, but it is Tottel, not the authors of these works, who—in parcelling up the poems and presenting them for sale as precious items worthy the purchase—is doing the hoarding: treasure is not treasure *unless* it is hoarded. Indeed, there is evidence that the rarity and unavailability of the courtly manuscripts to which the volume supposedly grants the reader unique access was greatly exaggerated (such material being in wide circulation and readily available at the time), in which case the supposed "hoard" of poems alluded to is no more than a printerly ploy craftily designed to raise their price.[14] Tottel needs to sell these poems as valuable commodities and the only way he can do this is by attributing his own mercantile practices to the courtly class: that is, by casting the gentle as "vngentle" or as like himself.

In the second place, Tottel's preface not only identifies contradictions between the two economic systems that clash here very visibly but also within the capitalist scheme that underwrites his whole project. For if treasure is treasure only by virtue of being hoarded, then it quickly ceases to be so once released and put into general circulation: when distributed for the "profit" of the many, those valuable items soon drop in price, their profitability compromised. Any attempt at marketing exclusivity runs into the same problem, for if the readers whom Tottel invites to buy into his scheme of social and economic self-advancement were actually to succeed in that end, the gentility to which they aspire would promptly vanish and they, no less than the salesman who got them there, could only be said to be the victims of their success.[15] As many critics again have noted, this contradiction surfaces in Tottel's shifty use of class terminology. On the one hand, he paints a straightforward picture of readerly self-improvement when, at the end of the preface, he addresses the reader as "vnlearned" and invites him, by reading the volume, to purge the "swinelike grossenesse" that, uncorrected, would otherwise characterize his condition ("swinelike"—a coinage of Tottel's own— suggests, perhaps, a surge of inspiration as the printer warmed to his theme).[16] This unlearned reader, moreover, can look to "the learned" for help (the printer asks the latter to assist in mediating the high style of the volume's "learned" authors down to the lower classes). The path to self-improvement, that is to say, is very logically

---

[14] See May, "Popularizing Courtly Poetry"; and Marotti, *Manuscript, Print*, pp. 211, 294.

[15] On the paradoxical aspect of marketing exclusivity, see Jonathan Crewe, *Trials of Authorship: Anterior Forms and Poetic Reconstruction from Wyatt to Shakespeare* (Berkeley, 1990), pp. 50, 61; William J. Kennedy, *Authorizing Petrarch* (Ithaca, 1994), p.234; W.A. Sessions, *Henry Howard: The Poet Earl of Surrey* (Oxford, 1999), p.274; Wall, *Imprint of Gender*, pp. 95–7; Marotti, *Manuscript, Print*, pp. 214–16, 222–3, 295–6; Lerer, *Courtly Letters*, pp. 31–2; and May, "Popularizing Courtly Poetry," p. 419.

[16] Antedating the *OED*'s first citation for "swinelike" dated 1585.

presented as a move from low to high, from the unlearned to the learned state, rather as Puttenham would later trace the aspirant's trajectory from the cart to the court via the school.[17] That this change in status is fully achievable, moreover, is reassuringly conveyed by the fact that, only a few lines earlier, that same reader is addressed—apparently *post facto*—as "gentle reder" and "good reder," as if he has already bought, read, and mastered the volume in hand, learned its lesson, purged himself of any swinishness, and become a fully paid up member of the gentlemanly class. On the other hand, the members of that class are, as we have seen, themselves described as "vngentle" and charged with a niggardly behaviour that, according to poems within the volume itself, has swinish characteristics all its own: "Such hordyng vp of worldly welth, such kepyng muck in store" (251/218.26). What this suggests is that the unlearned and ungentle reader might educate himself, improve his lot, move up in the world, and join the class of the learned, gentle, and good … only to find when he got there that it was populated by thoroughly ungentle types and full of people much like his former self. This is not Tottel's selling point but it does display with impeccable logic what the consequences of that selling point are: the erosion of the class exclusiveness that is up for sale as its defining borders become porous to the point of invisibility, and as gentle and ungentle prove so interchangeable that they to cease to be opposing terms.

As if to deny or delay the inevitable (or perhaps even to acknowledge the contradiction), Tottel's *Miscellany* is punctuated at regular intervals with poems on the "mean estate" in which the volume appears to try to control, rein in, and discourage with one hand the very social mobility it promotes with the other. Many of these poems caution the reader *not* to look to improve his lot but rather to content himself with a modest station such as that of the herdsman who is humble but happier by far "Then he, which ought [owned] the beastes, he kept" (170/140.20) or of the poor man advised to "Eschue the golden hall, thy thatched house is best" (200/169.14).[18] Other poems allow a degree of progression from these humble beginnings upwards, but only on strictly delimited terms since they identify as the perfectly balanced position a point between social extremes:

Who so gladly halseth [embraces] the golden meane,
Voyde of dangers aduisdly hath his home
Not with lothsom muck, as a den vncleane:
Nor palacelyke, wherat disdayn may glome. (28/32.5–8)

Surrey's translation of Horace's *Carmina* 2.10 (other versions of which appear elsewhere in the volume at 194/163, and Q2 253) here presents as an ethical ideal the place of the middling sort: the type, indeed, who might well be cast

---

[17] *Arte of English Poesie*, p. 298.

[18] The second of these two poems forms an acrostic on the name of the Protector, Edward Seymour, Duke of Somerset, executed in 1552, suggesting that the poem is to be read as a cautionary tale on the downfall of an ambitious courtier (see Rollins, ii. 277–8). For other "mean estate" poems, see: 27/31, 150/274, 191/160, and 251/218.

as the ideal reader of the *Miscellany*, since—addressed as variously "gentle," "good," "vnlearned," and "swinelike"—that reader might be taken to occupy an indeterminate position precisely midway between the pigsty and the palace.[19] In order for each of those terms to be applicable to Tottel's reader, that reader must remain staked to the place that defines his middling station: he will not, in the end, seek to go any higher since that station is ethically unimprovable. In which case, Slender—who does not, after all, win Anne Page in the end or move any higher up the social scale—might be a better reader of his "Book of Songs and Sonnets" than we originally thought, or at least be more attentive to the *Miscellany*'s endorsement of fundamentally conservative values in poems such as these.[20]

Alternatively, Slender (not to mention his creator) might also have taken note of other poems within the volume's pages in which injunctions to stay modestly put between the pigsty and the palace are thrown aside for advice on how to leave the one behind to get to the other as fast as possible—to get rich quick and make one's way up in the world by, for example, marrying for money—only to find, if they do so, that the palace is pretty much a pigsty after all. In Wyatt's satire, "A Spendyng hand," for example, the traditions of Horatian and Chaucerian satire combine to suggest that, corrupted by the alien values of self-interest and personal avarice, the court is indeed a pigsty already. To the speaker's proposal that he adopt such values and "Fede thy selfe fatte, and heape vp pounde by pounde," his interlocutor, Bryan, indignantly replies that that is how pigs behave:

> ... For swine so groines
> In stye, and chaw dung moulded on the ground.
> And driuell on pearles with head styll in the manger,
> So of the harpe the asse doth heare the sound.
> So sackes of durt be filde. The neate courtier
> So serues for lesse, then do these fatted swine. (126/136.17–23)

These last two lines (which in the Egerton manuscript read "So sackes of durt be filled vp in the cloyster,/That servis for lesse then do thes fatted swyne") were revised so as to suppress their implied criticism of the monasteries in deference to the Marian regime. In the context, "neate"—a relatively new word meaning clean, smart, well apparelled (from Latin *nitēre*, to shine, gleam)—serves to point

---

[19]   Horace has "*obsoleti/sordibus tecti*" and "*invidenda ... aula*," *Horace: The Odes and Epodes*, ed. and trans. C. E. Bennett (London, 1929), p. 130. In other versions of Horace's ode, the middle way is positioned between "sluttishe coates" or "filthines," on the one hand, and "hye estate," on the other (194/163.11,12,13); or, more alliteratively, between "carlishe coate" and "carefull court" (Q2 253. 6). Marotti, *Manuscript and Print*, p. 295, comments that Tottel's preface "locates the reader midway between the nobility of Surrey and the commonness of the rude multitude."

[20]   One might add that the only other Shakespearean character to cite the *Miscellany*— the Gravedigger in *Hamlet* who quotes extensively from poem 212/182 (probably by Lord Thomas Vaux)—clearly did not rise far up the social scale either. The Gravedigger's song is discussed in greater detail in this volume by MacFaul (p. 134ff.) and Lerer (p. 159ff.).

up the contrast between the spruce courtier and the dirty beasts from whom he self-righteously distances himself. But the shiny new adjective also carries with it the shadow of a much older, Anglo Saxon noun—neat, "an animal of the ox-kind; an ox or bullock, a cow or heifer"—suggesting that such protestations might be taken with a pinch of salt and that the neat courtier might not in fact be so very far from the manger after all.[21] As the poem proceeds, moreover, the speaker's ironic advice to Bryan on how he best might fill his coffers could be read as a manual in the ungentle art of hoarding—"How to bring in, as fast as thou doest spend" (29)—as courtly freehandedness becomes just one side of the accountant's ledger and as Bryan is counselled to "Seke still thy profite" (42) and to lend only on very profitable terms: "By which returne be sure to winne a cant/Of halfe at least" (45–6).[22] This is the first use of "cant" in the sense of "a portion, a share, a parcel, a division," the new word making a noun out of a very old verb but in so doing also adapting its original meaning—"to part, divide, share, parcel out, apportion"—so as better to fit the new, capitalist times being described. In this world, "sharing" comes to mean the accrual of private profit: in this case a hefty interest payment of 50 percent (a development that might also remind us of the sense of Tottel's "parcelles" as down payments of a profitable kind).[23] The speaker's advice continues—cheat, steal, marry old widows for their money, prostitute your daughters, anything "so gold thee helpe and spede" (73)—only to be scorned by Bryan who laughs at "thy thrifty iest" (80). But the speaker's jest, perhaps, rings truer than he knows, for "thrifty"—like its cognate forms, a derivative of "thrive" and thus originally associated with qualities of prosperity, acquired wealth, fortune, and success—began to shift its meaning around the middle of the sixteenth century to designate the qualities of frugality ("thriftines"

---

[21] See *OED* neat, *a* and *adv*, sense 7a: clean; free from dirt or impurities (first citation 1494); sense 2a: of persons, inclined to refinement or elegance (first citation 1546); cf. *OED* neat *n*, an ox etc, current from early Old English. The same revision to the line is to be found in the Arundel Harington MS—see *The Arundel Harington Manuscript of Tudor Poetry*, ed. Ruth Hughey (2 vols., Columbus, 1960), i. 170–71—although, as Hughey notes (ii. 184), it is impossible to say whether the change was made in the *Miscellany* or in the MS first. If the former, the interpolation might well be taken as Tottel's own. Critics remain divided over the question of Tottel's personal interventions in the volume. For some, the printer's role remains uncertain and editorial decisions are attributed elsewhere: for example, both Paul A. Marquis, in his edition of Q2, and Elizabeth Pomeroy, in *The Elizabethan Miscellanies: Their Development and Conventions* (Berkeley, 1973), refer to "Tottel's editor" throughout. For others, Rollins, ed., ii. 93 and May, "Popularizing Courtly Poetry," p. 42, Tottel is the volume's "guiding spirit" who took, for Marotti, *Manuscript, Print*, p. 217, an "active role" in shaping it and was, according to Crewe, *Trials of Authorship*, p. 51, "no fool." I for one am inclined to agree with the latter assessments.

[22] Q2 reads "But if thou can be sure to winne a cant," which is also the reading in the Arundel Harington MS.

[23] *OED* cant n^2: a portion, a share, a parcel, a division (this, the first citation) from cant v^1: to part, divide, share, parcel out, apportion (first citation 1440, last citation 1533).

is Sir Thomas Elyot's translation of *Frugalitas* in his *Dictionary* of 1552), and by extension parsimony, niggardliness, hoarding.[24] As a sign of the times, the speaker's ambivalent "thrifty" could thus be taken in either sense as Wyatt's satire sets the "gentle," courtly world of the open, spending hand against the "ungentle," mercantile world of the grubby, usurious hand that brings the money in at a better rate. The speaker thus plays an ambidextrous hand—both "A Spendyng hand" (thriving, thrifty) and a hand that brings in as faster or faster (hoarding, thrifty)— thereby exposing rather neatly the masquerade of a courtly liberality that financed itself by just such means. Bryan declares that he would never trade his "honest name" for money (83) and protests that, if he did, "then take me for a beast" (84). But given his reputation for activities of just the kind Wyatt's poem catalogues— and the "vicar of hell" being the name by which he was perhaps most honestly known—he emerges as the perfect picture of the "neate" courtier: the fatted swine who chews on dung and dribbles on pearls while his snout is firmly in the trough. That it would take an insider's knowledge to know of Bryan's notoriety, furthermore, serves to emphasize the point that if any reader actually achieved the desired access to the court which Tottel's volume dangles before him, he might discover when he got there it was quite as "swinelike" as the low world he had ostensibly left behind.[25]

Gentlenesse

Tottel's claim that his volume will bring its readers "profit and pleasure" is not, therefore, as straightforward as it might at first have seemed, and both the *Miscellany*'s preface and the poems within its pages could be said to give those readers (assuming they actually bought the book) some very mixed messages indeed. Rise above your swinelike station, unlearned reader, and become a gentleman for your own good and the good of the nation. Do not rise above your middling station, good reader, but be content with your lot for, as worthy authorities have anciently attested, the mean estate is the ethical ideal where true gentility is to be found and is not, therefore, to be surpassed. If you do rise above your station, gentle reader, be warned that those who profit themselves in this way are niggardly, ungentle, hoarding swine. These mixed messages testify to the social and economic turmoil that characterized the sixteenth century's shift toward an incipient capitalism, and as many have noted that turbulence manifests itself perhaps most pointedly in Tottel's oscillatory uses of "gentle": a word whose

---

[24]   *OED* thrifty *a*, the semantic shift occurring between senses 3 and 4 (the first citation of the latter is 1526); the same occurs also in thrift *n*[1] between senses 2 and 3 (first citation 1553); in thriftily *adv*, between senses 1 and 2 (first citation 1581); and thriftiness between senses 1 and 2 (first citation 1552).

[25]   For Lerer, *Courtly Letters*, p. 202, Tottel's preface is a "guide to the flight from courtly swinishness exemplified by Bryan," although perhaps one should also add "the flight *to*."

shifting meanings combined the social and the economic with issues of status, value, worth, and class in a single fraught term.[26] If one of Tottel's authors wrestles with this key problematic more tortuously than any other, moreover, that author is arguably Wyatt (all three uses of the word "gentleness" in the volume are his). As they perused Wyatt's poems—and it was in the pages of the *Miscellany* that most sixteenth-century readers read their Wyatt—Tottel's readers would have found the poet harking back, in his lyric poems especially, to an idealized, archaic, feudal, precapitalistic gift-economy in which giving was matched by receiving and love by reward. Here is a typical example from the song, "Passe forth my wonted cryes":

> Wherfore my plaintes, present
> Styll so to her my sute,
> As ye, through her assent,
> May bring to me some frute.
> And as she shall me proue,
> So bid her me regarde,
> And render loue for loue:
> Which is a iust reward. (77/82.25–32)

In another poem "So feble is the threde"—a translation of Petrarch's *Canzoniere* 37—the speaker fondly recalls the gracious words with which his beloved once "gaue to me the curteis gift [*mi fer già di sé cortese dono*], that erst had neuer none" (104/108.74): a gift which he courteously returns by means of the adoration, praise, and ardent laments for her absence that constitute the long *canzone* which he, by way of tribute, is sending back to her.[27] In the idealized world of *amour courtois*, that is, love is indeed rendered for love, gracious words for gracious words, and such exchanges are wholly removed from anything that might resemble a transaction. When, elsewhere in the *canzone*, the speaker describes his absent beloved as both "my swete weale" (6) and "myne absent wealth" (58), Wyatt conflates two very old and etymologically related English words to suggest that his lady's worth is inestimable, beyond all price, and not quantifiable in any way (it does not work in the Italian).[28]

---

[26]   Chaucer, of course, had already gone head to head with the term "gentilese" in a world turned upside down in the aftermath of the Black Death and the Peasants' Revolt. One of the best accounts of the shift toward a capitalist economy, as it is registered in the literary texts of the sixteenth century, remains Richard Halpern's *The Poetics of Primitive Accumulation: English Renaissance Culture and the Genealogy of Capital* (Ithaca, 1991).

[27]   All references to Petrarch are to *Petrarch's Lyric Poems: The* Rime sparse *and Other Lyrics*, ed. and trans. Robert M. Durling (Cambridge, MA, 1976).

[28]   *OED* weal *n*[1], sense 2: welfare, well-being, happiness, prosperity (current from Old English); wealth, sense 1: the condition of being happy and prosperous (current from before 1300). Wyatt's "my swete weale" translates Petrarch's "*dolce mio bene*"; there is no equivalent in the original for his later phrase, "my absent wealth." For a similar example of such a gracious rendering and surrendering of love in Shakespeare's Sonnets, see MacFaul, above, p. 132.

Similarly, in the ballad "For want of will," Wyatt's speaker conjures the same courtly gift-economy so as to place his situation within a set of familiar rules and expectations: "Betimes who geueth willingly,/Redoubled thankes aye doth deserue" (80/85.8–9). This is not the language of usury but of grace and favor, and lyrics of this kind invoke the courteous world of suit, service, reward, redress, rendering, reciprocation, and requital that had already been deeply embedded in the national consciousness by *Troilus and Criseyde*. In this world, any benefit that might accrue to the courtly lover could not, by definition, be quantified. Rather, such a "return" was habitually romanticized, euphemized—"mystified" gives, perhaps, a better sense of its ideological function—by means of religious or agricultural metaphors such as pity, grace, "fruit," and so forth.[29] By the same token, the courtly lover naturally made no material gain from his loyal service to the Lady, except of course to prove himself the perfect Troilan lover: an intangible asset or symbolic capital that nevertheless won him moral standing of immeasurable price (a kind of "gentle" hoarding, if you will).

In "Synce loue wyll nedes" (another *canzone*, this time possibly inspired by Serafino), Wyatt's speaker makes clear that the moral qualities he accrues as a result of his refined suffering more than compensate for the lack of any actual return on the part of the Lady (the only thing that he gets from her—and that increases—is cruelty and grief), making the whole experience, he insists, unquestionably worth the effort:

> Yea though my grief finde no redresse:
> But still increase before mine eyes:
> Though my reward be cruelnesse,
> With all the harme, happe can deuise:
> Yet I professe it willingly
> To serue, and suffer paciently. (107/111.19–24)

---

[29]   I draw here on Pierre Bourdieu's analysis of gift-exchange in *Outline of a Theory of Practice*, trans. Richard Nice (Cambridge, 1977): "In every society it may be observed that, if it is not to constitute an insult, the counter-gift must be *deferred* and *different*, because the immediate return of an exactly identical object clearly amounts to a refusal ... Thus gift exchange is opposed on the one hand to *swapping*, which ... telescopes gift and counter-gift into the same instant, and on the other hand, to *lending*, in which the return of the loan is explicitly guaranteed by a juridical act and is thus *already accomplished* ... gift exchange [by contrast] presupposes (individual and collective) misrecognition (*méconnaissance*) of the reality of the objective 'mechanism' of the exchange, a reality which an immediate response brutally exposes: the *interval* between gift and counter-gift is what allows a pattern of exchange that is always liable to strike the observer and also the participants as *reversible* ... to be experienced as irreversible ... the lapse of time *separating* the gift from the counter-gift is what authorizes the deliberate oversight, the collectively maintained and approved self-deception without which symbolic exchange, a fake circulation of fake coin, could not operate" (pp. 5–6). Like the sense of honour that Bourdieu analyzes, courtly love is a classic example of such "symbolic exchange."

Indeed, in this recuperation of a negative economy—one that can only work when nonquantifiables are in play—the very fact that he gains nothing from her allows him, in turn, to prove himself the greater, the more patient, the more perfect a lover, and so, in terms of his moral standing as the worthiest of men, to "gain" incomparably more.

For Wyatt, the word that best sums up the highly complex set of relations, expectations, obligations, gifts, debts, and rewards that characterizes this courtly world—and that nets the Troilan lover a worthiness that cannot be counted—is "gentleness." Yet this word only appears in his poems when it is under imminent threat of erasure. In the world that his speakers most commonly occupy, gentleness is more evident in the breach than the observance. In "They flee from me," for example, the speaker is famously brought up short by the apparent obsolescence of his favorite word: "But all is turnde now through my gentlenesse/Into a bitter fashion of forsakyng" (52/57.16–17). This is not the usual stony-heartedness on the part of the Lady that will allow the lover to generate untold spiritual capital from his sufferings, but a flat rejection—worse, infidelity—an all-too-Troilan scenario in which the death toll of courtly love had already long been rung. In the new and unfamiliar regime to which the speaker wakes up—one characterized by the Lady's "newfanglenesse" (19)—the older meanings of gentleness have become thoroughly antiquated, irrelevant, and quaint.

As the relics of a vanishing world that was fading fast, those meanings badly need to be refreshed, revived, and brought back into circulation. To cite the ballad "For want of will" again, the speaker clearly feels it necessary to remind the Lady of the rules by which he is operating and—by jogging her memory with the heavy hint that the courtly lover's service deserves *redoubled thanks*—of the etiquette that should dictate her next move: "Awake therfore of gentlenesse./Regard at length, I you require,/The sweltyng paynes of my desire" (80/85.5–7). In the long *canzone*, "Myne olde dere enmy"—a rendering of Petrarch's *Canzoniere* 360 that stages a formal debate between the speaker and Love on the value of love that is arbitrated by the goddess Reason—"gentleness" is again the word that Wyatt deploys to define the quintessence of the courtly lover's art. To the speaker's complaint that his love has gained him nothing but "pain and smart" and that his master, Love—"false lyer" that he is—is the epitome of "vngentlenesse" (64/69.16, 18, 21), Love counters with all the spiritual benefits the experience has garnered him:

> Euermore thus to content his maistresse,
> That was his onely frame of honesty,
> I stirred him still, toward gentlenesse:
> And causde him to regard fidelity.
> Pacience I taught him in aduersity.
> Such vertues learned, he in my great schole. (99–104)

There being no equivalent in the Petrarchan original, "gentlenesse" is Wyatt's distinctive interpolation here, the word encapsulating for him the paradox of an amorous exchange that is definitively noncommercial and yet that makes something out of nothing and transmutes emotional suffering into spiritual gold.[30] The debate, however, remains unresolved—Reason reserves judgment on the *questione d'amore* laid before her—and, although it is unresolved in Petrarch as well, the effect of Wyatt's interpolation is to leave the meaning and value of his key-word unconfirmed.

As Wyatt's modern editors note, where he otherwise translates the *canzone* fairly closely, these lines represent one of his idiosyncratic but telling riffs on the original, for where Petrarch had emphasized the fame he won for his aureate verse—the immense cultural capital his love netted him making it, by implication, manifestly worthwhile—Wyatt's poem removes all such reference to poetic achievement and with it any sense of the personal recompense.[31] In his poem the whole question of what love is worth—and, indeed, whether it is worth it at all—thus hangs in the balance, and what was essentially a rhetorical question for Petrarch remains for Wyatt an urgently interrogative one.[32] In the cold wind of sixteenth-century commercialism, the language of courtly love—once the sputtering glow of its extinct values has been finally blown out—seems to translate rather readily into crudely economic, transactional terms after all.[33] In the final exchange of the

---

[30]   In the original, the speaker's initial charge of Love's "vngentlenesse" is Wyatt's rendering of Petrarch's "*ingrato*." The speaker accuses Love of being an ingrate, a charge that the latter swiftly turns round, twice describing the lover in those terms: on these occasions, Wyatt's translation of "*ingrato*" is "vnkinde" (74, 110).

[31]   See *Sir Thomas Wyatt: The Complete Poems*, ed. R. A. Rebholz (Harmondsworth, 1978), p. 384; and *Collected Poems of Sir Thomas Wyatt*, eds. Kenneth Muir and Patricia Thomson (Liverpool, 1969), pp. 271, 275. In Petrarch's original, Love claims that he rescued the speaker—who in his youth was given to merely selling words, "*l'arte/da vender parolette*" (360.80–81)—and delivered him to a sweet life ("*dolce vita*," 360.87) and the fame ("*fama*," 360.88) that came of the higher art and transcendent poetry inspired by love. In Wyatt's rendering, while Love still claims to have rescued the speaker "from that art,/That selleth wordes" (64/69.75–6) and delivered him to "delight" (64/69.77; "*diletto*," 360.83), there is no sense of a deliverance from a commercialized venture: on the contrary, the *dolce vita* is rendered "pleasant gain," 64/69.79) and any sense of poetic fame is completely obliterated: "*salito in qualche fama*" [risen to some fame] becomes "I brought him to some frame" (64/69.81).

[32]   The same question hangs in the balance in "Give place all ye that doth rejoice," Rebholz, CCXVII: "What vaileth faith or gentleness" (21), although this poem (in the Devonshire MS) does not appear in Tottel.

[33]   In Bourdieu's analysis, *Outline*, pp. 171, 172–3, 177, the mystifications of an idealized gift-economy are always waiting to be exposed: "the essence of the 'archaic' economy lay in the fact that economic activity cannot explicitly acknowledge the economic ends in relation to which it is objectively oriented"; "The historical situations in which the unstable, artificially maintained structures of the good-faith economy break up and make way for the *clear, economic* (i.e. *economical*) concepts of the undisguised self-interest economy reveal the cost of operating an economy which, by its refusal to acknowledge and confess itself as such, is forced to devote as much time to concealing the reality of economic acts as it expends in carrying them out: the generalization of monetary exchange,

poem, the speaker accuses Love of having taken the Lady away from him, to which Love replies "Not I but price: more worth than thou" (140). This highly problematic line is another of Wyatt's distinctive departures from the original (in the Petrarch poem, it is quite unambiguously God who gathers the Lady to himself: "*Io no, ma chi per sé la volse*'"). Wyatt's ambiguous "price"—which then as now could mean both "preciousness" (the word is etymologically related to "praise") and "the money paid for something"—suggests that the Lady's worth is indeed capable of being quantified in crudely monetary terms (she is described as his "wealth" only four lines previously, although again not in Petrarch). The effect of Wyatt's word is to create an interpretative crux, and especially so in this, the reading specific to the Tottel version. While the manuscript reading—"'Not I' quoth he; 'but price, that is well worth'"—could be interpreted as being closer to Petrarch's meaning (as if to say, "the reward she deserved at death was the reason she was removed from you"), the version that most readers would have read on the pages of their Tottel could be interpreted as "the price a richer rival paid."[34]

Gentleness has little place in this bleak modern world where love can be counted and where "Two thinges prevaile: money, and sleight," to cite a poem possibly by Sir John Cheke that Tottel added to the second and subsequent editions of the *Miscellany* and entitled "*Totus mundus in maligno positus*" (Q2 234.43). This is the debased world of the "now a dayes" of the Satire to Bryan (126/138.37) in which love can all too easily be bought and sold: "But if so chance, thou get nought of the man:/The wydow may for all thy charge deburs ... The golde is good" (59–60, 63). In this world, which after all is Tottel's world, the gift-economy of courtly love proves as unrevivable as Troilus's long buried corpse and the idealized relations and unquantifiable returns that, under its aegis, took on the warm glow of an earlier age, look, once the mystifying veils are torn away, like nothing more than the crude transactions they always perhaps were. In a world increasingly governed by the profit motive, words like "wealth" and "price" take on a whole new valence, such that the typically Troilan complaint in a song such as "I see, that chance hath chosen me," begins to sound more like that of someone who has been sold a bad investment: "chance hath ... to an other geuen the fee/ Of all my losse to haue the gayn" (113/117.1, 3–4), "fee" variously suggesting (as Rebholz notes) an estate, an office involving profit, a wage or salary, and a reward.[35]

---

which exposes the objective workings of the economy, also brings to light the institutional mechanisms, proper to the archaic economy, which have the function of limiting and disguising the play of economic interest and calculation (economic in the narrow sense of the word)"; "practice never ceases to conform to economic calculation even when it gives every appearance of disinterestedness by departing from the logic of interested calculation (in the narrow sense) and playing for stakes that are non-material and not easily quantified."

[34]   For Rebholz, p. 387 (and see note 38 below), this last gloss is the most probable; see also Muir and Thomson, pp. 276–7.

[35]   Rebholz, p. 425.

As if to draw attention to the lover's real motive here and to drive the lesson home, Tottel follows this (in the first edition of the *Miscellany*, at least) with a poem warning against avarice: he entitles it "Against hourders of money" (114/124).[36] "Innocent" exchanges that might try to pass themselves off as the virtuous cycles of a gift economy cut little ice in a world where commercial transactions are the order of the day.[37] Thus, to cite the *canzone* "So feble is the threde" again, if the lover repays the "curteis gift" which his Lady had bestowed on him in the form of the poem he returns to her—a poem he hopes she will treasure by nestling it "Betwene her brestes" (104/108. 98)—that hope is unceremoniously dashed and the cycle decisively broken in the poem placed immediately after it: "Svffised not (madame) that you did teare,/My wofull hart, but thus also to rent:/The weping paper that to you I sent" (105/109.1–3). The juxtaposition infers a female reader who might be perfectly capable of detecting—and rejecting—the manipulations of such a supposedly "innocent" exchange, or who might, indeed, be involved in other transactions (no doubt lucrative) of her own. Either way, the virtuous cycle of gift exchange soon converts into a vicious one—in every sense of that word—as the speaker goes on to trade spite for spite and to hope, vengefully, that the Lady will feel the same pain: "Fele as I do. This shalt thou gain thereby" (12). When they are exposed for what they really are—and their transactional purpose revealed once and for all—the pretty conceits of the courtly lover can look pretty ugly and his gentle trade in pleasantries, flatteries, and "no-strings-attached" gifts can rapidly convert into a very ungentle exchange of insults and threats.

[36]   In Q2, Tottel inserts the "extra" Wyatt poems he had appended at the end of the first edition (poems 266, 267, 268, 269, 270, and 271) between "I see that chance hath chosen me" and "Against hourders of money" so the juxtaposition is lost in the second and subsequent editions.

[37]   Compare the juxtaposition that Tottel makes between poems 237/206 and 238/207. In the first, "I read how Troylus serued in Troy," the speaker compares himself with Troilus and urges his Lady "To graunt me grace and so to do,/As Creside then did Troylus to" (71–2), although his reading has obviously not extended as far as the end of the Troilus narrative since he appears to be quite unconscious of what happens next. The poem that immediately follows this in Tottel, however—and that seems to provide the appropriate riposte—is Chaucer's "Truth." As Seth Lerer notes, "Receptions: Medieval, Tudor, Modern," in Susanna Fein and David Raybin (eds.), *Chaucer: Contemporary Approaches* (University Park, 2010), pp. 83–95, Tottel's title for the Chaucer poem—"To leade a vertuous and honest life"—is followed by a comma, effectively making it the conditional clause that leads straight in to the first line "Flee fro[m] the prese & dwell with sothfastnes." Lerer also emphasizes the juxtaposition between the two poems which "form, in the *Miscellany*, a kind of dramatic pair or dialogue ... The first text is a personalized reading of a great love poem; the second is an exemplary ballade now presented as a piece of practical advice. The first is private, the second public" (p. 88). What also needs to be emphasized, I think, is the irony of a juxtaposition in which the speaker's aspiration to be the archetypal courtly lover in 237/206 is immediately followed by Chaucer's injunction to avoid the court and any impulse to hoard or aspire, "For horde hath hate and climyng ticklenesse" (238/207. 3). This juxtaposition is also discussed below by Davis, pp. 77–9.

Indeed, the aggressiveness of the speaker here—it is very common in Wyatt's poems—exposes what the courtly love tradition otherwise conceals behind dazed accounts of the Lady's superlative beauty, worth, and so forth: namely, the sheer coerciveness of the courtly lover's demand. The powerful sense that his love for the Lady places her under a moral obligation to reciprocate creates a sense of right or entitlement that comes out in the speaker's threats, which, in the case of Wyatt, are not far off from the sinister tactics of the loan shark:

> Then if an hart of amorous fayth and will
> Content your minde withouten doyng grief:
> Please it you so to this to do relief.
> If otherwise you seke for to fulfill
> Your wrath: you erre, and shal not as you wene,
> And you your self the cause therof haue bene. (38/43.9–14)

The sense of menace is palpable. In another sonnet the barely veiled threats are once again in evidence: "Sins that disceit is ay returnable,/Of verye force it is agreable,/That therwithall be done the recompence" (39/44.10–12). And there are other examples, too, of the vicious turn that courtly love can take. In the song "My lute awake," the speaker warns the Lady: "Thinke not alone vnder the sunne/ Vnquit to cause thy louers plaine" (87/91.23–4). What these examples suggest, I think, with such locutions as "returnable" and "Vnquit," is that Wyatt was more attuned than most to the crudely monetary turn that the language of courtly love was capable of taking and thus of the cruel fate that awaited gentleness in an ungentle, mercantile world. This also suggests, I would argue, that Wyatt can truly be understood as the poet of requited love: but only where *requited* is understood in the absolute sense of pay back.[38]

---

[38] In "The answere that ye made"—a song in which the speaker reproaches the Lady for her refusal of "my pore hartes redresse" (83/87.2)—he continues that "of my wo, I can not so be quite" (8), "quite" meaning both quit (rid) and requited (avenged). For other uses of the word in poems attributed to Wyatt but not in Tottel, see: "Repentance now shall quit thy pain," Rebholz, CCXV. 28; and "I quit th'enterprise of that that I have lost/ To whomsoever lust for to proffer most," Rebholz, CCIV.29–30. Interestingly, the latter poem uses the highly ambivalent word "price" (24) also used in "Myne olde dere enmy" (140; see note 34 above). Rebholz's gloss is significant here: "The charge that the lady sells herself … is here reinforced by the impersonal tone of a business transaction: the speaker gives up his attempt to recover a piece of lost property ('that') and concedes to the highest bidder the option of trying to take possession" (p. 516). For other usages of "requite" in the *Miscellany*, see two poems (not by Wyatt) which Tottel added to the second and subsequent editions: "And if you can requite a man,/Requite me as you finde me than" (Q2 228.287–8, the closing lines of a long ballad); and "The lover complaineth his harty love not requited" (Q2 265, title). Holton similarly comments on the menacing sense of obligation that Wyatt's poetry can exude (p. 95), while MacFaul shows how Shakespeare Sonnets provide a contrasting picture of love's more gracious exchange (p. 139).

Redoubled Thankes

For the idealized circulations of courtly love to be exposed in this way—for its gentle operations to be outed as a trade in goods (or insults) that is sordid, competitive, aggressive, and very far from gentle—bears rather heavily on the claims Tottel makes in his preface that the readers who buy and use his volume will thereby gain access to a world of superior manners and, implicitly, make themselves substantial material gains. It suggests, rather, that far from launching themselves beyond the sordid sphere of the commercial world into a higher, gentlemanly, courtly class, those readers will (if they read the book they have bought) find instead that the world it portrays is commercial through and through, and that any "advance" they might hope to make will not, in the end, have taken them any great distance. They might also note that the transaction in which they have already engaged by exchanging money for the volume at the printer's shop or bookseller's stall in order to buy into the social advancement and economic success it sells is not, in fact, so different from some of the relations transacted within its pages: transactions, however, which are for the most part—and especially in the lyrics—presented as disappointing, loss-making, and fruitless (where they are not, as in the Satire to Bryan, they are excoriated). With its endless scenarios of rejection, the lover/investor in the *Miscellany* could be argued to net himself very poor dividends since he rarely gets back what he puts in and never, as a rule, the "Redoubled thankes" (80/85.9) that he feels his due. On the contrary, he is left with less than he started out with and, generally angry at the shortfall, retaliates by wishing the same on his partner—debt for debt, loss for loss—paying her back in kind with threats and insults. Seen in this cold light, as a cycle in which the only thing that is traded is debt—capitalism, in essence—love as it appears on Tottel's pages represents the classic bad deal and, with those odds, is definitely not worth the price: a thoroughly negative economy that can no longer be recuperated by such unquantifiable assets as moral standing, spiritual worth, or poetic fame once the mystifications of courtly love have begun to take on the colour of a commercial transaction. In which case Tottel's readers, by this stage somewhat disgruntled customers, might be entitled to ask what exactly the "profit and pleasure" his preface promised them actually amounts to.

In *Courtly Letters*, Seth Lerer found the answer to this question to lie in the art of impersonation: the ability to learn to speak and write like their betters. From the pages of the *Miscellany* such "vnlearned" readers would "learne to be more skilfull," as the preface put it, and ultimately become like those "studious of Englishe eloquence" for whose "profit" the volume (like Puttenham's, perhaps) is explicitly published. In Lerer's view, this educational project is enacted nowhere more visibly than in the lyric briefly adverted to earlier, "Svfficed not (madame) that you did teare,/My wofull hart, but thus also to rent:/The weping paper that to you I sent" (105/109.1–3). Here, the speaker's injunction to "Fele as I do" (12) is, the critic suggests, directed not only at the Lady but also at the reader; and, if the reader obeys the command, the speaker's closing statement—"This shalt thou gain thereby" (12)—will apply to him also. The reader will, that is, have discovered how to insert himself into the role of the poet/lover—how to imitate, how to ventriloquize lyric subjectivity—and he will have earned from what he has learned. "What we gain," the critic explains, "is the technique of the early Tudor lyric. To some degree, this had been Tottel's purpose: to provide his readers with the templates of poetic imitation. 'Feel as I do' becomes, in the project of the *Miscellany*, an injunction to write as I do, and what will be gained is what Tottel offers in the prefatory 'Printer to the Reader': 'to haue wel written in verse.'"[39] But what the reader also learns is that he might indeed write well in verse, yea and in small parcels, only to have them unceremoniously torn up and thrown back in his face, much as, in Tottel's juxtaposition, the "weping paper" that is decisively "rent" here is presumably the poem that immediately precedes it: the lover's tributary return to the Lady of her own "curteis gift" to him (104/108.74), which he hopes, no doubt as a sign of favors to come, "Betwene her brestes she shall thee put" (99). No luck there, then. The reader who successfully learns how to imitate Tottel's lyric speakers, that is, can look forward, in the main, to finding the courtesies of gift exchange rudely disrupted, the flow of goods back and forth blocked or averted, and any positive cycle of investment and increase replaced with the negative cycle of accumulated losses and looming debt. The speaker of this poem gains very little for his pains. Indeed, pain is more or less the only thing he does gain insofar as it is the only thing that shows any signs of increase: "Could not my present paines, alas suffise … But new and new must to my lot arise" (5, 8). If it is only "This shalt thou gain," then in the end neither the speaker, the Lady, nor the reader can be said to have profited a great deal.

As suggested by the uneasy shifts with which the poems of "the vngentle horders" were offered up to the "gentle" reader for sale, these contradictions between profits promised and losses incurred are largely a consequence of Tottel's project of putting gentility up for sale and peddling the courtly love lyrics of the courtly class in the pages of a commercial volume. The transactions entailed in the producing, marketing, selling, buying, disseminating, and circulating of such a volume—clearly successful ones if the brisk turnover the printer enjoyed is anything to go by—naturally had a bearing on the product itself, not least in presenting it and its contents as saleable commodities. If it was by virtue of appearing on Tottel's pages that courtly love could begin to look like the transactions of a capitalist economy, it was the same economy in which Tottel's openly commercial and mass-produced volume was directly participating. And if the very success of his volume, in terms of its voluminous sales, had the effect of cheapening the product it sold, it was not inappropriate, ultimately, that courtly love should appear on its pages as that capitalist economy stuck in a permanent phase of negative growth. It was the perfect downward spiral: a self-fulfilling prophecy, in the unfolding of its own, inexorable economic logic, except that it ended up proving the opposite of what the salesman prophesied—"thine own profit and pleasure"—thereby rather

---

[39] Lerer, *Courtly Letters*, p. 201.

queering his pitch.[40] Parcelled up and distributed on the pages of a trade book, poems that may once have been composed, circulated, and read in an entirely different setting—a hypothesized manuscript, coterie culture, for example— acquired a quite different resonance and floated readings that neither their authors nor those first courtly readers may ever have imagined. It was, nevertheless, via those readily available and inexpensive pages that those poems were supplied to the vast majority of sixteenth-century readers and as such that they were (in the circumstances, it is the most suitable world) consumed. There is an argument, therefore, for taking them thus—editorial juxtapositions, alterations, leading titles, and all—and for being open to interpretations that, however destructive of the courtly love ethos and its supposed "gentleness" they might be in the end, their appearance there made possible, even inevitable. In which case, one might say that the "profit" that Tottel's *Miscellany* sells is nothing so crude (*pace* Bryan) as the prospect of money in the bank or cash in hand but something that, in the middle of the sixteenth century, was arguably a whole lot more valuable: an elementary lesson in market economics. Notwithstanding the rhetoric of the preface to buy, reader, buy, this chary lesson was there, in the interstices of Tottel's volume, for the savvy reader to pick up. And if he was interested—interest being the operative word—then he might well learn something to his own advantage.

Let us go back, then, to the wary buyer still dithering at the bookseller's stall, not yet a disgruntled customer because he has not yet committed to parting with his shilling. He has read the preface and—un-persuaded but intrigued, perhaps, and wanting to know more about what is on offer—turns to the first page and finds a long lyric by the Earl of Surrey, in fashionable *terza rima* (this reader is not entirely unlearned), an *excusatio* in which, as Paul Marquis has suggested, the poet's excuse for writing also serves as a borrowed justification for the volume as a whole.[41] What our careful buyer finds himself reading about is a natural cycle unnaturally arrested, its seasons stalled, as the speaker of the poem bleakly subsists in a permanent winter of discontent: the paradigmatic situation of the courtly lover and in stark contrast to the gushing flow of April showers that inaugurates that other great monument of the national literature, *The Canterbury Tales* (our reader might have small Latin and less Greek but he knows that much at least). In the

---

[40] In order to see through the mystifying veils of an archaic gift economy, Bourdieu, *Outline*, p. 178, argues, it is necessary "to extend economic calculation to *all* the goods, material and symbolic, without distinction, that present themselves as *rare* and worthy of being sought after in a particular social formation—which may be 'fair words' or smiles, handshakes or shrugs, compliments or attention, challenges or insults, honour or honours, powers or pleasures": a list to which one might add "small parcelles, [that] deserueth great praise." That is, as Tottel's volume materializes and quantifies the otherwise symbolic "rewards" of courtly love (by selling them for a shilling), so its own claims to an incalculable cultural value—as a national "treasure"—are at the same time quantified (as cheap).

[41] Paul A. Marquis, "Politics and Print: The Curious Revisions to Tottel's *Songes and Sonettes*," *Studies in Philology*, 97 (2000): 145–64, esp. 153–5; and his *Tottel's* Songes and Sonettes, pp. xxxix–xl.

blasted, frozen world presented by Surrey's poem—a metaphor for the lover's lamentably unremunerated state (his love goes unreturned, his pleas unheard, and so on)—there is neither production nor reproduction. Where, in the natural world, time always heals—spring follows winter and "time in time reduceth [brings back] a returne" (1/1.14)—for the lamenting lover the only return he receives and the only thing that grows is pain: "In time my harm increaseth more and more" (15). So far so conventional (our reader knows more than we thought), and so the poem continues in kind, piling up the metaphors of emptiness, depletion, and loss (for the most part drawn from the natural world: ice, fire, night, day, the storm-tossed ship, the wounded deer), until the reader—his interest by now well and truly aroused—turns over the page and reads the following:

> ... and I may plaine my fill
> Vnto my selfe, vnlesse this carefull song
> Printe in your harte some parcell of my tene [grief]. (49–51)

While "your" ostensibly interpellates the object of the lover's complaint (the Lady, referred to as "she" only four lines earlier), the classic shift from third to second person also incorporates the reader in the address, so that he—as much as the typically nay-saying Lady—here finds himself on the receiving end of the lover's typically vengeful wish. Indeed, the very fact that he is reading those lines at all indicates that the lover's laments *are* being heard on this occasion and that the solipsistic cycle of a complaint otherwise unheard, self-echoing, and narcissistic has been broken simply by virtue of being made available on the pages of Tottel. With the poem in print, the reader who might otherwise never have come across it is able to obey the lover's instruction and dutifully to commit the complaint to his own, empathic, memory. The "parcell of my tene" that he is invited to take to heart in this way has an authentically Chaucerian ring to it: in *The Franklin's Tale*, for example, Dorigen experiences "a parcel of hire wo" (852), and the speaker of the *Complaint unto Pity* complains of the "parcel of my peyne" (106).[42] For all Surrey's deep indebtedness to the Chaucerian idiom, however, the phrase "parcell of my tene" is, in this case, not his. Indeed, it is most likely to be Tottel's, for the manuscript reads "parcell of my *will*" (my emphasis) and "will" indeed fits the scheme required by the *terza rima* (still/fill/will). In which case, it is the enterprising printer who is requiring the reader to take to heart a parcel of tene, and not only that but to "Printe" that parcel there, as if his own processes of reproduction were to reproduce themselves, in turn, on the experience of the reader, and his own volume to become, in effect, another printing press: its pages

---

[42]   A number of the contributors to this volume also comment on Surrey's lines, including MacFaul (p. 138) and Lerer (p. 153). All references to Chaucer are to *The Riverside Chaucer*, gen. ed. Larry D. Benson (Oxford, 1987). Both these and the later citations from Chaucer are also to be found in sixteenth-century editions of Chaucer's works.

the forme and chase with which to reproduce an indefinite quantity of pain and grief on the quire of the reader's heart.

This serves as a neat example of the way in which a new context can make possible an entirely new understanding of a word. To "print" something on the heart or mind is also, as it happens, a highly Chaucerian phrase: to cite *The Franklin's Tale* again, "Men may so longe graven in a stoon/Til som figure therinne emprented be," such that Dorigen receives the "emprentyng" of her friends' consoling remarks on her troubled mind (830–31, 834); in *The Merchant's Tale* January tells May that she is "depe enprented in my thoght" (2178, although, somewhat ominously, she has not long before "emprented" in warm wax the key to his love garden so as to make a copy for her lover. 2117); at the end of *The Clerk's Tale*, Chaucer urges his readers to "Emprenteth wel this lessoun in youre mynde" (1193); and Criseyde "gan to prenten in hire herte faste" every word of Antigone's song about love (*Troilus and Criseyde*, 2.900). In examples such as these, "print" indicates the action of exerting of pressure on a surface in order to make a more or less permanent mark. For those who came after Caxton, however, to "print" acquired meanings that were simply unavailable to Chaucer. It is quite possible—quite likely, even—that when Surrey's speaker first urged his reader and the Lady to "Printe" his suffering in their hearts, what he had in mind was a wholly pretechnological operation, and there would certainly be every justification for taking it that way if reading the poem in manuscript. But that injunction reads entirely differently when it appears on the pages of a mass-produced volume that the relatively new technology of the printing press was able to produce on what, by the standards of the time, was an industrial scale. By the same token, the instruction to "Printe in your harte some parcell of my tene" also acquires a quite new valence when found in a volume where, on only the preceding verso, "small parcelles" were proffered by "The Printer to the Reader" explicitly for the "profit and pleasure" of the latter. The small parcels advertised there as precious bundles and as leading to bountiful rewards ("great praise," cultural capital, public and private abundance, "and moe"), however, are now—no more than a page later—being presented as parcels that will lead explicitly to the reader's "tene," this being (probably) the printer's own substitution for the poet's original word. And not only are these parcels to be printed on the individual, private heart of our good reader, but also on the hearts of the hundreds of other readers whose demand for such products the volume is busy creating and supplying, and whose insatiable appetite would be stoked and fed as, over the decades, copies of the *Miscellany* flew off the shelves.

Whatever Surrey may have intended when he wrote his poem (and given his deep immersion in the Chaucerian idiom, not to mention the stigma of print, the mechanics of the London printing presses were arguably very far from his mind), when it appeared on the pages of Tottel—which is where it appeared for virtually everybody—the lover's private message to his reader to print his personal suffering upon his own individual heart becomes an instruction to a mass audience: in an instant his grief is given exponential increase. This is courtly love in an age of mechanical reproduction. There is no escaping the processes of this production (the volume announces its provenance as "Imprinted at London in flete street ... by Richard Tottel"), nor the fact that it is produced for the profit of the printer whose monopoly is clearly endorsed by the authorities ("*Cum priuilegio ad imprimendum solum*"): a licence to print money, as it turned out.[43] In the long run, however, the effect of all this would be to debase the value of the product for sale.

In Tottel's *Miscellany* the symbolic capital of courtly love gets cashed in and everyone is rushing for this must-have buy: at a shilling a share, it is the flotation of the century. In the process, however, the truth of courtly love gets told, the reality of its economic transactions revealed, and its value—its "gentleness"—indeed, the whole concept of symbolic or cultural capital that makes that kind of love "worth it," gets debased and destroyed.[44] With the old rewards of grace or virtue now thoroughly debunked, the courtly lover's emotional shortfall converts directly into a negative balance, a loan unpaid, an overdraft he can ill afford and that he "repays" only with debts and threats. In printing his volume Tottel popularized courtly love and the net result was to drive down the price to the point where it began to look very uncourtly indeed. And in buying into Tottel's scheme—in clamoring for his volume and creating the demand for edition after edition—his readers, knowingly or otherwise, contributed to the selfsame process, each purchase bringing down the value a little bit more, to the point at which verses were grown "such merchantable ware/That now for Sonnets sellers are and buyers."[45] It is only logical, therefore, that the one thing that can truly be said to increase all round is loss, and that what Tottel was actually reproducing was, indeed—as the word he inserted into Surrey's parcel—"tene." Given the mechanics of a protocapitalist system in which Tottel was an early speculator, this output represents perhaps a more honest version of what was actually for sale than the glossy promises of "profit and pleasure" trailed in the preface. For all that, however, the prospect of increased indebtedness—if

---

[43] From the colophon. The fact that, in the second and subsequent editions, Tottel removed the reference to himself from the preface—now entitled simply "To the reder" (Q2, p. 1)—might be taken as a gesture of modest self-deprecation or as a desire on his part to suppress his own "ungentle" part in the book's physical manufacture: either way, a classic move on the part of the capitalist to prove himself a "gentleman."

[44] Richard Halpern's brilliant reading of *King Lear* provides a similar example of the way in which an exaggerated and nonreturnable gesture of generosity—the kind of giving away or *dépense* that asserts aristocratic values at the same moment as sacrificing them utterly—represents one reaction to the shift from a feudal to a capitalist economy, *Poetics of Primitive Accumulation*, Chapter 6. What Jonathan Crewe aptly styles "The Suicidal Poetics of the Earl of Surrey" might well be interpreted along similar lines, *Trials of Authorship*, Chapter 2.

[45] From *The Epigrams of Sir John Harington*, ed. Gerard Kilroy (Farnham, 2009), p. 123 (Book 1, epigram 82). Although first published in 1618, Harington's epigrams were circulating in manuscript from the 1590s.

that is what the pain and grief of "tene" can be taken to mean—could be a valuable lesson if only for the forewarned.[46]

Our reader, meanwhile—who by this stage has bought the volume (no question but this is a book he must own)—might wonder as he walks off with his new purchase whether these verbal coincidences, however revealing, might not be the result of mere accident or chance. As he reads on, however, other poems seem to press home the same theme. On the first eight pages alone—all still part of the Surrey section—he finds lyrics in which the natural and economic cycles of growth and return are again, as in the first, arrested, stifled, and stalled. In the sonnet immediately following the first poem, the joys of spring are enumerated through a host of natural examples only to end—the *volta* is delayed to the last possible moment, half-way through the final line—with the utterly depleted and unspringlike state of the speaker: "and yet my sorow springes" (2/2.14). The bathos is all the more powerful for the copious *amplificatio* of the preceding thirteen and a half lines in which examples of "these pleasant thinges" (13) are piled high only to point up their contrast with the speaker's utter lack of pleasure, the paucity of his experience also being mirrored in the unusually small number of rhymes (only two; the typical Surrey sonnet has seven).[47] As Jonathan Crewe remarks, this alienated speaker is "absolutely perverse," a figure of "pure melancholy" who lacks "any apparent recourse to a compensatory or therapeutic poetics": an example of what happens when the normal flows and returns of the natural and economic cycles are abnormally blocked.[48]

The same scenario appears over the page in "When som[m]er toke in hand the winter to assail" (where winter again prevails in the lover's heart in the midst of spring: "My harmes haue euer since increased more and more," 5/5.45), as it does in the sonnet where "Brittle beautie" is blasted as flowers and fruit are by winter frosts (9/9.1). In the Windsor sonnet, the memory of springs past is held in bleak contrast with the speaker's bereft and wintry present in which the only thing resembling a spring is his welling tears: "My vapord eyes suche drery teares distill,/The tender spring whiche quicken where they fall" (11/11.12–13). In the pastoral elegy, "In winters iust returne" (18/18), this apparently perpetual winter provides the setting for a suicidal lover whose story the shepherd speaker hears and whose body he inters.

Amid these poems of unrecuperable loss, moreover, the indelible impact of that painful experience on the speaker's mind and heart seems frequently to be metaphored as something *printed*. One of the sonnets that Surrey wrote lamenting

---

[46] Lerer, *Courtly Letters*, p. 203, proposes rereading Tottel's preface "through Surrey's lines" in "W[yatt] resteth here" (31/35), in order to appreciate the *Miscellany* as a "Tudor book of the dead." I am proposing that we reread Tottel's preface through Surrey's lines in its opening poem, "The sonne hath twise brought forth his tender grene," in order to understand the volume as, ultimately, a testament to the pitfalls of a capitalist economy which it exemplifies at every level.

[47] On the use of *amplificatio* in this sonnet see May, "Popularizing Courtly Poetry," p. 428.

[48] Crewe, *Trials of Authorship*, p. 69.

the death of Wyatt, for example—and specifically mourning the loss to the nation of the poet who had translated the *Penitential Psalms*—is a tormented combination of wish-fulfillment, grief, and displaced rage in which the speaker's profound sense of personal loss is hysterically (suicidally?) transferred onto the pain he wishes those same *Psalms* to engender in the breast of one (barely disguised) king: "In princes hartes gods scourge imprinted depe,/Ought them awake, out of their sinfull slepe" (29/33.13–14). The penitence of a concupiscent king, shamed by the example of King David, would be a worthy "graue" (5) for Wyatt's *Psalms* were they to find themselves engraved there (the implicit pun on the printed prince also serving to the emphasize the point).[49] To give another example, at the end of "Suche waiward waies hath loue"—a long poem in poulter's measure—the world-weary speaker concludes the extensive catalogue of disappointments, contradictions, and unpleasant surprises that he has learned, from bitter experience, love to be, with the following lines:

> The hidden traines I know, and secret snares of loue:
> How soone a loke wil printe a thought, that neuer may remoue.
> The slipper state I know, the sodain turnes from wealth,
> The doubtful hope, the certain woe, and sure despeire of health (4/4.47–50)

The same argument made about the opening poem, with its injunction to "Printe in your harte some parcell of my tene," also applies to these examples: a word quite possibly intended in the pre-technological, "Chaucerian" sense, acquires—by virtue of the medium in which it is communicated on Tottel's pages—a quite new resonance. And again it is the experience of "tene," grief, sorrow, and loss—in the last case, explicitly, the sudden "turnes" from wealth to woe, the negative cycle of emotional outlays unrepaid, loans not honoured, and mounting debts incurred—that, in being reprinted on the thoughts and hearts of Tottel's many readers, is being mechanically reproduced, at their own expense and to their own detriment, many times over.

Similarly, in the elegy "In winters iust returne," the suicidal lover imparts to the speaker the narrative of his unhappy love—essentially a rerun of the Troilus story, this time right to the end (the speaker buries him next to Troilus's grave)—and bids him, along with all those who are reading the poem, to "Come, hie the fast at ones, and print it in thy hart:/So thou shalt know, an I shall tell the, giltlesse how I smart" (18/18.39–40). This request is intended to preserve and disseminate a story that would otherwise go unheard, much as the speaker of the opening poem would "plaine my fill/Vnto my selfe" *unless* his lament were so reproduced in the reader/ Lady's heart. In the case of the elegy, moreover, the suicidal lover's request that his story be reproduced in this particular medium contrasts directly with the medium that had characterized all his productions to date: namely, manuscript poems that

---

[49]   Picking up, perhaps, on Wyatt's prologue to the first Penitential Psalm, CLII in Rebholz, not in Tottel, which describes how David was first struck by sight of Bathsheba and impressed by "The form that Love had printed in his breast" (15). This is Wyatt's only use of the verb "to print" in his poetry.

he had written by hand and sent to his unyielding Lady, all to no avail. Thus the first thing the speaker overhears when he encounters the suicide is the latter bitterly cursing his pen (the bird that bore the quill, the man and knife that sharpened it) and the hand (which he wishes unjointed) with which he wrote those manifestly ineffective, scribal texts: "Wo worth the time, and place, where I so could endite./ And wo be it yet once agayne, the pen that so can write" (18/18.17–18). As reproduced on the pages of Tottel's *Miscellany*—a text which, more than any other, dramatizes the transition from manuscript to print culture—the poem rather neatly proves its own point: that the new medium is much more effective than the old one (unlike the faithless Lady, the speaker is deeply affected, as, presumably, are the many readers invited to imitate his example).[50] Effective, that is, but not in the positive way that Tottel had floated in his preface where learning the art of writing well in verse and producing poems of this kind was supposed to net the reader impressively increasing yields. Rather, print makes the poem widely available and disseminates it far beyond the reach of a coterie manuscript circulation with the result that anyone (anyone who can afford a shilling) is able to sympathize, imitate, and enter into the role. In the process, however, as the poem finds itself literally being printed in the hearts of its many readers, courtly love becomes less gentle, less courtly, less exclusive with each sale until, like the lover himself, the reader ends up with precisely nothing. What is hammering off Tottel's Fleet Street press in multiple editions, therefore—and reproducing itself on the hearts and minds of its customers who seem strangely eager for more—is the message that Troilan, courtly love is a very bad deal and that the investor who buys into it for "profit and pleasure" can look forward, in the end, to nothing but diminishing returns.

---

[50]   Our reader would be entitled to think that "print" and its variants seem to cluster in the opening pages of Tottel. For other uses of "print" in the *Miscellany*, see the elegy by Nicholas Grimald on one A.W. "Who printed liues yet in our hertes alway" (159.5; the poem was dropped in Q2), and a long song by one of Tottel's "uncertain authors" in which Cupid's dart is found to be "So depe imprinted in my thought" (185/154.74). Otherwise, all the uses of the word are Surrey's and all are in the opening pages of Tottel's volume. For other words that convey the same sense of pressure being applied to a surface in order to make a mark—and to which the same shift from a pre- to a posttechnological sense might also apply—see also Surrey's uses of [im]pressed: "mine empressed mynde" (5.41; Q2 reads "mine expressed minde"); "Endlesse despeyre longe thraldome hath imprest" (7/7.8); Wyatt is exceptional in possessing "A hart, where drede was neuer so imprest" (31/35.25); and [en]graved: "The frosen thoughtes grauen by loue" (262/28.18), "Thus I within my wofull brest her picture paint and graue" (265/30.32). "Grave" and its cognates is also Wyatt's suitably melancholy preference, and conveys the sense of a mark that, once made, is quite immovable: see "in my hart, also,/Is grauen with letters depe/A thousand sighes and mo" (65/70.5–7); "So in her stony hart/My plaintes at last shall graue" (77/82.21–2); and "As lead to graue in marble stone:/My song may pearse her hart as sone" (87/91.7–8). See also "But naught availeth faithfulness/To grave within your stony heart" (Rebholz, CX.3–4) and, perhaps most famously, "And graven with diamonds in letters plain/There is written her fair neck round about:/'*Noli me tangere* for Caesar's I am'" (Rebholz, XI.11–13), although neither of these two poems appears in Tottel.

Chapter 3
Tottel's Troy

Alex Davis

The colophon of the first edition of Richard Tottel's *Songes and Sonettes* dates the volume to 5 June 1557. The revised second edition dates from 31 July of the same year, eight weeks later. In between, Tottel published *Certain bokes of Virgiles Aenaeis turned into English*, dated 21 June. It is likely, therefore, that the work of revising, setting and printing the *Songes and Sonettes* was carried on concurrently with that of preparing the translation of the *Aeneid*.[1] Sheets from one volume would have been hung to dry, stacked and assembled alongside those from the other.

As Peter Herman notes elsewhere in this collection, Tottel is usually thought to have been motivated by profit, rather than expansive artistic ambitions. His main business throughout his career was legal texts, and his 1557 activities might plausibly be understood as commercial ventures first and foremost. Nonetheless, there is more than mere chronological coincidence at work here, and there exist a number of similarities and connections between these publications. The Earl of Surrey, translator of the *Aenaeis*, is foregrounded in the *Songs and Sonnets*, in the title ("the right honorable Lorde Henry Haward") and through his positioning as the premier poet in the collection. The 1557 volumes look similar, sharing an elegantly minimal title page format, and, within, verse presented in close-printed black letter script under Italic running titles. Most significantly for what follows, though, there is the matter of Troy.[2] Surrey's translation opens not with the first book of Virgil's poem, but its second. The effect is to plunge his readers almost directly into scenes of devastation and ruinous loss, as Aeneas narrates the fall of his city to the besieging Greek army. The catastrophe is described by the priest of Apollo, Panthus:

> The later day and fate of Troy is come,
> The which no plaint or prayer may auaile.
> Troyans we were, and Troye was somtime,
> And of great fame the Teucrian glorie erst:

---

[1]   See Paul A. Marquis, "Editing and Unediting Richard Tottel's *Songs and Sonettes*," *The Book Collector*, 56.3 (2007): 360–61.

[2]   Earlier, Tottel had also published his edition of Lydgate's *Fall of Princes*, which contains a chapter on Troy. See *A treatise excellent and compendious, shewing and declaring, in maner of tragedye, the falles of sondry most notable princes and princesses* (London, 1554), "Of Priamus king of Troy," F6v.

Fierce Ioue to Grece hath now transposed all.
The Grekes ar Lordes ouer this fired town.
Yonder huge horse, that stands amid our walles,
Sheds armed men. And Sinon victor now,
With scorne of vs, doth set all things on flame.
And rushed in at our vnfolded gates
Are thousands moe, than euer came from Grece.
And some with weapons watch the narrow streetes,
With bright swerdes drawn to slaughter redy bent.[3]

In passages such as these, Surrey's translation rises to an almost hallucinatory intensity: the vast wooden horse, impossibly birthing adult men (elsewhere in the poem, the chamber in which they are concealed is repeatedly described as a "womb"),[4] or indeed casually "shed[ding]" them like so much waste matter; and the scorn of Sinon, the Greek who persuaded the Trojans to admit the horse within the city walls, setting "all things on flame" as if his very contempt were possessed of an incendiary force. It is a nightmarish vision of what it might mean to be the ones from whom the gods have "transposed all," history's losers, and it is embedded within an array of other stories that variously offer to repeat or to redeem this primal scene of loss: Aeneas' destiny as the founder of Rome; Rome's rise to imperial preeminence; Dido's death and Carthage's fall. Surrey's translation, and Richard Tottel's printing of it, repeat the question in relation to changed circumstances. Where might the energies and aspirations of Tudor England, political or cultural, belong on this Virgilian scale of success and failure?

This essay will argue for the fall of Troy as the imaginary point of origin, the crippling yet endlessly productive *ur*-trauma that is replayed and repeated throughout Tottel's publications of 1557: in the second half of Surrey's translation, which skips to Book Four of Virgil's epic and his account of the failed attempt to establish a new Trojan kingdom in Carthage; but also in the lyric verse of the *Songes and Sonettes*. Troy is a constant point of reference in the miscellany: particularly, perhaps, in Surrey's verse; but regularly throughout the rest of the volume. The serviceable anthology of quotably witty love poetry that Slender longs for in *The Merry Wives of Windsor* is marked by a puzzling rhetorical excess—excessive beyond even the hyperbolic conventions of the lyric format, which *Songes and Sonettes* did so much to establish—that has constant recourse to images of loss, betrayal and death; of dynastic ruin; and of a city on fire.

The Matter of Troy

Trojan allusions are threaded throughout the collection. In one of Surrey's poems, a dying lover "refused upon his ladies injust mistaking of his writing" bewails the loss of former happiness:

---

[3]   *Certaine Bokes of Virgiles Aenaeis turned into English meter by the right honorable lorde, Henry Earle of Surrey* (London, 1557), sig. B3r.

[4]   See sigs. A1v, B1v, B2r, B4r.

> Who joied then, but I? who had this worldes blisse?
> Who might compare a life to mine, that never thought on this?
>   But dwelling in this truth, amid my greatest joy,
> Is me befallen a greater losse, then Priam had of Troy.[5]

An almost identical construction appears in the same author's "So cruell prison." Most likely composed during a period of imprisonment in Windsor Castle in 1537, this poem mourns Surrey's childhood friend Henry Fitzroy, Duke of Richmond and bastard son of Henry VIII:

> So cruell prison how could betide, alas
> As proude Windsor? where I in lust and joy,
> With a kinges sonne, my childishe yeres did passe,
> In greater feastes than Priams sonnes of Troy ... (15: 1–4)

Once again, the Trojan allusion compactly evokes past felicity and the inevitability of its loss.[6]

Often the tragic associations are so strong as to scarcely require emphasis. Consider the ominous undertones that a reference to the judgment of Paris imports into the following short poem, "Of the token which his love sent him":

> The golden apple that the Troyan boy,
> Gave to Venus the fayrest of the thre,
> Which was the cause of all the wrack of Troy,
> Was not received with a greater joy,
> Than was the same (my love) thou sent to me,
> It healed my sore it made my sorowes free,
> It gave me hope it banisht mine annoy:
> Thy happy hand full oft of me was blist,
> That can geue such a salve when that thou list. (201: 1–9)

The poem is structured around the baffling disjunction between the situation it describes and the comparison used to elucidate it. "The golden apple ... was not received with greater joy/Than was the same (my love) thou sent me": the lover

---

[5]   See *Tottel's Miscellany: Songs and Sonnets of Henry Howard, Earl of Surrey, Sir Thomas Wyatt and Others*, eds. Amanda Holton and Tom MacFaul (London, 2011), poem 18, ll. 49–52. I will be referring to this edition throughout, which prints the second, revised quarto of 1557. Further references, to number of poem and then line numbers if relevant, appear parenthetically. I have also consulted *Tottel's Miscellany, 1557–1587*, ed. Hyder Rollins (2 vols., Cambridge, 1965), which takes the first quarto as its copy text.

[6]   For an analysis of the transgressive force of the Trojan allusions in this poem, see Candace Lines, "The Erotic Politics of Grief in Surrey's 'So Crewell Prison'," *Studies in English Literature, 1500–1900*, 46.1 (2006): 1–26. As Lines notes, p. 4, Surrey "writes himself into the royal family" by comparing himself to a king's son (inadvertently anticipating his execution for encroaching upon the privileges of the crown). He also imaginatively encompasses Henry VIII's death by recasting him as the doomed Priam.

seems naively delighted by the gift of this "token," yet the reference to Troy suggests that disaster is in imminent prospect. What kind of "salve" is it that might coherently be compared to the apple "which was the cause of all the wrack of Troy"?

Elsewhere, a forsaken lady compares herself to Dido, the central figure in the second half of Surrey's *Aenaeis*:

> Alas poore Dido now I fele
> Thy present painful state,
> When false Eneas did hym stele
> From thee at Carthage gate.
> And left thee slepyng in thy bed,
> Regarding not what he had sed. (192: 31–6)

In Virgil, the bed in which Dido sleeps becomes her funeral pyre, as she ends her life in despair at Aeneas' betrayal. The allusion is appropriate, for the poem develops in an increasingly suicidal direction, with the lady declaring that her tears will "moist the earth in such degree,/That I may drowne therin," and ending with the declaration that she is "lyke to dye" (192: 45–6, 54).

The *Songes and Sonettes* include "The song of Iopas," a poem by Thomas Wyatt that supplies words to a song mentioned in Book One of Virgil's epic (137), and a poem (omitted from the second edition) in praise of the *Aeneid*.[7] The miscellany also extends its range of Trojan allusion well beyond the merely Virgilian. It contains a translation from Ovid's *Heroides*, with "The beginning of the epistle of Penelope to Vlisses, made into verse" (225), and, in particular, it contains a rich seam of references to Geoffrey Chaucer's *Troilus and Criseyde*, which is intensively mined for scenes of romantic abjection and despair. Once again the Earl of Surrey provides a paradigmatic brief example. The poem mentioned above, on the suitor "refused upon his ladies iniust mistaking of his writing," concludes with the initial Trojan allusion having run its predictable, lethal course, and with the narrator seeking to bury the now-dead lover:

> Then as I could devise, to seke I thought it best,
> Where I might finde some worthy place, for such a corse to rest.
> And in my minde it came: from thence not far away,
> Where Creseids love, king Priams sonne, the worthy Troilus lay.
> By him I made his tomb, in token he was true:
> And as to him belongeth well, I covered it with blew.
> Whose soule, by angels power, departed not so sone,
> But to the heavens, lo it fled, for to receive his dome. (18: 75–82)

We might be teased by the slight grammatical uncertainty, as to who the "he" who "was true" is: the dead suitor, or Troilus? But of course it doesn't matter. Each, as an equivalently faithful lover, can stand as the other's "token." The final

---

7   Rollins, vol. 1, p. 99.

lines of this piece recall the ending of Chaucer's poem, with its sudden shift into a supermundane perspective, as the spirit of dead Troilus, having ascended to heaven, laughs at the "wo" of those who mourn him and damns the "blynde lust" of earthly lovers.[8] *Troilus and Criseyde* provides the source for the unexpectedly consolatory description of the soul's flight to the "heavens," but Surrey's poem modifies Chaucer's flat rejection of earthly concerns. Here, the lover's tomb is strewn with the blue flowers (Emrys Jones notes that Troilus had sent Criseyde a "blewe rynge"), and he seems to be predicted a heavenly reward for his faithfulness.[9]

One could multiply examples. However, it is worth noting that the second, post-*Aenaeis* edition of the *Songes and Sonettes* adds a number of particularly forceful pieces alluding to the matter of Troy. Most substantially, there is a poem (discussed at length below) "Of the troubled comon welth," which seems to condemn the rebellion of Sir Thomas Wyatt the younger in 1554 by reworking into rhymed verses a scene from Book Two of the *Aeneid*. But there is also a general heightening of the density of Trojan references. Thus, we have the "praise" of an anonymous lady, "M":

> In court as I behelde, the beauty of eche dame,
> Of right my thought from all the rest should .M. steale the same.
> But, er I ment to iudge: I vewed with such advise.
> As retchelesse dome should not invade: the boundes of my devise.
> And, whiles I gased long: such heat did brede within
> As Priamus towne felt not more flame, when did the bale begin. (266: 1–6)

The lady is so fair, "That Paris would have Helene left, and .M. beauty chose" (266: 12), had he known her. Would that mean disaster amplified or disaster averted, we might wonder? In another poem the lover, undeceived, finds himself to be no Ulysses, wedded to a faithful Penelope, but instead bitterly situated in "Troylous case" (232: 5). And in the final lines of this short lyric, Helen of Troy is deployed as an emblem "Of the vanitie of mans lyfe":

> Where is become that wight
> For whose sake Troy towne:
> Withstode the grekes till ten yeres fight,
> Had rasde their walles adowne.
> Did not the wormes consume,
> Her caryon to the dust?
> Did dreadfull death forbeare his fume
> For beauty, prise, or lust? (257: 13–20)[10]

---

[8]   See *Troilus and Criseyde*, in *The Riverside Chaucer*, ed. Larry D. Benson (Oxford, 1987), 5: 1821, 1824. Further references are to this edition.

[9]   See *Henry Howard, Earl of Surrey: Poems*, ed. Emrys Jones (Oxford, 1964), p. 117 and *Troilus and Criseyde*, 3: 885.

[10]   With their combined references to Helen, dust, and death, these are lines that might lie somewhere in the background to Thomas Nashe's famous song beginning "Brightnesse

Helen, and the war fought over her, enjoy a paradoxical status here, simultaneously evoked as sources of exceptional "prise" (such beauty, and so many lives lost) and positioned as mere instances of a universal fate. "Dreadfull death" is indifferent, even to Helen—and, we may therefore be assured, to us too.

Troy, then, is a significant presence throughout the collection—and one with a structural, as well as an ornamental function. Allusion to the matter of Troy in the *Songes and Sonettes* harbors the potential to expand beyond its merely local contexts and to begin first to draw in, and then ambiguously position itself in relation to, earlier versions of the Troy myth. It is to this expansive, self-referential, and also powerfully revisionary quality that this discussion will now turn.

Troy and *Translatio*

What might happen if we were to follow Troy as a motif recurring throughout Tottel's activities of 1557? These references are individually often small; conceivably even of no more than passing interest. Cumulatively, though, they resolve themselves into a roadmap that can guide us through the various interests of the collection and the kinds of cultural work it performs. In the first place, one is struck by the sheer mobility of the motif. If it exists within a certain publishing venture of 1557, Troy is also very much part of a past, inasmuch as the *Songes and Sonettes* repackage Wyatt and Surrey's literary activities from the 1530s and 40s. And beyond these decades, further histories still disclose themselves, always marked by their engagement with the Trojan theme: the fourteenth century, evoked through references to Chaucer's *Troilus and Criseyde*; further back again, the Rome of Augustus and then the mythic origins that Virgil imagined for it in the *Aeneid*; and finally the Homeric literary tradition that he reconstructed in the process. The Greek, the Roman, the medieval, the Henrician, the Marian: Troy establishes lines of connection between zones of history (distant and proximate, real and imagined) that we might otherwise seek to keep conceptually distinct.

Troy therefore speaks to the debate over the literary significance of the *Songes and Sonettes*, and provides a lens through which this question can be understood as, in essence, one of the collection's temporality. Is this a ground-breaking document in the history of English literature and a stimulus to future literary production? For Hyder Rollins, the miscellany ignited a "poetic fire" that blazed brightest during the reign of Elizabeth I.[11] Or is it, as C.S. Lewis claimed, a "neo-medieval" collection, forward-looking only in its promotion of a certain metrical regularity?[12]

---

falls from the ayre ..." See *The Works of Thomas Nashe*, ed. Ronald B. McKerrow, rev. F.P. Wilson (5 vols., Oxford, 1958), vol. 3, p. 283. Tottel's poem is also noteworthy for those interested in the collection's religious positioning: it reappears in British Library Sloane MS 1896, among a series of poems commemorating Protestant martyrs (fol. 42).

[11]   Rollins, vol. 2, p. 3.

[12]   C.S. Lewis, *English Literature in the Sixteenth Century Excluding Drama* (Oxford, 1954), pp. 237–8.

Might it even, as James Simpson has suggested, exemplify an "elegiac" mode that articulates a form of historical consciousness even in its very solipsism and absence of reference to anything outside of the lover's anguished subjectivity?[13] Troy, I want to suggest, not only exists within various different time zones within the miscellany; it also provides an array of scripts through which to understand the traffic between these zones. It evokes narratives that constantly threaten to surge outwards and rewrite the entire collection in their image, contextualizing the volume's ambitions in relation to past and present. For above all, Troy is a motif that signifies translation, both in the narrow sense of movement between languages, and also in the larger one of cultural transmission, *translatio*, from the past and into the future.

This is how Troy figures in W.A. Sessions's recent readings of the *Songes and Sonettes*'s dominant presence, the Earl of Surrey. For Sessions, both Wyatt and Surrey can be understood as pursuing a conscious project of humanistic *renovatio*.[14] Surrey is therefore not only the translator of Virgil, but also a poet with Virgilian cultural aspirations. As Sessions's biography of the poet explains, for Surrey

> the poet could be … a protector of the community, the guardian of language as Aeneas had guarded the household gods, as Virgil had glorified Augustus and the new empire, and as Petrarch, a diplomat like Wyatt, had worked to unify Europe and renew Rome, even receiving his laureate there. Troy—and its genetic offspring in the new city of Rome and the revived new Rome—now stood in the protection of the poets, to paraphrase Anchises' farewell to Troy in Book II of Surrey's *Aeneid*: "O native Gods, your family defend!/Preserve your line! This warning comes of you,/And Troy stands in your protection now."[15]

The reference here is to the *Aeneid*'s powerful weaving together of a political narrative (about the *imperium sine fine* of Rome) and a literary one (the reworking of Homeric epic into Latin) through its description of the flight from Troy. The Aenean exodus simultaneously founds a new empire and models the westwards transfer of literary authority.[16] These ambitions in turn find their echo in the *Songes and Sonettes*, which, on Sessions's account, blends old and new in a "progressive logic" that mirrors the Marian work of religious restoration and that was to produce a publication "as revolutionary as that of the *Lyrical Ballads* in 1798."[17]

---

[13] See James Simpson's chapter on "The Elegiac" in *The Oxford English Literary History, Volume 2, 1350–1547: Reform and Cultural Revolution* (Oxford, 2002), pp. 121–90.

[14] W.A. Sessions, "Surrey's Wyatt: Autumn 1542 and the New Poet," in Peter C. Herman (ed.), *Rethinking the Henrician Era: Essays on Early Tudor Texts and Contexts* (Urbana, 1994), pp. 168–92.

[15] W.A. Sessions, *Henry Howard The Poet Earl of Surrey: A Life* (Oxford, 1999), pp. 245–6.

[16] On this latter theme, see Édouard Jeauneau, *Translatio Studii: The Transmission of Learning. A Gilsonian Theme* (Toronto, 1995).

[17] Sessions, *Henry Howard*, pp. 273, 177.

In what follows, I would like to take seriously Session's proposal regarding the relevance of a Virgilian framework to the *Songes and Sonettes*, while developing a slightly modified account of what this might involve for the collection. The raw materials for a narrative of *renovatio* certainly exist in Tottel's 1557 publications. The printer's preface to the *Songes and Sonettes* advertises the volume as one showing that English can finally hold its own as a medium of cultivated expression, alongside "divers Latines, Italians, & other." These poems have been published "to the honor of the english tong, and for the profit of the studious of Englishe eloquence" (p. 3). Within the collection, we find Surrey's elegies for Wyatt, which celebrate him as an author whose daily labor was for "Britaines gaine," and who eventually "reft Chaucer the glory of his wit" (35: 8, 14). And Surrey's *Aenaeis* too might be understood as contributing to a project of national revival through the revival of eloquence. Yet in both the *Songes and Sonettes* and in the *Aenaeis* we find the matter of Troy systematically reworked into a narrative of disaster and loss, and in particular into a lexicon of tragic love stories. Troy acts here almost exclusively to pinpoint moments of exclusion, alienation and grief (the heavenward surge at the end of the poem on the "refused" lover is entirely untypical). This is also the case in Surrey's translation. As David Carlson points out, by focusing in on Books Two and Four of the *Aeneid*, "Surrey elected to concentrate on both the prototype and the antitype—Troy and Carthage—of Vergil's *imperium sine fine*, power without end, built on the ruin of these others."[18] Tottel's 1557 publications work to evoke scenarios in which cultural achievement is always built out of—is profoundly embedded within—some antecedent catastrophe. This is an order of progression that involves repeated returns to destruction—one in which, to quote Benjamin Péret, "one ruin drives out the one before and kills it."[19]

Recall Panthus' lament, that "of great fame the Teucrian glorie erst:/Fierce Ioue to Grece hath now transposed all." Here, the poem forcibly suggests that this is what *renovatio*, or *translatio*—or, as Surrey would have it, "transposition"—must always emerge out of: dispossession and loss. A translation like Surrey's mines the past for new literary models and sources of cultural authority, such as might in turn become templates for future cultural production; but in so doing it propagates a poetics of ruination. It brings out the sense in which, rather than simply or complacently functioning to celebrate the rise of Roman world power, there is something doubled and melancholic about the *Aeneid*, meditating throughout the losses incurred by empire. These are the "further voices" of the poem beyond

---

[18] David R. Carlson, "The Henrician Courtier Writing in Manuscript and Print: Wyatt, Surrey, Bryan, and Others" in Kent Cartwright (ed.), *A Companion to Tudor Literature* (Chichester, 2010), p. 155. And see also Stephen Guy-Bray, "Embracing Troy: Surrey's *Aeneid*" in Alan Shepard and Stephen D. Powell (eds.), *Fantasies of Troy: Classical Tales and the Social Imaginary in Medieval and Early Modern Europe* (Toronto, 2004), pp. 177–92, for a powerful meditation upon the thematics of memory and loss at work in Surrey's translation of Virgil.

[19] 'Ruines: Ruine des Ruines', *Minotaure*, 12–13 (May, 1939): 58, cited in Hal Foster, *Compulsive Beauty* (Cambridge, 1993), p. 166.

that of imperial celebration, comprehensively explored by modern criticism and intermittently present (as Craig Kallendorf has argued) in Renaissance readings of Virgil.[20] Certainly one must concede the presence of much that is entirely straightforwardly affective and impressive and serviceable in all these texts. But it is at the very moment of offering these poems for use that Richard Tottel's 1557 publications also foreground all that is least digestible, least easily assimilated in the myth of Troy. They represent a paradoxical attempt to assemble a Virgilian moment of cultural *renovatio* out of the fragments of Virgilian counternarrative.

"Raging Love": Lyric Voices and Literary Inheritance

We can see these contradictory dynamics at work in one of Surrey's most compelling and popular poems from the *Songes and Sonettes*:[21]

The lover comforteth himselfe with the worthinesse of his love.

> When raging love with extreme payne
> Most cruelly distrains my hart:
> When that my teares, as floods of rayne,
> Beare witnes of my wofull smart:
> When sighes have wasted so my breath,
> That I lye at the point of death.
>
>   I call to minde the navie great,
> That the Grekes brought to Troye towne:
> And how the boysteous windes did beate
> Their ships, and rente their sayles adown,
> Till Agamemnons daughters blood
> Appeasde the Gods, that them withstood.
>
>   And how that in those ten yeres warre,
> Full many a bloodie dede was done,
> And many a lord, that came full farre,
> There caught his bane (alas) to soone:
> And many a good knight overron,
> Before the Grekes had Helene won.
>
>   Then thinck I thus: sithe such repaire,

---

[20] See for example Oliver Lyne, *Further Voices in Vergil's Aeneid* (Oxford, 1987), David Quint, "Repetition and Ideology in the *Aeneid*," in *Epic and Empire: Politics and Generic Form From Virgil to Milton* (Princeton, 1993), pp. 50–96; and Craig Kallendorf, *The Other Virgil: Pessimistic Readings of the Aeneid in Early Modern Culture* (Oxford, 2007).

[21] "When raging love" was registered as a ballad three times before 1569. It also became a productive source for parody and further ballad production. There exists a "Ballad of Unthrifts" beginning "When raging louts …," whilst Richard Jones's collection of broadside ballads, the *Handefull of pleasant delites*, contains "The complaint of a woman Louer, To the tune of, Raging loue." See Rollins, vol. 2, p. 109–10, 142–3.

So long time warre of valiant men,
Was all to winne a lady faire:
Shall I not learne to suffer then,
And thinck my life well spent to be,
Serving a worthier wight than she?
      Therfore I never will repent,
But paines contented still endure.
For like as when, rough winter spent,
The pleasant spring straight draweth in ure:
So after raging stormes of care
Joyful at length may be my fare. (16: 1–30)

This is a poem that uses the image of Troy to rework the trauma of cultural translation into an idiom of love poetry. Having called Troy "to minde," the anguished poet reasons by comparison that his own story might eventually have a "joyful" conclusion. The poem thus looks back to a vanished Trojan past and recovers a strange consolatory potential from its disasters. But it is also profoundly engaged in the meditation of a more strictly literary kind of pastness. It is a formally inventive piece, yet it is also one dense with history, with allusion to its own precedents; it aims to evoke the sedimented history of transmission that provides the foundation for its achievement.[22]

"When raging love" harks back to antique accounts of the matter of Troy, of epic battle and the tragedy of the house of Atreus. It also evokes medieval redactions of this tradition, with its talk of "knight[s]," of "valiant men" competing "to winne a lady faire." These parallel strains of influence are then combined with a more up-to-date model of graceful, continental verse composition: the verse structure of tetrameter stanzas rhymed *a b a b c c* had been used for musical renderings of Petrarchan verse.[23] The form of the poem might thus be described as that of a palimpsest: antique legend; medieval diction; modern form, each marked by its successive engagement with Trojan subject matter and each superimposed upon its predecessor without ever totally obscuring it—although the relations between these literary strata are more involved than this description might suggest, since Chaucerian Troy itself represents an earlier point of connection between these different temporal levels, incorporating as it does the first translation of Petrarch into English.[24]

Celebrating the productivity of the past as a resource to "call to mind," then, the poem simultaneously evokes a history of transmission, of past resourcefulness. To the extent that it does so, it represents an exemplary instance of humanist *translatio*, and for W.A. Sessions it is, therefore also, logically, a Virgilian poem.

---

[22] In Sessions's first study of Surrey, "When raging love" is the showpiece poem that introduces his discussion of the poet's works by articulating a poetics of "translation." See William A. Sessions, *Henry Howard, Earl of Surrey* (Boston, 1986), pp. 27–39.

[23] See Sessions, *Henry Howard, Earl of Surrey*, p. 29.

[24] See *Troilus and Criseyde* 1: 400–420.

He writes of the lover that, by the end of the poem, "as an integrated human being, he is now at peace and resolute":

> The pilgrimage of the lover is … heroic. To use Surrey's own residual myths, it is an Aeneas-progression towards the lover's own destiny with a possible ("may be") happy ending, a personal destiny mirroring the larger Rome of human continuity, which itself recapitulated and transformed the losses of Troy, the oldest subtext in Surrey's mythologizing.[25]

But this is perhaps only half the story. For the achievement of "When raging love" in yoking romantic abjection to a genealogy of poetic styles is radically unstable. To the extent that the flight from Troy is available as *the* model for humanist translation, the poem exists, and shows itself to exist, in a state of tacit bad faith. Its affective force develops out of the way it evokes grief, not so much directly, but instead via allusion to the fall of Troy, marked by the double absences produced by death in battle on the one hand and the long passage of time on the other. Yet even while "When raging love" mourns Greek lives spent in pursuit of Helen and strongly suggests the futility of the siege of Troy, it shows itself to be all too aware, in its layering of literary histories, of just how productive the city's fall has been: of the seeds scattered and sown though space and time by its destruction, not just in terms of the different national traditions that the exodus from Troy supposedly founds (Aeneas and Rome, Brutus and Britain, Francion and France), but also of the richly interlaced networks of cultural production that spring up in its wake.

To this fundamental short circuit in the poem's logic, we might add a supplementary one, which develops along the faultline provided by the poem's account of gender relations, and which acts to call into question its attempt to establish a secure source of "worth" (poetic or social value) in the past. Jonathan Goldberg has argued in his discussion of the "Tottelization of Henrician verse" that we need to be attentive to the narratives of desire in these poems beyond those heterosexual scenarios proposed by their repackaging in 1557, when virtually every lyric text seems to be conceived of as dealing with the interactions of a male lover and his female mistress.[26] "When raging love" provides a striking example:

> Then thinck I thus: sithe such repaire,
> So long time warre of valiant men,
> Was all to winne a lady faire:
> Shall I not learne to suffer then,
> And thinck my life well spent to be,
> Serving a worthier wight than she? (16: 19–24)

---

[25] Sessions, *Henry Howard, Earl of Surrey*, p. 38.

[26] Jonathan Goldberg, *Sodometries: Renaissance Texts, Modern Sexualities* (Stanford, 1992), p. 59.

The archaic word "wight" could signify either a man or a woman.[27] The more conventional reading would select the latter option, in which case the poem's underlying argumentative structure would read as follows: "considering the lives prematurely lost in pursuit of Helen, I can surely 'learne to suffer,' given that my mistress is "worthier" than she was." But in the context of an allusion to service, and within the chivalric field of reference established by the rest of the poem, we might also plausibly read it as offering a different, fully misogynistic logic: "considering the lives prematurely lost in pursuit of Helen—only a woman, after all—I can surely 'learne to suffer,' given that I serve, or love, a worthy man." (The "valiant *men*," in this reading, would exist in clear opposition to the "*lady* faire," and in alignment with the "wight," rather than the comparative "worthier" simply relating the latter two as women, more and less good.) Later lyric conventions may have rendered this second option comparatively illegible, but there is at least one telling piece of evidence in its favor. As Hyder Rollins notes, the initial letters of each stanza form an acrostic: WIATT.[28]

In each case, the poem might be seen to anticipate the debate scene in *Troilus and Cressida*, with its use of the question of Helen as a platform from which to broach questions of value more generally. As Shakespeare's Hector puts it, "Brother, she is not worth what she doth cost/The holding."[29] But if the ambiguity alerts us to the different ways in which the poem might seek to mobilize the values provided by a heroic past, it also calls these efforts into question. There is something off-kilter about the order of knightly "worth" envisaged in "When raging love." Consider the reference to the sacrifice of Iphigenia, "Agamemnons daughters blood," coupled with the parallel emphasis on the performance of "bloodie dede[s]' on the fields of Troy. Rather than operating through the exchange of women, the homosocial order envisaged in this poem commits itself instead to their expenditure (Iphigenia) and abduction (Helen). Women, here, seem unable to facilitate or secure interaction between men; instead, they are placed in opposition to those interactions. The consequence seems to be a kind of collapse of genealogical continuity: murdered daughters and prematurely dead sons. "Many a lord," we read, "… caught his bane (alas) to soone" at Troy. The lines of literary inheritance evoked by the poem find their negative image in the lineages extinguished in the Trojan expedition, even while they issue from it.

These intimations are further developed through the poem's positioning in the *Songes and Sonettes* (both the first and second edition), where it is followed by the "Complaint of the absence of her lover being upon the sea," beginning "O happy dames …" This poem identifies a voice of complaint as the inevitable companion to the chivalric order evoked in the preceding poem. It picks up the metaphor of

---

[27]   We have already seen the word used of Helen of Troy, above (257: 13). For an example of a male "wight," see the poem on the "lover refused," who is asked, "What woful wight art thou?" (18: 29).

[28]   Rollins, vol. 2, p. 143.

[29]   *Troilus and Cressida*, ed. David Bevington (Walton-on-Thames, 1998), 2.2.51–2.

the sea voyage, present throughout "When raging love," in order to invoke a "ship, freight with remembrance/Of thoughts, and pleasures past" in which the speaker's lover sails (17: 8–9). When, the speaker wonders, will he return? The general ruin of chivalry envisioned in the preceding poem cannot fail to lend this question an ominous edge. And once again these intimations of disaster are sharpened through allusion to the Trojan myth:

> Drowned in teares to mourne my losse,
> I stand the bitter night,
> In my window, where I may see,
> Before the windes how the clowdes flee.
> Lo, what a Mariner love hath made me. (17: 24–7)

Emrys Jones notes that these lines echo Surrey's description of the just-abandoned Dido in his *Aenaeis*: "by her windowes the Queen the peping day/Espyed, and nauie with splaid sailes depart" (F4v).[30] Dido wakes to see Aeneas' fleet fleeing Carthage; the faithful narrator of "O happy dames" longingly waits for the lover's return. The poem also recalls the Penelope of Ovid's *Heroides*, and it thus evokes a composite of women abandoned by their menfolk as a consequence of events at Troy.

"O happy dames" has often been read as Surrey's ventriloquization of his wife's voice during one of his periodic absences on military service in France between 1543 and 1546.[31] Such a narrowly biographical reading may seem reductive, but debate over the poem's narratorial politics continues, energized by its appearance in the Devonshire manuscript, which is substantially compiled by women.[32] Perhaps we might note that, Tottel's title aside, the speaker of the poem is never overtly identified as female. We have an appeal to "happy dames," but with no necessary implication that the poem is composed by an unhappy one, and the option of a man longing the return of his male love might be considered fully open. What is clear, though, is that "O happy dames" aligns itself—from whatever subject position—with a tradition of female-voiced complaint that has often been understood as standing in opposition to epic values.[33] It ironizes the gender politics

---

[30]   See Jones, *Henry Howard*, p. 119. Sessions further develops the parallel: *Henry Howard, Earl of Surrey*, p. 79.

[31]   The claims to imperial status of Henry VIII—the Caesar of Wyatt's "Who so list to hunt"—were buttressed with reference to Trojan mythology. To this extent, we might understand Surrey's campaigning in Northern France to have been undertaken in the service of a "New Troy," founded by Brute, Aeneas' grandson.

[32]   See Elizabeth Heale, "'Desiring Women Writing': Female Voices and Courtly 'Balets' in Some Early Tudor Manuscript Albums," in Victoria E. Burke and Jonathan Gibson (eds.)., *Early Modern Women's Manuscript Writing: Selected Papers From the Trinity/Trent Colloquium* (Aldershot, 2004), pp. 9–31.

[33]   Although, given the status of Book Four of the *Aeneid* as a touchstone for this tradition, it should be evident that it is fully contained by and emerges out of epic forms, too.

of "When raging love" by fully bringing out what the earlier poem only hints at: the extent to which that poem's investment in masculine worth is bound up with the prospect of its loss; the inevitability of its going away never to return, so to speak. It suggests that the poetic order adumbrated in the earlier poem is grounded in the elegizing of lost honor and the sacrifice of women to the interests of "good knight[s]" and "valiant men." And finally, it emphasizes the costs of that loss, whereas the former poem leans more towards emphasizing its productivity.

Allusion to Troy, here, stands for a more complex mobilization of the past than W.A. Sessions would always allow. It *is* about wholeness and integrity—but it also permits us a view into the historical sources that underpin that vision, and exposes them as a fantasy. These paired lyrics self-consciously evoke a poetic tradition that reproduces itself as much through absence and negativity as through presence. Troy is both the name of what is lost and the motif that keeps loss in play, endlessly productive. They therefore propose an ironic or dialectical relation between ruin and achievement, and while Tottel's pairing of "O happy dames" with "When raging love" certainly serves to position the former poem as the desolate, yearning counterpoint to projects of national self-aggrandizement, whether military or cultural, one would not, in the end, want to read it as the merely "oppositional" antithesis of its companion poem. It is itself too comprehensively embedded in the procedures of humanistic *renovatio* to disclaim liability for the costs that project might incur, and if it longs for the return of what has been swallowed up in the Greek expedition to Troy, this only repeats the Trojan thematics of "When raging love" in a different key. Loss is what allusion to Troy is all about; not its opposite. If, then, there is something here that might want to disavow the disseminative movement produced by Troy's fall, that wishes itself undone, there is something too that also allows us to intuit the compromised character of Trojan literary production—the perfect model, as it might be, for the moral flexibility required of what Greg Walker has described Surrey's poetry as: writing under tyranny.[34]

What is "Trouth"? Troy, Chaucer, and Didactic Verse

It might be thought that these are just the complexities proper to a certain kind of lyric verse, and that they therefore have little bearing upon the comfortable middle range of "drab," moralizing texts that dominate the *Songes and Sonettes*: poems in praise of "The meane estate" (160, 163); poems declaring that "All worldly pleasures vade" (166); poems written "Against wicked tonges" (147); and such like. In what follows, I want to show much the same uncertainties at play in relation to another two poems. These are both taken from the section of the miscellany devoted to "uncertain auctors", but are centrally related to its Chaucerian antecedents. What they suggest is the capacity of Trojan thematics

---

[34] Greg Walker, *Writing Under Tyranny: English Literature and the Henrician Reformation* (Oxford, 2005).

to extract ambiguity from even the most apparently coherent and authoritative didactic verse.

One of the most substantial, and most strikingly corrosive deployments of the Troy legend in the *Songes and Sonettes* comes in "A comparison of his love wyth the faithful and painful love of Troylus to Creside." The poem opens:

> I read how Troylus served in Troy,
> A lady long and many a day,
> And how he bode so great anoy,
> For her as all the stories say. (206: 1–4)

The emphasis, made at the very head of the poem, falls upon the firmly established character of the legend of Troilus, on antecedent literary production. (From the poem immediately following "A comparison," it will become clear that it is Chaucer in particular who is relevant here.) And yet, having alluded to this bedrock of familiar "stories," the poem proceeds to give a deliberately partial account of them. Troilus' demeanor was changed by his love for Criseyde, we read. He kept to his chamber, he sighed, he called her name, he wept. But all was well in the end:

> … she that was his maistresse good,
> And lothe to see her servant so,
> Became Phisicion to his wo. (206: 40–42)

Therefore, the poem argues, let the lover's mistress do the same:

> … if you can compare and way,
> And how I stand in every plight,
> Then this for you I dare well say,
> Your hart must nedes remorce of right
> To graunt me grace and so to do,
> As Creside then did Troylus to. (206: 67–72)

"Set me," the poem concludes, "in as happy case,/As Troylus with his lady was" (206: 83–4). Of Criseyde's forced removal to the Greek camp, her new relationship with Diomedes, Troilus' despair and death, we read nothing whatsoever. Chaucer's Criseyde had predicted, more or less accurately, that "of me, unto the worldes ende,/Shal neyther ben ywriten nor ysonge/No good word, for thise bokes wol me shende" (5: 1058–60) "A comparison" seems determined to make a liar of her. The poem has sardonically excised the second half of Chaucer's poem from its field of reference, an act of willed amnesia that plays out to calculatedly provocative effect:

> And truth it is except they lye,
> From that day forth her study went,
> To shew to love him faithfully,
> And his whole minde full to content.
> So happy a man at last was he,
> And eke so worthy a woman she. (206: 49–54)

To which, one can only respond that this really is not the "truth" at all (the carefully selected verb "to shew" notwithstanding), unless "all the stories" referred to at the opening of the poem "lye" in recording Criseyde's lack of faith and in ascribing to Troilus, not happiness "at last," but rather abandonment, heartbreak and premature death. And that if they do lie about this, then the poem has no business in pretending that it is authorized by them; for that too would be a kind of untruth.

In both 1557 editions of the *Songes and Sonettes*, "A comparison" is immediately followed by a poem entitled "To leade a vertuous and honest life":

> Flee from the prease and dwell with sothfastnes
> Suffise to thee thy good though it be small,
> For horde hath hate, and climing ticklenes
> Praise hath envy, and weall is blinde in all
> Favour no more, then thee behove shall.
> Rede well thy selfe that others well canst rede,
> And trouth shall thee deliver, it is no drede.
>
> 　　　Paine thee not eche croked to redresse,
> In hope of her that turneth as a ball,
> Great rest standeth in litle businesse,
> Beware also to spurne against a nall,
> Strive not as doth a crocke against a wall,
> Deme first thy selfe, then demest others dede
> And trouth shall thee deliver, it is no drede.
>
> 　　　That thee is sent, receive in buxomnesse,
> The wrestling of this world asketh a fall:
> Here is no home, here is but wildernesse.
> Forth pilgryme forth, forth beast out of thy stall,
> Looke up on hye, geve thankes to God of all:
> Weane well thy lust, and honest life ay leade,
> So trouth shall thee deliver, it is no dreade. (207: 1–21)

This, unattributed, is one of the most widely copied of Chaucer's poems, the *Balade de Bon Conseyl*. We are more or less obliged to read this poem in the light of the outrageous claim made in the preceding Trojan piece: "truth it is" that Troilus and Criseyde lived happily together until the end of their lives. The deliberate assertion of the truth of a transparent lie—a lie made, moreover, in relation to another Chaucerian text—exerts a distorting force on the second poem, bending quite out of shape the apparent confidence of its biblical refrain (which derives from John 8: 32: "the truth shall make you free"). Read in the light of the double dealing of "A comparison," *Truth* (the poem's modern title) emerges as an unexpectedly provocative and even disorienting piece of writing.[35]

---

[35] This is not how the poem is usually read. Paul Strohm's *Social Chaucer* (Cambridge, 1989) claims that were it not for the destabilizing perspective provided by the manuscript envoy to "thou Vache" (not printed by Tottel), the poem "would pose no … interpretative problems," p. 74. Similarly, in his discussion of Chaucer's uses of the word "trouthe,"

"A comparison" begins with the words, "I read"—before proceeding to systematically travesty what the poet must, in truth, have been reading about events in Troy. The first stanza of *Truth* urges us: "Rede well thy selfe that others well canst rede." "Rede," this time, signifies good counsel. We might take the line to mean something like, "govern yourself that you may govern others well" (or, conceivably, "that you may be virtuously transparent and legible to them"). How might this second kind of reading look when read against the first? "A comparison" is certainly untruthful. Does it offer good advice? To the extent that it urges that the poet's love should imitate Criseyde, one would have to say that it does not. And after such a spectacularly ill-considered recommendation, just how much trust should one place in the advice about advice offered in *Truth*? These are both poems that explore intuitions about betrayal and uncertainty through the figure of a fickle woman: Criseyde on the one hand, and Fortune ("her that turneth as a ball") on the other. The first poem does so implicitly, and might therefore be said itself to enact a kind of witty betrayal of its readers. The second seems all candor and simplicity. Yet—following the thread laid down by the homophonic pairing, "read" and "rede"—the guidance it offers emerges as really quite peculiar, even contradictory.

Despite its exhortatory tone ("Forth pilgryme!") and its apparent concern for a kind of exemplary, even communal, virtue (for "others ... rede"), the poem might be described as actually advising its readers as follows: be pleasant only when it is profitable ("Favour no more, then thee behove shall"); best not try to right wrongs ("Pain thee not eche croked to redresse"); take whatever comes to you but don't exert yourself particularly ("That thee is sent, receive in buxomnesse"); do little ("Great rest standeth in litle businesse"). Lower your expectations, be prudent, wait and see. The poem's advice is formally consistent with its Christian theme, but, sensitized by the proximity of the bad advice offered by "A comparison," the "rede" of *Truth* begins to read somewhat dubiously. We get warnings against the vicissitudes of courtly life produced in an eerily *politique* vein; a wary, ambassadorial Chaucer folded into a religious one, to disorienting effect. Comparison with the manuscript tradition is revealing here. Of the lines discussed above, the edited text in the *Riverside Chaucer* offers the following significant variants (with my emphasis): "*Reule* wel thyself that other folk canst rede" (6); "*Savour* no more than thee bihove shall" (5); "Tempest thee noght *al* croked to redresse" (8). The loss of the doubling of "rede" dampens the connection with "A comparison." Courtly cynicism regarding "favour" is revealed as an exhortation to temperance. And the recommendation not to attempt to redress all wrongs specifies something lost in its 1557 reworking: *some* wrongs, even if not *all*, as opposed

Owen Boynton, in "The *Trouthe/Routhe* Rhyme in Chaucer's *Troilus and Criseyde*," *The Chaucer Review*, 45.2 (2010): 227, writes that "Chaucer's poem *Truth*, or *Balade de Bon Conseyl*, might seem the obvious place to focus our attention, but that poem is of limited use here, insofar as it tethers itself to the word in its refrain rather than explicitly making it an object of discussion."

to an exasperated rebuke offered to attempts to court fortune by righting "eche" wrong. Tottel's rendering of line five may look like a simple misreading ("f" for "s"), but taken as a sequence these discrepancies may be enough to induce the suspicion that his version has selected between available variants, or modified the text, in ways that deliberately sharpen it into paradox.[36] Further thoughts follow: given the apparent ubiquity of untruth that it describes, might the poem itself not "spurne against a nall" when urging its readers to turn to heavenly things? Does it instill in us any confidence that its own advice is likely to be followed? And if it doesn't, it is not therefore, once again but at a still more involved level than previously, just another instance of the world's "ticklenes"? To what extent does its framing in the *Songes and Sonettes* undermine Chaucer's literary authority, for which *Truth* had, by the sixteenth century, become a virtual shorthand?[37] Just how subversive is this poem?

"Truth," in the fourteenth century (when Chaucer's poem was composed), might signify either something like integrity and dependability, or conformity to fact.[38] Both meanings of the word seem to be put under pressure in these two poems as they are paired together in the *Songes and Sonettes*. They act to induce almost comic levels of uncertainty, set off by the confident narration of the former and the clarity and assurance of the refrain to the latter. And, once again, they produce these effects through the reconstruction of an antecedent literary authority, a medieval-Trojan past, which they both bend out of shape and use as a benchmark against which to measure their own distortions.[39]

---

[36]   Tottel's version of *Truth* corresponds precisely to no known manuscript or print version of the poem. According to Seth Lerer, his line 20 is unique—see his *Courtly Letters in the Age of Henry VIII* (Cambridge, 1997), p. 244, nn. 29, 30.

[37]   See Seth Lerer, "Receptions: Medieval, Tudor, Modern," in Susanna Fein and David Raybin (eds.), *Chaucer: Contemporary Approaches* (University Park, 2010), pp. 83–95, which argues that the poem gradually came to act as a synecdoche for "Chaucerian authority," p. 87. Lerer's longer account of the juxtaposition of these two poems in *Courtly Letters*, pp. 170–72, notes the latter's relevance to Wyatt, and that its advice "resonate[s] ironically with Pandarus' exhortations to his bedridden friend" in *Troilus and Criseyde* 1: 729–35. Tottel's positioning of the poems side by side, Lerer argues, "distill[s] the entire range of Chaucerian writing into two small texts: the one, a personalized reading of his great love poem, the other, an exemplary ballad presented now as a piece of practical maximal advice."

[38]   Richard Firth Green's *A Crisis of Truth: Literature and Law in Ricardian England* (Philadelphia, 2002) argues that the fourteenth century saw a broad reorientation of the meaning of the word from the former towards the latter meaning.

[39]   One further interpretative option is opened up by the *Songes and Sonettes*' publication of the *Balade de Bon Conseyl*. This is that its first line, "Flee from the prease," might now acquire significance in relation to its appearance in a printed book. The suggestion might seem outlandish. However, the essays by Catherine Bates, Seth Lerer, and others in this volume should give a sense of the intensity with which the *Songes and Sonettes* engages with its own mediation. The Trojan resonances of print are not confined to the miscellany, furthermore. At the start of his rendition of Book Four of the *Aeneid*, Surrey describes

"Repugnant Kindes": Undoing Epic

We have looked at Troy's presence in lyric and didactic verse. *Songes and Sonettes* also contains a number of slightly longer works that might seem to be where the collection could most forcefully stake its claims for the kind of "weightinesse" and "depewitted" cultural importance that Richard Tottel speaks of in his preface "To the reder" (p. 3). This category would include the two blank verse poems by Nicholas Grimald that occupy the penultimate and antepenultimate positions in the second Quarto of 1557, on "The death of Zoras" (278) and "Marcus Tullius Ciceroes death" (279). It might also contain the texts that form the focal points for the final section of this discussion, Thomas Wyatt's "Song of Iopas" (137) and the anonymous "Of the troubled comon welth" (229). These are both poems that bear a particularly close relationship to the matter of Troy in its epic manifestations. The former expands upon a reference in Virgil's *Aeneid*, while the latter, introduced into the second printing of the *Songes and Sonettes*, returns to the fall of Troy in the wake of Surrey's translation of the same poem. They mark the clearest attempts in the miscellany to harness Trojan themes to the assertion of a certain ideal of ethical and political order, embedded in the very structure of the cosmos. But, here as elsewhere, the Trojan material resists being marshalled into the kind of coherent statement it aspires towards. These are, in the end, compositions every bit as mired in uncertainty and skepticism as their shorter lyric and didactic companion poems. In both cases, the weightiness of epic remains tantalizingly, tellingly, out of reach.

The "Song of Iopas" takes its cue from Virgil. When Aeneas is welcomed into Carthage in Book One of the *Aeneid*, the feast culminates in song. In Robert Fagles's translation:

> Then Iopas,
> long-haired bard, strikes up the golden lyre
> resounding through the halls. Giant Atlas
> had been his teacher once, and now he sings
> the wandering moon and laboring sun eclipsed,
> the roots of the human race and the wild beasts,
> the source of storms and the lightning bolts on high,
> Arcturus, the rainy Hyades and the Great and Little bears,
> and why the winter's suns so rush to bathe themselves in the sea
> and what slows down the nights to a long lingering crawl ...[40]

Wyatt's poem, which concludes the section of *Songes and Sonettes* dedicated to his verse and which remains unfinished, fills out this summary with an account in

the impact of Aeneas' narrative upon Dido: "in her brest," we read, "imprinted stack his wordes" (D4ʳ). For examples of "trouth" as a key term in discussions of the reproduction of Chaucer's works as they moved between manuscript and print, see Stephanie Trigg, *Congenial Souls: Reading Chaucer From Medieval to Postmodern* (Minneapolis and London, 2002), pp. 116, 119–21.

[40] *The Aeneid*, trans. Robert Fagles (London: Penguin, 2007), 1: 886–96.

poulter's measure of the nature and movements of the Ptolemaic heavens derived from Johannes de Scarobosco's *Tractatus de Sphaera*: the elements, the fixed stars, the seven planets.

The "Song" is both a celebration of the order of the universe, and of the imaginative activity that apprehends this order. Thus, the line connecting north to south poles is "by imaginacion, drawen"; it is a line "that we devise" (137: 21, 25). The cosmos is described as a "frame" (137: 7), an ordered structure; but "frame" is also the word that Wyatt uses in other contexts to designate ingenious thought ("My Poyns," he notes ruefully, "I can not frame my tune to fayn" [135: 19]).[41] Iopas, meanwhile, functions as a surrogate for the poet. Wyatt's adaptation makes this transparently clear when he refers to the planet Venus, "that governd is by that, that governs mee:/And love for love, and for no love provokes: as oft we see" (137: 55–6). As Chris Stamatakis notes, the phrase "love for love" is a common verbal motif in the poetry of the period.[42] The lines embed an allusion to Wyatt's lyric persona within his epic adaptation, almost as if to suggest some sort of logic of progression leading from the one to the other, in the manner of the Virgilian *cursus*. More generally, the poem tacitly asks us to identify the sheer regularity of its format—the tendency of poulter's measure to produce a powerful medial caesura, for instance—with the "even continuall cours" (137: 16) of the heavens. The vision is one of controlled energies. Towards the start of the poem, we read that the universe holds in productive tension the opposing elements, naturally "repugnant kindes" to each other (137: 8). The adjective was a revision: Wyatt had originally written of "dyuerse" kinds, but he evidently wanted to heighten the sense of the powerful antagonisms that could be harnessed within his cosmology— as also within his writing. Condemning "The song of Iopas" as "Wyatt's worst poem," David Scott refers to its "struggling lines"; yet it is not clear that at least some of this effortfulness is not a deliberate effect.[43]

---

[41]   On "framing" in Renaissance verse, see Rayna Kalas, *Frame, Glass, Verse: The Technology of Poetic Invention in the English Renaissance* (Ithaca, 2007).

[42]   Chris Stamatakis, *Sir Thomas Wyatt and the Rhetoric of Rewriting: "Turning the Word"* (Oxford, 2012), p. 179.

[43]   David Scott, "Wyatt's Worst Poem," *The Times Literary Supplement* (13 September 1963), p. 696. Scott identifies the poem's source in Scarobosco, and suggests that the poem is an occasional one, embarked upon as part of the celebrations for welcoming Anne of Cleves to England. He is also fully alive to the ironies of the Trojan allusion: "It would have pleased Henry VIII's taste to be cast as Great Aeneas (the man of Destiny), and that the roles of guest and host, visitor and native, superior and subordinate, at the banquet to his foreign queen should be reversed in complement to her. And then his character as a lover! Aeneas, too, had got tired of a queen he had turned the country upside down to marry, and had caused her death casually." But Scott finds it hard to believe that Wyatt might be similarly knowing. On revisions to the poem in the Egerton manuscript, which bear witness to Wyatt's efforts to coordinate his thought with his chosen form, see the notes in Amanda Holton and Tom MacFaul's edition of the *Songes and Sonettes*, pp. 445–7.

In many ways, "The song of Iopas" should be regarded as a companion piece to Surrey's *Aenaeis*. Both are unfinished adaptations of Virgil in unusual or innovative verse forms: poulter's measure in Wyatt's case, and blank verse in Surrey's. In retrospect, Surrey's choice may seem obviously the correct one, Wyatt's self-evidently eccentric, but this would not have been so clear at the time. The moment at which blank verse became the default medium for epic poetry in English lay far in the future. Surrey's translation was in many ways an oddity: the initial 1554 printing, consisting of Book Four only, describes it as having been "translated into English, and drawne into a *strange* metre."[44] "The song of Iopas" thus invites us to imagine possible future for epic in what was to become the common metre of English hymns.

This future went unrealized, of course; the Carthaginian setting is, in retrospect, all too apt. But even within the poem itself, Wyatt's vision is less confident than it may seem at first glance. Increasingly, his account finds itself punctuated by curious omissions, hesitancies and redundancies. The planets exhibit "repugnant" motions contrary to the general progression of the firmament, but also "smaller bywayes ... skant sensible to man": "To busy worke for my poore harpe," Iopas comments (137: 33–4). There is a sphere between the first two heavens: yet, "I name it not for now" (137: 40). The planets move in "bywaies," "as I afore have said" (137: 67). Are these simply intricacies too small to be worth bothering with, or might they represent something too complex to be contained within the grand cosmological scheme Wyatt is proposing? Furthermore, as it appears in the *Songes and Sonettes*, "The song of Iopas" is all too obviously not only unfinished, but unfinishable. The author is (as the miscellany signs the poem, ending the section devoted to his verse) "T. WYATE the elder," already superseded by his namesake. There will be no new entries in this "Tudor book of the dead."[45] The message of the poem is not, this time, ironized to the point of cancellation; but it is rendered poignant and remote, both by virtue of Wyatt's death and of the very cosmological vastness of the perspectives evoked within the poem. Temporal distance from the pagan past acts, here, as a surrogate for the absence of the more recently deceased.

This is even more emphatically the case when one considers that Thomas Wyatt the younger is a very real Trojan presence in the miscellany. The anonymous poem "Of the troubled comon welth" (229) recounts in rhymed verse the fall of Troy to the Greeks, blaming the catastrophe on the treason of Sinon and Trojan conspirators. It then draws a contemporary parallel: as in Troy, so "Like in our time," we read, "wherein hath broken out./The hidden harme that we suspected least" (229: 37–8). But the poem ends on a note of cosmic assurance. "He on hye that secretly beholdes/The state of thinges" (229: 55–6) promises to visit shame and retribution upon the traitors. This poem is thought to allude to Thomas Wyatt the younger, who was executed in April 1554 for having attempted rebellion following the announcement of Mary Tudor's marriage to Philip II.[46]

---

[44] *The fourth boke of Virgill,* (London, 1554), titlepage. My emphasis.

[45] This is Seth Lerer's description, in *Courtly Letters*, p. 203.

[46] Rollins, vol. 2, p. 322, raises the possibility that Lady Jane Grey may be the target of the poem.

Once again, then, this is a poem that takes its bearings from Virgil's *Aeneid*—or, rather, from both the *Aeneid* and from Surrey's translation, with which it shares a number of details of imagery and phasing. "Of the troubled comon welth" describes how

> ... their king the aultar lay before
> Slain there alas, that worthy noble man.
> Ilium on flame, the matrons crying out,
> And all the streets in streames of blood about (229: 21–4)

This seems to echo Panthus' phrase about "all things on flame" from the *Aenaeis*, quoted above, and Surrey's description of Polites' death in "streames of blood" (C2r), immediately preceding the scene of Priam's murder at the altar in his palace (C2v). However, there is one glaring difference between the poem from the *Songes and Sonettes* and its predecessors. In Virgil, Aeneas figures as the savior of Troy by virtue of his transplantation of the remnant of his people to a new home in Italy, later to become Rome. Here, "Of the troubled comon welth" alludes to the story that Aeneas was, on the contrary, the betrayer of his native city, along with Antenor and Sinon. As Troy burns

> Then rose the rore of treason round about ...
> Then was the name of Sinon spred and blowne,
> And wherunto his filed tale did tend.
> The secret startes and metinges then were knowne,
> Of Troyan traitours tending to this end.
> And every man could say as in that case:
> Treason in Anthenor and Eneas. (229: 7–18)

These are lines that violently invert Virgil's conception of a heroic Aeneas. To the extent that the poem echoes Surrey's translation—to the extent that it seems to belong to a shared project, of Trojan matter reworked for a sixteenth-century audience and concerns—they may prompt the suspicion that, far from being a reverent Englishing of its Latin original, the *Aenaeis* might share something of their revisionary impulse. They retroactively raise the possibility that Surrey's poem might have been, not incomplete, but designedly selective, deliberately focusing in upon Aeneas' flight from Troy and his betrayal of Dido to the exclusion of other, more conventionally heroic books of the poem. The primary effect, however, is that of the violent contradiction of an authoritative original: Surrey's Virgil, just published, here revised within the pages of a book that bears his name on its very title page.

This, then, is not only a political poem, but also an intensely literary one. Following its description of "Ilium on flame," we read there were those—like Cassandra, although she is not mentioned by name—who warned of the betrayal of Troy, "if our stories certein be and just" (229: 27). And yet, when "Of the troubled comon welth" is placed in relation to the predecessor that it itself invokes, the suggestion is that these "stories" are neither certain nor just. But then again, and just to add a further layer of self-referential complexity, this is an accusation that the poem might also legitimately turn against itself. For inasmuch as Virgil's poem remains the dominant point of reference for the collection's account of Aeneas' character and actions, his identity as a traitor cannot, in fact, have been made definitively "knowne" to "every man" in the way suggested above (as Sinon's has been). The divine punishment promised in the second half of the poem, which is that of merited "shame" and public humiliation (229: 70), has not obviously been meted out in this instance. "Of the troubled comon welth" is marked by a kind of fractional indeterminacy, perhaps even by a certain slipperiness, such as might actually echo the elusive, unreliable natures of the traitors it condemns, and the literary predecessors it revises.

In their different ways, then, both the "Song of Iopas" and "Of the comon welth" seem ultimately repugnant to the "kinds" of epic assertion they aspire towards. They collapse and fail. And in each case, it is the poem's Trojan affiliations that provide the focal point for these moments of ruination. We have seen Troy sharpen our sense of the possibilities in Richard Tottel's publications of 1557 for a certain cultural ambition, and for its collapse. What is new here, though, particularly when set against the Virgilian and Chaucerian landmarks that structure this tradition, is the fragmentary and small-scale character of Tudor literary production. These failed epics suggest how, in 1557, Troy might be taken as an emblem for forms of poetry that are self-consciously minor, deliciously compromised in advance of the fact: that know they can never be what they hope to be. To the extent that Tottel's miscellany founds something new, then, it does so by embracing the diminishment and loss of integrity hinted at within the Trojan theme. The movement from the courtly manuscript verse collection to the *Songes and Sonettes* as a mechanically reproduced array of small-scale, portable "parcelles" of verse, for instance: is this *renovatio*, or does it seem to echo, just a little to closely for comfort, the Trojan counternarratives of betrayal that thread through the volume? Spreading outwards along the networks of transmission opened up by a nascent print culture, Tottel's miscellany thus announces an entirely new way in which the Trojan tradition might seek out its ruination. "Of great fame the Teucrian glorie erst:/Fierce Ioue to Grece hath now transposed all": he has "transposed" it, ultimately, via the offices of Richard Tottel, into the hands of Master Abraham Slender. Like some second Cassandra, the *Songes and Sonettes* saw it coming, but could do nothing to prevent it. In truth, it never really wanted to.

Chapter 4
Chaucer's Presence in *Songes and Sonettes*

Amanda Holton

In some respects, *Tottel's Miscellany* is a profoundly Chaucerian collection. In its interest in courtly love poetry and in Petrarch, it follows a trajectory in English poetry set by Chaucer. Its courtly verse is saturated with words, phrases, and tropes from a wide range of Chaucer's writing from *Troilus and Criseyde* and the *Canterbury Tales* to his prose translation of Boethius' *De consolatione philosophiae*. The collection rings with Chaucerian allusion from the first poem, Surrey's "The sunne hath twise brought furth his tender grene,"[1] which instantly and richly echoes Book V of *Troilus*.

The fact that Chaucer had a strong influence on the collection is not surprising. In 1557, when *Tottel's Miscellany* was first published, Chaucer's reputation had been high for a century and a half, and he was embedded in print. The *Canterbury Tales* had been printed in four different editions between 1483 and 1526,[2] and the first complete edition was printed by William Thynne in 1532, two more editions by Thynne appearing in 1542 and 1545.[3]

Chaucer's prestige is explicit in the *Miscellany*. In poem 35, Surrey's elegy to Wyatt, "W. resteth here, that quick could never rest," Chaucer's role is to stand as England's greatest poet—until he is displaced by Wyatt. Wyatt is characterized as "A hand, that taught, what might be said in rime:/That reft Chaucer the glory of his wit" (13–14). Chaucer is thus invoked as a pillar of the literary tradition in which Surrey wishes to locate Wyatt (the fifteenth century is silently passed over). His prestige is also reflected in the way that the *Canterbury Tales* has been fully assimilated in the collection and can be referred to allusively with the same confidence of the audience's knowledge as is the case when referring to classical

---

[1]   This and all subsequent quotations from the *Miscellany* are from Amanda Holton and Tom MacFaul (eds.), *Tottel's Miscellany: Songs and Sonnets of Henry Howard, Earl of Surrey, Sir Thomas Wyatt and Others* (London, 2011).

[2]   See James Simpson, "Chaucer's Presence and Absence, 1400–1550," in Jill Mann and Piero Boitani (eds.), *The Cambridge Companion to Chaucer*, 2nd ed. (Cambridge, 2004), pp. 251–69, p. 269, note 21.

[3]   For a discussion of sixteenth-century editions of Chaucer, see Stephanie Trigg, *Congenial Souls: Reading Chaucer from Medieval to Postmodern* (Minneapolis, 2002), pp. 109–43. See also Alexandra Gillespie, *Print Culture and the Medieval Author: Chaucer, Lydgate, and Their Books 1473–1557* (Oxford, 2006), and Simpson, "Chaucer's Presence and Absence."

myth; in Wyatt's "Myne owne Jhon Poins" (poem 135), the speaker, disclaiming deceitfulness, says that he cannot

> say that Pan
> Passeth Appollo in musike manifold:
> Praise syr Topas for a noble tale,
> And scorne the story that the knight tolde. (48–51)

Structurally, Chaucer's liking for leaving works unfinished is reflected in the fact that the Wyatt section of the *Miscellany* ends with an unfinished poem (poem 137). [4] Its incompleteness is stressed by the title it is given, "The song of Iopas unfinished," and by its ending with "&c.". Interestingly it maintains these features and its position in both the first and second editions of the *Miscellany*, despite the fact that there is some rearrangement of the Wyatt material between the editions: in the first edition, although most Wyatt poems appear together after the Surrey section, there is another tranche of poems by Wyatt at the very end. These poems were removed to the main Wyatt section in the second edition, but they were not attached to the end of the section; they appeared as poems 118–123, leaving the Wyatt section to close with an unfinished poem.

The single poem of Chaucer's which is included in the *Miscellany* is the ballade usually known as "Truth" (poem 207). This moral lyric survives in 22 manuscripts and two early editions, which suggests it was a particularly popular poem. Even though Chaucer's major influence on the other poets in the volume is as a poet of love and springtime, and even though he wrote love lyrics which could have been included, the editor of the *Miscellany* chose instead to include one of his moral lyrics. This reflects the emphasis with which many sixteenth-century readers read Chaucer; as Alison Wiggins has shown, sixteenth-century annotations on editions of Chaucer show particular interest in his work "as a source for sententious wisdom."[5] The poem, which is discussed at length elsewhere in this volume,[6] plays an important part in the *Miscellany*, setting the tone for many of the other moral lyrics. It is, for instance, the model for poem 122, Wyatt's "If thou wilt mighty be."[7]

---

[4]   In Thynne's 1532 edition of Chaucer's works (STC 5068), *The House of Fame* was supplied with an ending (a version of Caxton's), although other incomplete works are allowed to stand; the *Squire's Tale*, for instance, is followed by the note "There can be founde no more of this foresaid tale/whiche hath ben sought i dyvers places" (f. 32ᵛ).

[5]   Alison Wiggins, "What Did Renaissance Readers Write in Their Printed Copies of Chaucer?," *The Library: The Transactions of the Bibliographical Society*, 9 (2008): 3–36.

[6]   See Alex Davis's illuminating discussion of the poem pp. 78–80 above.

[7]   For a discussion, see Robert J. Meyer-Lee, *Poets and Power from Chaucer to Wyatt* (Cambridge, 2007), p. 221. For a comparison of this poem and "Myne owne Jhon Poins" with "Truth," see John Watkins, "Wrastling for this World: Wyatt and the Tudor Canonization of Chaucer" in Theresa Krier (ed.), *Refiguring Chaucer in the Renaissance* (Gainesville, 1998), pp. 26–30. Watkins interestingly argues that "[a]lthough Wyatt repeatedly echoed

Yet Chaucer's role in the *Miscellany* is not a straightforward one. Surrey's comment that Wyatt "reft Chaucer the glory of his wit," which both lauds and resists Chaucer, is a microcosm of the way Chaucer is treated throughout the book. Remarkably, "Truth," the only poem of his which appears in the volume, is found in the "Uncertain Authors" section. This may be because the editor was genuinely unsure of its authorship, but given that the text was probably taken from Thynne's edition of Chaucer, this seems unlikely. It is more probable that the poem was deliberately anonymized in the interests of foregrounding Surrey, Wyatt, and to a lesser extent, Grimald, in a demonstration of the supersession which Surrey claims above, and in a sly challenge to Chaucer.

As this suggests, the poetry of the *Miscellany* interacts with Chaucer's work in a conscious and purposeful way; it does not simply echo Chaucer. Simpson comments of fifteenth-century responses to Chaucer, "Precisely by virtue of building onto his achievement, without underrating or monumentalizing it, these responses reveal a confident readiness to enter into often competitive and productive conversation with Chaucer, freely adding to his works,"[8] and sixteenth-century responses are similar in this respect.[9] As I will show in this essay, some of the most important aspects of Chaucer's work are strongly resisted in the *Miscellany*, either ignored, dismissed or challenged. These elements include Chaucer's interest in variety of voice, his sympathetic engagement with women, particularly wronged women, and his interest in female speech and particularly female complaint.

The *Miscellany* represents work by a number of different poets (we can confidently identify around a dozen, although others remain anonymous), and this might lead us to expect variety of perspective and tone, yet on the whole it is a rather monologic work in comparison with Chaucer's *oeuvre*. One of Chaucer's major interests is voices and narrators, as the *Canterbury Tales*, with its numerous different narrators, attests. The love poems in the *Miscellany* are almost all male voiced, and almost invariably protest the suffering that women cause them. A frequent preoccupation is the lady's faithlessness, expressed compactly in an invective by Vaux (poem 187):

> O temerous tauntres that delights in toyes
> Tumbling cockboat totring to and fro,
> Janglyng jestres depravers of swete joyes,
> Ground of the graffe whence al my grief doth grow,
> Sullen serpent environned with dispite,
> That yll for good at all times doest requite.

Chaucer's Boethian counsels, he never fully heeded them. Throughout his career, he broke his resolutions to flee from the press of courtly preoccupations almost as soon as he made them" (p. 27). The reason Watkins gives for this is that "[a]s a Tudor new creation, he had no other place to turn," unlike Chaucer with his "multiple social identities" (both quotations p. 26).

[8] Simpson, "Chaucer's Presence and Absence," p. 257.

[9] There is some excellent critical work focusing on sixteenth-century "productive conversation" with Chaucer, such as Dennis Kay, "Wyatt and Chaucer: They Fle from Me," *Huntington Library Quarterly*, 47.3 (1984): 211–25.

There is often a strong emphasis on the cruelty of women. Poem 109, which is by Wyatt, has a characteristically huffy and resentful tone:

> Suffised not (madame) that you did teare,
> My woful hart, but thus also to rent:
> The weping paper that to you I sent.
> Wherof eche letter was written with a teare.
> Could not my present paines, alas suffise.
> Your gredy hart? and that my hart doth fele,
> Tormentes that prick more sharper then the stele,
> But new and new must to my lot arise.
> Use then my death. So shall your cruelty:
> Spite of your spite rid me from all my smart,
> And I no more such tormentes of the hart:
> Fele as I do. This shall you gain thereby.

The speaker here sets his lady's greedy heart against his own (which is torn, rent, woeful, and pricked with torments). He rains down rhetorical questions upon her, and eventually announces her punishments: the withdrawal of his love, and perhaps also the receipt of the angry poem.

The *Miscellany*, then, is dominated by male-voiced lyrics preoccupied with the pain inflicted on the lover by a lady who is frequently unfeeling, cruel, or faithless.[10] It is true that this position can be found in some of Chaucer's lyrics: the subject position of "A Complaint to his Lady" is similar to many of the male-voiced lyrics in the *Miscellany*, and parts of the poem can be paralleled with Wyatt's "Suffised not (madame)" above. One stanza in part IV of Chaucer's poem, for example, reads

> My dere herte and best beloved fo,
> Why lyketh yow to do me al this wo?
> What have I doon that greveth yow or sayd,
> But for I serve and love yow and no mo?
> And while I lyve I wol ever do so,
> And therfor, swete, ne beth nat yvel apayd.
> For so good and so fair as ye be
> Hit were right gret wonder but ye hadde
> Of alle servantes, bothe of goode and badde;
> And leest worthy of alle hem, I am he. (58–67)[11]

There is much more open subservience to and praise of the lady here than in the Wyatt poem (Wyatt's speaker has nothing good whatever to say of the lady), and the tone of Chaucer's speaker is gently reproachful rather than resentful and

[10]   For a discussion of the way Wyatt's male speakers take on the sensations and experiences of the women they describe, see Barbara L. Estrin, "Becoming the Other/The Other Becoming in Wyatt's Poetry," *English Literary History*, 51.3 (1984): 431–45.

[11]   This, and all subsequent quotations from Chaucer, are from Larry D. Benson, *The Riverside Chaucer* (Oxford, 1987).

angrily accusatory. Yet there are also similarities; again the lover positions himself as the object of the lady's deliberate ill-will; again he stresses his own good faith; again he questions the lady about the reasons for her causing him suffering. And again we find a deixis; in Wyatt's poem there is a reference back to the poem itself ("This"), and in Chaucer's to the speaker ("I am he").

However, in other poems by Chaucer the male lover is satirized. This is clear in the third stanza of Chaucer's ballade beginning "Madame, ye ben of al beaute shryne," conventionally titled "To Rosemounde":

> Nas never pyk walwed in galauntyne
> As I in love am walwed and ywounde,
> For which ful ofte I of myself devyne
> That I am trewe Tristam the secounde.
> My love may not refreyde nor affounde,
> I brenne ay in an amorous plesaunce.
> Do what you lyst, I wyl your thral be founde,
> Thogh ye to me ne do no daliaunce. (17–24)

The speaker here compares himself with a fish in a jellied sauce. This unexpected comparison stresses not only his helplessness but his very undignified state. It reduces him to a comically specific ("pyk"), uncommunicative comestible, mouth and eyes perhaps agape. The idea that the speaker should conclude from this ("For which ful ofte I of myself devyne") that he is the second Tristram is outstandingly silly, given that Tristram, while certainly a lover, is also a famously macho and resourceful figure with a reputation for military prowess. The comparison with Tristram only undermines the speaker's pathetic piscine proneness. This is a poem which could never be integrated into *Tottel's Miscellany*, as its satirical take on the posturings of the male lover would undermine those posturings which are taken so seriously in the *Miscellany*.

The poems in the *Miscellany* are generally decorously respectful in their presentation of male voices, whereas Chaucer takes more risks with his presentations of masculinity, as "To Rosemounde" suggests. This becomes sharply visible if we compare, say, poem 182, written by Lord Thomas Vaux and titled "The aged lover renounceth love" with the Prologue to the *Reeve's Tale*. The speakers of both are old men talking about their own age and diminished physical state. The *Miscellany* speaker bemoans his grey hair, his increasing baldness, the perishing of his poetic ability, his wrinkles, "[t]he cough, the cold, the gasping breath" (27), and the impedimenta of death, from shroud and spade to tolling bell. But these decorous losses and conventional props of death are nothing compared to the indignities age has inflicted on the Reeve. Seething about the *Miller's Tale* (which he takes as a personal insult), the Reeve declares that he would retaliate with a story about the tricking of a miller, "[i]f that me liste speke of ribaudye./But ik am oold" (3866–7).[12] He proceeds to work through a

---

[12] In terms of variety of voice, it is also notable that the Reeve, unlike the other pilgrims, speaks in a Northern dialect, as indicated by his use of the pronoun "ik" for "I."

rapid sequence of metaphors to describe the state of being old, which he sees as a mixture of helplessness, decay, and undiminished desire. First he presents himself as an animal: "Gras tyme is doon; my fodder is now forage" (3868), and then compares himself and other old men to medlars, fruit which is not ripe to eat until it is rotten. The debasement is stressed by the nasty conditions under which the medlars rot—"in mullok or in stree" (rubbish or straw, 3873), and by the word denoting the fruit: "open-ers" (3871). Yet even these rotting dirty lumps of vegetation are driven by a humiliating lust; "in oure wyl ther stiketh evere a nayl" (3877). Like leeks, they have green tails despite their white heads (3878), and the Reeve declares that he has always had "a coltes tooth" (3888). Desire here is an involuntary and seemingly unquenchable physical irritant, a more brutal situation than is found in the Tottel poem, which states simply "My lustes they do me leave" (5). Finally, according to the Reeve, in the ashes of old age, there are four embers, "[a]vauntyng, liyng, anger, coveitise" (3884)—boasting, lying, anger and greed—none of which appear in the *Miscellany* poem. The Chaucer extract thus presents a male speaker admitting to much more debasement and vulnerability than is the case in its counterpart—or indeed any other poem—in the *Miscellany*.

Chaucer's use of male voices is therefore more various than is the case in the *Miscellany*. But the most important difference between Chaucer and the *Miscellany* is Chaucer's interest in women and in female perspectives and voices. He is particularly alert to the covert power and the potential for dangerous deceit in the male lover, the intimidation of women that can lie under the rhetoric of *fin'amor*. Gavin Douglas, objecting to Chaucer's pro-Dido retelling of the *Aeneid*, famously charged Chaucer with being "euerr ... wemenis frend."[13] This sympathy for women is almost entirely absent from most of the love poems in the *Miscellany*. These poems, by contrast, are almost exclusively concerned with the perspective of the self-absorbed male speaker,[14] and do not show Chaucer's compassionate engagement with the plight of the Petrarchan mistress.

This lack of sympathy, and a cold skepticism about female fidelity, can be seen in the pairing of poems 154 and 155, which strongly recalls and resists Chaucer. The former is titled "The lover here telleth of his divers joyes and adversities in love and lastly of his ladies death." C.S. Lewis describes it as "almost exactly an

---

[13]   Gavin Douglas, *Eneados* I, Prologue, 449. See *The Poetical Works of Gavin Douglas*, ed. John Small (Edinburgh, 1874), vol. 2, p. 17.

[14]   Rebholz argues that Wyatt "denies his speakers his own understanding, or he limits them to a knowledge of the most proximate cause—fancy's arbitrariness or subjection to appetite. They therefore at times resort to facile explanations, blaming 'womankind' or Fortune for their unhappiness. In other instances they become the victims of ironies latent in their statements but not perceived by them. Where the poems give us clues to a level of understanding different from the speakers', the speakers approximate to dramatis personae." See Ronald A. Rebholz, "Love's Newfangleness: A Comparison of Greville and Wyatt," *Studies in the Literary Imagination*, 11:1 (1978): 17–30, quotation 24–5.

abridged version of the mourner's narrative in the *Boke of the Duchesse*,"[15] and it does indeed share the same trajectory of hope, disappointment, suffering, joy, and grief. This parallel is strengthened by the subject of the following poem, "Of his love named White," which begins "Full faire and white she is, and White by name." The lady in the *Book of the Duchess*, who commemorates John of Gaunt's wife Blanche, shares this name: "goode faire White she het;/That was my lady name ryght" (948–9). However, despite similarities in name and beauty, the two ladies are very different. In Chaucer's poem, the Black Knight's grief for his deceased lady White is intensified by his certainty of her fidelity and truth. In the later poem, however, the speaker crows over his cuckolding of White's husband, the "nerer gaser" (7) who is treated with "chilling cold" (8) by the lady, with the result that "White [i.e., the husband], all white his bloodlesse face will be:/The asshy pale so alter will his cheare" (9–10).[16] It is difficult to see the placing of this "White" poem with poem 154 as anything other than a deliberate recalling of Chaucer's poem. Yet the nature of lady White in poem 155 is provocative. Is the fidelity of Chaucer's lady White being brought into question, with the implication that the Black Knight is deluded, his complaint and grief ironically misplaced? If so, this is a cynical and misogynistic comment on the faithlessness and unreliability of women, and the sincere, abusable love of men. And if we read it in those terms, it is also a challenge to Chaucer, perhaps a knowing suggestion that he too is the fond dupe of women.

Chaucer is particularly alert to the manipulation and blackmail of women within *fin'amor*, and he is interested in the way the conventional props and rituals of love can be manipulated by men to falsify love. This is made particularly clear in the description of Aeneas' courting of Dido in the *Legend of Good Women*:

> Tak hede now of this grete gentil-man,
> This Troyan, that so wel hire plesen can,
> That feyneth hym so trewe and obeysynge,
> So gentil, and so privy of his doinge,
> And can so wel don alle his obeysaunces,
> And wayten hire at festes and at daunces,
> And whan she goth to temple and hom ageyn,
> And fasten til he hath his lady seyn,
> And beren in his devyses, for hire sake,
> Not I not what; and songes wolde he make,
> Justen, and don of armes many thynges,
> Sende hire lettres, tokens, broches, rynges—
> Now herkneth how he shal his lady serve! (1264–76)

---

[15] C.S. Lewis, *English Literature in the Sixteenth Century Excluding Drama* (Oxford, 1954), p. 238.

[16] For a very different reading of this poem as an encomium, see Paul A. Marquis (ed.), *Richard Tottel's Songes and Sonettes: The Elizabethan Version* (Tempe, AZ, 2007), p. xliv.

The majority of these amorous activities can be found, described by their enactors, in the *Miscellany*. A lover fasts in poem 255. There are many references to love songs, for instance poem 72, in which the lady hears "my plaint, in piteous song" (3). We hear of jousts and deeds of arms in poem 15, Surrey's "Windsor Elegy," in which the two young men compete "[o]n foming horse, with swordes" (18) in the sight of the ladies, and in particular "our dame," wishing to "baite her eies" (15–16). The same poem mentions "daunces" (10). Love letters are sent, as in Wyatt's poem 109. A number of tokens and gifts are given and exchanged; in poem 201, a lady sends one, and in 199, a 'flowring hart' (3) is given in exchange for a rosemary branch. No brooches are mentioned, but we do hear of a ring, engraved with a message of unchangeable love, in poem 173. In the *Miscellany*, these items are usually presented as sincere conventional expressions of love, but to Chaucer, they are signifiers which have the potential to be misused in a deliberate attempt to deceive women. This means that in Chaucer they carry a freight of skepticism about male motivation which is not present in the *Miscellany*.

Chaucer is also interested in exploring the cruelty and intimidation which the rhetoric characteristic of a male lover is fully able to contain.[17] This can be seen clearly in the *Franklin's Tale*, a story which raises the issues of "maistrie," of dominance and power in a love relationship, and deals with attempts to negotiate these within both courtship and subsequent marriage. Aurelius, the squire who falls in love with Dorigen while her husband is away, deploys the usual range of courtly behaviors, singing complaints, taking to his bed, staring at her piteously and so forth (925–78). Dorigen, who is in love with her husband, jokes that she will love Aurelius when he has removed all the rocks along the coastline, upon which he enlists the help of a magician to create the illusion that the rocks have disappeared. Aurelius' speech, when he comes to tell Dorigen that he has fulfilled her condition, is a thoroughly nasty piece of threat and menace presented under the guise of humility and devotion. He has a "dredful herte" (1309); he grovels to "his sovereyn lady deere" (1310), "Whom I moost drede and love as I best kan,/And lothest were of al this world displese" (1312–13). Yet this sycophantic and hypocritical exaggeration of the lady's power and suggestion of his own inadequacies in the face of her perfection is qualified by the underlying threat: "Avyseth yow er that ye breke youre trouthe" (1320). He repeatedly euphemizes what he is demanding, at the same time creating the spurious intimacy of a shared secret: "Ye woot right wel what ye bihighten me" (1327). Then he caps this with the now almost ludicrous, "Al be that I unworthy am therto" (1330), which maintains the forms of courtliness emptily, as he has shown the strength of his hand. His speech proceeds in a similar vein, dwelling unpleasantly but unconvincingly on how she will be responsible for his death if she insists on perjuring herself, and claiming that he is reminding her of her promise for her own honor. The brutality of this speech, made by a courtly lover knowingly exerting his power over a vulnerable woman, is stressed by the

---

[17] See also Catherine Bates' discussion of "the sheer coerciveness of the courtly lover's demand" in Wyatt, p. 53 above.

fact that Aurelius is in effect lying (because the rocks have not vanished), and by Dorigen's candidly horrified response:

> she astoned stood;
> In al hir face nas a drope of blood.
> She wende nevere han come in swich a trappe.
> "Allas," quod she, "that evere this sholde happe!
> For wende I nevere by possibilitee
> That swich a monstre or merveille myghte be!
> It is agayns the proces of nature."
> And hoom she goth a sorweful creature;
> For verray feere unnethe may she go.
> She wepeth, wailleth, al a day or two,
> And swowneth, that it routhe was to see. (1339–49)

This is followed by an extended complaint of over a hundred lines. The lover's speech is thus thoroughly embedded in an account of the lady and her own responses of shock, sorrow, and fear, which emphasize the cruelty of the speech. Her horror is manifested physically in her sudden pallor, and it is clear that she has been tricked and taken in a "trappe" by Aurelius' use of a "merveille" to accomplish something which she had thought physically impossible.

Similar speeches to Aurelius' are found throughout the *Miscellany*. Poem 94, for instance, Wyatt's "Al in thy loke my life doth whole depende," combines statements of the lady's value (as in the first line) with an emphasis on the speaker's mortal suffering at her hands ("Thou hydest thy self, and I must dye therfore," 2). He reproaches her ("Why dost thou stick to salve that thou madest sore?" [4]), and claims that she has obligations towards him because of his suffering and because she could "so easily" (3) help him. Finally there are threats: not only does he threaten her with his death, and the fact that his death will be her doing, but he also threatens her own death, on the grounds that she currently lives for his grief, so that if he dies, depriving her of this, she will also die. The speaker of this poem thus shares some strategies with Aurelius. However, in sharp contrast to Chaucer, this speech, and other similar *Miscellany* speeches, are not embedded in contexts stressing the lady's response, and their aggression can thus be downplayed rather than highlighted.[18]

Chaucer has a particular interest in women whose trust in men has been abused, women who have been treated cruelly and deserted. There is a high concentration of stories about these women in *The Legend of Good Women*. Dido is abandoned

---

[18] A.C. Spearing also compares Wyatt's characteristic persona with Aurelius', but develops the point in a different direction: rather than considering the absence of the woman's response in Wyatt, he argues that the fear typically felt by the lover had, in Wyatt's time, more pressing reasons: "The politics of amatory relations under Henry VIII might make love's pains deadly indeed, its perils all too abundant" (p. 287), given the executions of those accused of being involved with Anne Boleyn. See A.C. Spearing, *Medieval to Renaissance in English Poetry* (Cambridge, 1985).

by Aeneas; both Hysipyle and Medea are betrayed by Jason; Lucrece is raped by Tarquin; Ariadne is abandoned by Theseus, who as he leaves takes her sister Phaedra "in his hond" (2173) because she was more beautiful than Ariadne; Philomela is raped and has her tongue cut out by her brother-in-law Tereus; Phyllis is deserted by Demaphon; Hypermnestra is abandoned (if unmaliciously) by her husband Lynceus. Even the story of Cleopatra is refigured into a tale of Cleopatra's undying faithfulness to Antony, who causes her death; after his suicide, she too kills herself in accordance with her previous covenant with him, "[t]hat ryght swich as ye felten, wel or wo ... The same wolde I fele, lyf or deth" (689, 692). The story of Thisbe and Pyramus is the sole tale where men are blameless, and it seems to have been chosen to highlight by contrast the general male depravity in the work; the narrator comments:

> Of trewe men I fynde but fewe mo
> In alle my bokes, save this Piramus,
> And therfore have I spoken of hym thus.
> For it is deynte to us men to fynde
> A man that can in love been trewe and kynde. (917–21)[19]

Neither is Chaucer's interest in the suffering of classical women limited to the *Legend*. The story of Philomela, for example, is evoked in Book II of *Troilus*: after a restless night for the lovesick Pandarus,

> The swalowe Proigne, with a sorowful lay,
> Whan morwen com, gan make hire waymentynge
> Whi she forshapen was; and evere lay
> Pandare abedde, half in a slomberynge,
> Til she so neigh hym made hire cheterynge
> How Tereus gan forth hire suster take,
> That with the noyse of hire he gan awake[.] (II, 63–70)

Once he is awake, Pandarus sets off to promote Troilus to Criseyde and to persuade her to accept his love. The reference to the story of Procne and Philomela forms a troubling gloss on Pandarus' actions. Tereus' abuse of a close female relative casts an unflattering shadow on Pandarus' treatment of his niece. In a story which deals with a woman's betrayal of a man, it is striking that Chaucer goes to considerable lengths to explain the extenuating circumstances which led to that betrayal, and Pandarus' eager exploitation of Criseyde and her vulnerability contributes to that.

There is a telling contrast between Chaucer's interest in classical women who suffer as a result of untrustworthy and often malicious men, and those classical women who are favored in the *Miscellany*, namely Helen, Criseyde, and Penelope.

---

[19] It is notable that Surrey uses the story in one of his poems to Wyatt (poem 34), picturing himself weeping over Wyatt's grave as Pyramus did over Thisbe's breast. For a discussion of the implications of this, see Seth Lerer, *Courtly Letters in the Age of Henry VIII: Literary Culture and the Arts of Deceit* (Cambridge, 1997), pp. 204–5.

All of these women are presented in such a way as to cast men in a good light. Helen is associated not only with great beauty (as in poems 233 and 266), but also with prostitution ("Helenes trade") in poem 243, which also emphasizes her part in the Trojan War ("For one yll wife Grece overthrew/The towne of Troy," 11–12). The following poem objects "Not Helenes face,/But Paris eye did raise the strife" (12–13), but cannot remove her association with the fall of Troy. Other poems too stress her perceived role in the destruction of "valiant men" (16. 20). She is also, as in poem 16, sometimes aligned with the ladies who cause the speakers of poems to suffer and lament.

Criseyde is presented as a foil to the acme of loyalty and faith, Troilus, in poem 18, and in 232 her infidelity is alluded to in lines 5–6.[20] The speaker of Poem 206 compares his love to that of Troilus for Criseyde as a way of persuading his lady of his love. He draws attention to his omission of Criseyde's infidelity from his summary of the story by pointing up issues of truthfulness, closing his account of their love affair with her acceptance of his love:

> And truth it is except they lye,
> From that day forth her study went,
> To shew to love him faithfully,
> And his whole minde full to content.
> So happy a man at last was he
> And eke so worthy a woman she. (49–54)

The poem's apparent praise of the lady who is paralleled with Criseyde is therefore a knowing implication about the lady's anticipated infidelity. It may also represent a mocking exaggeration of Chaucer's reluctance to dwell on Criseyde's betrayal and to spare her blame where possible.[21]

Penelope is a woman who suffers, but whose husband is not to blame. She can thus be unflinchingly praised without casting any aspersions on a guilty man. She crops up several times in the *Miscellany*, and her faithfulness is stressed in poems 20, 168, and 232. Poem 225 is a translation of the first 12 lines of Ovid's *Heroides*

---

[20]   For a discussion of medieval and Renaissance presentations of the figure of Criseyde, see Hyder Edward Rollins, "The Troilus-Cressida story from Chaucer to Shakespeare," *PMLA*, 32 (1917): 383–429. Poem 206 is considered on p. 390.

[21]   Seth Lerer comments on poems 206 and 207 ("A comparison of his love wyth the faithful and painful love of Troylus to Creside" and Chaucer's "Truth"), "Taken together, these two poems are stories about reading Chaucer. They are accounts of how the force of Chaucer's poem can provoke the writing of a verse epistle to a lover, and an epistolary response of a friend. The two poems thus form, in the *Miscellany*, a kind of dramatic pair or dialogue. But what they also form is something of a mid-sixteenth century distillation of the essentially Chaucerian: *Troilus* and 'Truth'". See Seth Lerer, "Receptions: Medieval, Tudor, Modern," in Susanna Fein and David Raybin (eds.), *Chaucer: Contemporary Approaches* (University Park, PA, 2010), pp. 83–95, quotation from pp. 87–8. This is true, but I would take the point further; the pairing of the two poems irresistibly recalls Chaucer, only to resist his presentation of Criseyde.

I, an epistle from Penelope to Ulysses. But Chaucer shows little interest in her, mentioning her on only five occasions, and only in passing in each case. This is particularly striking given her emphatic presence at the beginning of the *Heroides*, because this was a work which was highly influential on Chaucer; he uses it as a basis for several of his stories in the *Legend of Good Women*, for instance, and Penelope was a good candidate for inclusion in that work, given the fact that she was famous for her constancy.[22] Her absence can be explained by her status as a woman whose suffering is not caused by a faithless or neglectful lover, Chaucer's particular area of interest.

The kind of interest Chaucer shows in women and their suffering in love is effaced from the *Miscellany*, then. What is more, words and images Chaucer often associated with suffering vulnerable female lovers and predatory deceitful men are in the *Miscellany* repeatedly usurped to describe female duplicity and male suffering and victimhood. This can be exemplified through an examination of the words "change" and "newfangle(ness)," and of images of baits, hooks, nets, and traps.

Change is almost invariably negative in the *Miscellany*,[23] and male lovers are anxious to defend themselves against charges of changeability. Poem 173, for instance, presents the engraving on a ring sent to a lady:

> … sooner shall the sunne not shine by day,
> And with the raine the floods shall waxen lesse.
> Sooner the tree the hunter shall bewray,
> Then I for change, or choyce of other love,
> Do ever seke my fansy to remove. (5–8)

Poem 51, "Eche man me telth, I change most my devise," is unusual in that its male speaker admits his changeableness; it emerges, however, that he is changeable only because he is "treated after a divers fashion" (7) by his lady. His changeableness is thus not regarded as a fault, but as punishment for hers; she is its source, she is to blame for it, and she has the power to bring it to an end. The poem ends with the speaker instructing her:

> Change you no more, but still after one rate
> Treat you me well: and kepe you in that state,
> And while with me doth dwell this weried gost,
> My word nor I shall not be variable,
> But alwaies one, your own both firme and stable.

---

[22]   The *Legend*, of course, appears to be unfinished, though it is an open question whether it was left uncompleted or whether Chaucer purposefully closed the work where he did, mid-sentence ("This tale is seyd for this conclusioun—").

[23]   The exception is the hope that the lady will change from cruelty to pity, as in poem 82, "Passe forth my wonted cries," 13–14.

In this poem, as elsewhere, change is primarily a property of women. [24] Poem 230, "The bird that somtime built within my brest," for instance, charges the lady that "in change her choise doth chiefe consist" (7). Similarly, in poem 57, "They flee from me, that sometime did me seke," the women are characterized by changeableness: in the first stanza they are "[b]usily seking in continuall change" (7), and in the final stanza the lady has given herself leave "to use newfangleness" (19). This latter word appears on one other occasion in the *Miscellany*, where it also characterizes a woman: this is in poem 190, "Cruel unkinde whom mercy cannot move," an invective against a lady in which she is described as "Net of newelty, neast of newfanglenesse" (18).

For Chaucer, however, newfangleness is differently gendered.[25] In *Anelida and Arcite*, Arcite takes up with another lady "of his newfanglenesse" (141). In the Prologue to the *Legend of Good Women*, the dreamer witnesses birds' choosing of their mates on Valentine's Day, and among the birds are those who have previously "doon unkyndenesse" (F153), among them the (implicitly male) "tydif," a small, famously inconstant bird, who has been guilty of "newfangelnesse" (154). On two occasions Chaucer reflects on newfangleness in the context of a borrowing from *Le roman de la rose* which describes the irrational instinctive desires of animals; one example is a bird abandoning its furnished cage and rich supply of food to eat worms in a cold wood. The betrayed female falcon in the *Squire's Tale*, telling of her desertion by her tercelet lover, reflects on this example as a metaphor for male desire for sexual novelty. She comments that birds who desert their manmade home for the woods and worms do so because "[s]o newefangel been they of hire mete" (618), and comments "Men loven of propre kynde newefangelnesse" (610). The desire for novelty, and particularly for amorous novelty of a debased or savage kind, is here regarded as a property natural and innate to men. The *Manciple's Tale* is also interested in newfangleness and draws on the same material but in a different way. Here, in a story telling of a woman's infidelity, Chaucer places a series of exempla about animals which cannot control their instinctive bestial desires, commenting, in a contrarian way, "Alle this ensamples speke I by thise men/That been untrewe, and nothyng by wommen" (187–8). When the narrative voice goes on to conclude that "[f]lessh is so newefangel" (193), the gender of the betraying flesh has been brought into question; the body responsible for newfangleness in the story is female, but the narrative voice asserts that newfangleness is a property of men. So even in the one case when Chaucer associates the idea of newfangleness with a woman, the association is not straightforward. Furthermore, it is interesting

[24]   Indeed, Odabashian identifies "change, in particular the changefulness of women" as Wyatt's "primary theme" (p. 287). See Barbara Odabashian, "Thomas Wyatt and the Rhetoric of Change" in Mario Di Cesare (ed.), *Reconsidering the Renaissance: Papers from the Twenty-First Annual Conference* (Binghamton, NY, 1992), pp. 287–300.

[25]   Although "newefangelnesse" is identified with a lady in "Against Women Unconstant" (line 1), this lyric is of disputed authorship and is not ascribed to Chaucer in any manuscripts.

to note that the newfangleness of the female is implicitly set against the male's constancy, which, born of jealousy and obsession, is not in this case presented as a positive, resulting as it does in a vengeful domestic killing. The woman's newfangleness is a minor matter compared to the murderous rage of her partner.

In the love poems in the *Miscellany*, images of baits, hooks, nets, traps, and constraining briars are common. Poem 247, urging suspicion of women, has a full set:

> ... he that blontly runnes, may light among the breers,
> And so be put unto his plunge where danger least apperes:
> The bird that selly foole, doth warne us to beware,
> Who lighteth not on every bush, he dreadeth so the snare.
> The Mouse that shons the trap, doth shew what harme doth lye:
> Within the swete betraying bait, that oft disceives the eye.
> The fish avoydes the hooke, though hunger bids him bite,
> And hovereth still about the worme, whereon is his delite.
> If birdes and beastes can see, where their undoing lies:
> How should a mischief scape our heades, that have both wit & eyes? (5–14)

Images of the "bayted net" (108.46) and its like invariably express the male lover's sense of powerlessness and victimization. In accordance with this, the lover frequently aligns himself with small, frail, vulnerable objects of prey. In poem 184, for instance, the speaker identifies himself with "the beaten fowle/That from the net escaped" (37–8), in contrast to his lady, who is "lyke the ravening owle/That all the night hath waked" (39–40). In poem 232, the lover compares himself with a mouse, and a female one at that:

> Where I sought haven, there found I hap,
> From daunger unto death:
> Much like the Mouse that treades the trap,
> In hope to finde her foode,
> And bites the bread that stops her breath,
> So in like case I stoode. (13–18)

Sometimes the emphasis falls entirely on the lover's experience rather than exploring who has set the trap; in poem 227, the speaker comments "I had the bayte, the hooke and all" (5), without speculating on its source. Sometimes Love itself, occasionally in the form of Cupid, is seen as responsible for the trapping; poem 103, a renunciation of love, begins "Farewell, Love, and all thy lawes for ever,/Thy bayted hookes shall tangle me no more."

Often the baits, hooks and nets are not deployed by Love but by the lady herself. In poem 161, for instance, the lover is tied by the lady; he "laced is within her chaine" (28), and he expresses his sense that love is sweeter after suffering through a stanza of parallels:

> For who covets so high to clim,
> As doth the bird that pitfoll toke,

> Or who delightes so swift to swim,
> As doth the fish that scapes the hoke,
> If these had never entred wo:
> How mought they have rejoysed so. (31–6)

In this poem, then, the lover is metaphorically constrained by chains, and compared with a bird caught in a pitfall trap and a fish caught on a hook.

Sometimes the agent of the trapping is more complex. Poem 145 opposes the lover's previous freedom ("My hart and I might leape at large," 8) with his experience of being snared by love. Cupid "set him self to lye in wait:/And in my way he threw a bait" (35–6), namely the lady. The bedazzled lover immediately, "Or ever I had the wit to loke:/… swalowed up both bait, and hoke" (47–8). The poem ends with a warning not to despise lovers lest Cupid take revenge and "Lest you be caught within his snare" (60). There are several interesting things here. Firstly, the lady is herself the bait, placed on the hook by Cupid; in other words she is as helpless as the lover, and worse, has been consumed by him. Secondly, although stress is laid on the speaker's initial freedom (he is "free," 13, and "at libertee," 18), paradoxically he is already trapped by his own limitations and susceptibilities; he entertains himself "in the net of my conceit" (25). The snares which will trap him are thus half internalized.

Chaucer also deploys the imagery of nets, hooks and snares, but he uses it very differently. The *Miscellany* poets always use these metaphors to describe a man's experience of powerlessness in love. Chaucer does occasionally do the same; Troilus, for example, having fallen in love with Criseyde, says to himself, "O fool, now artow in the snare,/That whilom japedest at loves peyne./Now artow hent, now gnaw thin owen cheyne!" (I, 507–9). In the short poem "The Complaint of Mars," Mars laments the power of the god of love:

> Hit semeth he hath to lovers enmyte,
> And lyk a fissher, as men alday may se,
> Baiteth hys angle-hok with som plesaunce
> Til many a fissh ys wod til that he be
> Sesed therwith; and then at erst hath he
> Al his desir, and therwith al myschaunce;
> And thogh the lyne breke, he hath penaunce;
> For with the hok he wounded is so sore
> That he his wages hath for evermore. (236–44)

What is interesting about this instance, however, is the care the speaker takes to emphasize that his lady is not the wielder of the line and hooks. He says explicitly, "thogh my lady have so gret beaute/That I was mad til I had gete her grace,/She was not cause of myn adversite" (264–6).

Most often, however, Chaucer uses these metaphors to evoke women's vulnerability and exploitation at the hands of men. The most famous example of this can be found in *Troilus and Criseyde* in a description of the conniving Diomede, deliberately preying on Criseyde in the Greek camp:

> This Diomede, of whom yow telle I gan,
> Goth now withinne hymself ay arguynge,
> With al the sleghte and al that evere he kan,
> How he may best, with shortest taryinge,
> Into his net Criseydes herte brynge.
> To this entent he koude nevere fyne;
> To fisshen hire he leyde out hook and lyne. (V, 771–7)

The premeditated deliberateness of his determination to catch Criseyde is chilling. In the light of his desire to ensnare her with line and net, it is striking that in the previous stanza, she herself is considered in terms of ropes and knots; the narratorial voice heavily predicts that "bothe Troilus and Troie town/Shal knotteles thoroughout hire herte slide" (V, 768–9). Although in Book III, Troilus had called her eyes "[y]e humble nettes of my lady deere" (III, 1355), by Book V there is no longer even any pretence that she is the predator; the net is Diomede's, and Criseyde's lack of control over the situation is one of the things figured by her knotlessness.

The connection between women and nets is also made in the story of Dido in the *Legend of Good Women*. Here, it is a woman who is literally a deployer of nets; heading out to hunt with Aeneas, Dido "chargeth hire meyne/The nettes dresse" (1189–90). Ironically, though, it is she rather than Aeneas who is trapped by love. When they are forced to flee into a cave for protection from a sudden storm, Dido is deceived by Aeneas' protestations of love, which he makes "as a fals lovere so wel can pleyne" (1236).

A similar irony is found in the use of the word "chain" in Anelida's complaint in *Anelida and Arcite*. The forsaken Anelida asks her absent lover

> Which is the wey to doon yow to be trewe?
> For either mot I have yow in my cheyne
> Or with the deth ye mote departe us tweyne[.] (283–5)

It is painfully clear that she does not have him "in my cheyne," given that he has abandoned her for another woman. Interestingly, though, the lady he has chosen in preference wields a similar form of metaphorical restraint but much more successfully:

> His newe lady holdeth him so narowe
> Up by the bridil, at the staves ende,
> That every word he dredeth as an arowe;
> Her daunger made him bothe bowe and bende[.] (183–6)

Arcite's besottedness with this harsh lady anticipates the obsession many of the lovers have with cruel and heartless ladies in the *Miscellany*. But where Chaucer's poem differs sharply from the *Miscellany* is in the clear sense of Arcite's incomprehensibly bad judgment in choosing such a lady at the price of the loyal, loving, and cooperative Anelida, whom he is so ready to betray. The narrative voice notes cynically, "That for her liste him "dere herte" calle/And was so meke, therfor he loved her lyte" (199–200).

Some of the key terms and tropes which Chaucer uses to convey the predicament of suffering women are therefore usurped to express male suffering in the *Miscellany*. Another important way in which Chaucer's interest in and sympathy for women is manifested is his use of female voices, and particularly complaint. In this he is inspired by the *Heroides*, in which Ovid offers female characters the opportunity to renarrate famous stories from their own perspectives, allowing women voices and with them, the power to control narrative.[26] Chaucer's interest in women's perspectives and women's voices is exemplified by his summary of the *Aeneid* in *The House of Fame*. This summary occupies some 330 lines, of which around 215 are dedicated to the story of Dido, despite the fact that the episode takes up only one of the twelve books of the *Aeneid*. In Chaucer's version, Dido's voice, protesting against her treatment by Aeneas, fills some 60 lines, and it is her interpretation of events which leads the narrative. Aeneas, by contrast, does not have a single line of speech and is entirely unable to defend himself against her charges.

For Chaucer, women's voices and particularly women's complaints are so absorbing that at times a narrative seems to be provided for the sole purpose of setting up a female lament, and after it has been delivered, the rest of the poem shrivels away. The *Squire's Tale* (discussed further below) is 663 lines long, of which around a third deal with the abandoned female falcon's suffering and lament, her speech occupying some 150 lines (479–629). The text is terminated shortly after her lament, interrupted by another pilgrim. Similarly *Anelida and Arcite* seems to have been set up to showcase a woman's distressed voice. The poem begins with a formal three-stanza invocation, which suggests that a lengthy, perhaps epic, text will follow. The next section of the poem (22–210), the "Story" tells the tale of Arcite's betrayal and abandonment of Anelida. This followed by Anelida's complaint, which is told in different stanza forms from the rhyme royal used in the rest of the poem. This complaint absorbs a little under half of the poem (211–350), and ultimately it consumes it; the Story is resumed for a single stanza, after which it comes to a halt unfinished.[27]

In sharp contrast to the situation in Chaucer, there are only a handful of women speakers in the *Miscellany*. The *Heroides* has a much less profound influence,

---

[26]   Elizabeth Harvey considers Linda Kauffman's theory that the *Heroides* challenges the values of Augustan Rome just as its epistolary genre challenges the epic genre, but points out that Ovid "uses the metaphor of woman as a lever for dismantling certain patriarchal values, but, unlike the heroines he ventriloquizes, he simultaneously partakes of the very privilege he seeks to expose"; see Elizabeth Harvey, *Ventriloquized Voices: Feminist Theory and English Renaissance Texts* (London, 1992), p. 40.

[27]   For an extended discussion of Anelida's complaint, see Stephen Stallcup, "With the Poynte of Remembraunce: Re-Viewing the Complaint in *Anelida and Arcite*" in Bonnie Wheeler (ed.), *Representations of the Feminine in the Middle Ages* (Dallas, 1993), pp. 43–67.

which is limited mainly to two poems, 17 and 225, discussed elsewhere in this essay. In some poems there seems to be a deliberate turning down of an opportunity for female complaint. Poem 150, for instance, describes a love triangle: Harpalus loves Phillida, who does not reciprocate his love; instead she loves Corin, who "forst her not a pinne" (12). The poem features a detailed account of Harpalus and his physical state, and includes a lengthy complaint from him, but Phillida, whose love is also unrequited, is not accorded the same treatment, and is not given a word to speak.

On the rare occasions when female voices occur in the *Miscellany*, they are usually restricted. One means of restriction is to feature a woman's voice within a poem voiced and governed by a male speaker, which makes the account of her voice unreliable (as in poem 57, "They flee from me"). Another means of restriction is to tie the woman's voice tightly into a dialogue with a man's voice in a debate in which the man either sets the terms of the argument, and/or wins it. This debate can take place either between poems or within them. An example of the latter is poem 113, Wyatt's "It burneth yet." This is a dialogue between a lover and his lady, in which the lady is brought round to the lover's point of view. The poem begins with the lover's description of his burning desire, and the lady's attempt to make him take responsibility for his suffering (she asks "What may I do, if thy self cause thy smart?" [6]). Finally she is worn down, and agrees to accept his love: "Thou wilt nedes so: be it so: but then be trew" (30). Where Anelida forges her own stanza forms in her complaint, the lady in Wyatt's poem is forced to fall in with his *ottava rima* stanzas. Her opposition might be figured through her use of *b*-rhymes in contrast to his *a*-rhymes, but it is he who introduces the *c*-rhyme in each case, deciding when the run of cross-rhymed couplets will come to an end, and she has a structural obligation to echo his *c*-rhyme with her own. In the final stanza, she does not even have this: her turn to speak is usurped by the triumphant final line, "Thus, hartes be wonne, by love, request, and mone" (32), which may be spoken by the male lover in a self-satisfied vein, or by a narrative voice approving of the lover's technique.[28]

Women's voices in the *Miscellany* are also placed on the back foot when they appear in the secondary position in a pair of linked poems. Poem 27, for instance, "Girt in my giltles gowne," is framed as a reply "in the behalfe of a woman" to poem 26, "Wrapt in my carelesse cloke," a male tirade against "the suttle usage of women towarde their lovers." The first poem sets the terms; it decides the subject-matter, the structure, and the poetic form of the exchange. The second poem begins with an echo of the alliterating apparel which opens the first poem, and, mimicking its poulter's measure, proceeds to engage with the topic of "craft" as set by the first poem.

---

[28]   Rebholz considers this poem "one of the most amusing seduction poems of the century" ("Love's Newfangleness," p. 20, fn 10), presumably because of the ease with which the lady's objections are shot down.

The first woman speaker in the collection is the speaker of poem 17, Surrey's "O happy dames," entitled in the *Miscellany* "Complaint of the absence of her lover being upon the sea." An interesting feature of this poem is its relationship to *Heroides* II, the letter from Phyllis to Demophoon. The *Heroides* letter is the ultimate source for the poem, although the immediate source was Serafino's fifth epistle. What is missing from Surrey's poem is the Ovidian material identifying the classical story, resulting in a much less specific lament, an effect supported by the decontextualizing title which the compiler of the *Miscellany* has added. This shearing has two effects. Firstly, it removes the power of the Ovidian female speaker to take possession of a famous story and re-narrate it from her own perspective. Secondly, it removes the attack on the treacherous male character who caused the suffering, and in *Heroides* II, that attack is made in anger as well as sorrow. Ovid's text is about a woman betrayed and deserted by a reprehensible man. Surrey's is about a woman who is worried about her sea-going lover. What Surrey maintains from Ovid is the scene of Phyllis looking out to sea (*Heroides* II, 121–8), although in Ovid she is on the shore and in Surrey inside behind a window. Both women gaze out into clear air; Surrey's speaker watches at night when "Before the windes … the clowdes flee"(27), while Ovid's watches "sive die laxatur humus, seu frigida lucent/sidera" ("whether by day the soil is loosened [by warmth], or whether stars shine coldly"; 123–4). [29] Ovid's speaker is "[m]aesta" (sorrowful; 121); Surrey's, more elaborately, is "[d]rowned in teares to mourne my losse" (24). The ending of Surrey's poem also echoes the cluster of rhetorical questions in the middle of the Ovidian epistle: Surrey's reads "Now he comes, will he come? alas, no no." (42) Ovid's reads

> Expectem, qui me numquam visurus abisti?
> expectem pelago vela negata meo?
> et tamen expecto—redeas modo serus amanti[.]
>
> (Am I to wait, when you went away never to see me again? Am I to wait for the rejecting sails in my seas? But I do wait nevertheless—come back, even if you're late). (99–101)

One of the major differences between the texts is Surrey's removal of the resentment and rage of Ovid's Phyllis, which can be summarized by the epitaph she drafts for herself: "Phyllida Demophoon leto dedit hospes amantem;/ille necis causam praebuit, ipsa manum" (Phyllis' loved guest Demophoon caused her demise; he supplied the cause for her death; she supplied the hand; 147–8).

It has been suggested that Surrey wrote this poem in the voice of his own wife during his military service at Boulogne in 1546; if this is the case, Surrey's usurpation and sanitation of Phyllis' voice, raging and protesting about her betrayal by her lover, is even more remarkable. He is not only taking over Phyllis' voice, he

---

[29] Ovid, *Heroides* II, Latin text here and henceforth from G.P. Goold (ed.), *Heroides; Amores* (Cambridge, MA, 1977); translations mine.

is also occupying the persona of another woman, his wife, in order to write about himself.[30]

The same suggestion about voice and situation has been made about poem 19, another piece by Surrey on the same theme.[31] Here again, the speaker may miss her beloved, but there is no sense he is at fault; indeed she addresses other women whose husbands are away, and stresses that their love for these men, "whose good deserts none other wold require" (6). Poem 159, which seems to imitate the two Surrey poems discussed, is on the same subject, and the majority of the poem is occupied by the speaker's longing for her beloved and her fears for his safety. In this poem, however, the possibility of betrayal is raised, albeit at the end of the poem:

> But if thou slip thy trouth and do not come at all,
> As minutes in the clocke do strike so call for death I shall.
> To please both thy false hart, and rid my self from wo,
> That rather had to dye in trouth then live forsaken so. (19–22)

It is possible that there is a mild joke about the lady's lack of patience at the end of this poem, but nevertheless the final lines raise one of Chaucer's major concerns, the forsaken woman.

This poem is of uncertain authorship, as are the two poems which resemble Chaucer most strongly in their use of female complaint. The speaker of poem 192, "To love, alas, who would not feare," protests about her abandonment and compares herself to Dido, a figure entirely absent from the rest of the *Miscellany*

---

[30]   Tottel clearly identifies the writer of this poem as Surrey, and its speaker as a woman, but there has been debate about the gender and identity of both speaker and composer. Jonathan Goldberg, who appears to consider that the gender of the speaker is an indication of the gender of the poet, advances the peculiar argument that because this poem appears in the Devonshire MS in the hand of Mary Shelton—a fact which others dispute—it is likely to have been composed by her. See Jonathan Goldberg, "The Female Pen: Writing as a Woman," in Jeffrey Masten, Peter Stallybrass, and Nancy J. Vickers (eds.), *Language Machines: Technologies of Literary and Cultural Production* (New York, 1997), pp. 17–38. For a more subtle and convincing discussion, see Elizabeth Heale, "'Desiring Women Writing': Female Voices and Courtly 'Balets' in Some Early Tudor Manuscript Albums." in Victoria E. Burke and Jonathan Gibson (eds.), *Early Modern Women's Manuscript Writing: Selected Papers from the Trinity/Trent Colloquium* (Aldershot, 2004), pp. 9–31. Heale points out that over-focusing on the gender of the author can lead us "to obscure a more interestingly gender-fluid use of amorous topoi in the period. In the social circumstances in which these poems circulated, poems lamenting a beloved's absence offered a conventionally female subject position as easily appropriated by men wishing to please female companions or patrons, as, potentially, by women able to participate by composing balets themselves" (pp. 13–14).

[31]   Line 22 is sometimes taken as evidence for this argument, with "his faire little sonne" taken to be Surrey's son Thomas, born in 1536. The version of this poem in the Arundel Haringdon MS reads "with T. his lytle sonne," strengthening the association.

except for her brief scene-setting appearance in the first line of Wyatt's "Song of Iopas" (poem 137). She reproaches her lover for deceit and heartlessness, besieging him with rhetorical questions:

> And can you thus breake your behest
> In dede and can you so?
> Did you not sweare you loved me best,
> And can you now say no?
> Remember me poore wight in paine,
> And for my sake turne once againe. (25–30)

Just as male lovers threaten to die, leaving reputations or tombs which will forever reproach their cruel ladies, so the speaker of this poem imagines herself, dead from grief at her abandonment, being a lesson to others. After drowning in her own tears, she hopes "[t]hat by my death al men may say,/Lo women are as true as they" (47–8). Unfortunately, however, this message is thoroughly muffled by the volume of male speakers making very different claims.

Poem 259, "A cruell Tiger all with teeth bebled," is another poem which shares some of Chaucer's interests but which is uncharacteristic of the *Miscellany*. This piece, which does not appear in the first edition of the *Miscellany*, again has a female speaker who protests against the cruel way she has been treated by a man, although in this case the mistreatment has been more extreme. Here the speaker describes how she was raped when a virgin, and how she and the child she conceived were then murdered "for cloking of his crime" (15). The poem's description of a degrading and deadly assault on a woman is matched by the choice of form: a 15-line poem amounting to a distorted sonnet (the poem rhymes *ababbcbcbcbcbdd*). Heather Dubrow argues that the sonnet is "the verse form now considered one of the central markers of Petrarchism,"[32] and it is appropriate that this violently anti-Petrarchan episode is expressed through a disruption of the form. However, as with poem 192, discussed above, the effect of the cruelly-treated woman speaker is diminished by the volume of complaining male voices which surround her. She may accuse her killer of being a "cruell Tiger," for example, but there are so many more instances of male voices associating women with tigers that her protests are hard to hear.[33]

Not only does the *Miscellany* include very little in the way of female voices and female complaint, two particular poems by Surrey in the *Miscellany* appear to level a deliberate challenge to the claims of female complaint in the *Squire's Tale*. The *Squire's Tale* is incomplete because it is interrupted by the Franklin. It begins with a knight visiting King Cambyuskan (Genghis Khan) on his birthday, bringing several magical gifts, one of which, a ring which gives the wearer the

---

[32]   Heather Dubrow, *Echoes of Desire: English Petrarchism and Its Counterdiscourses* (Ithaca; London, 1995), p. 6.

[33]   In poem 115, for instance, the lady is a "Fierce Tigre" (15); in poem 82, the lady seems to have been nourished by tigers (line 11).

power to understand the language of birds, is sent to his daughter Canacee. The following day she discovers a very distressed self-harming female falcon. Because of the ring, Canacee is able to communicate with the falcon, who utters a long complaint about her ill treatment by a tercelet, who has abandoned her for a kite. This complaint, uttered by a bird fainting from loss of blood where she has savaged herself with her own beak, is one of Chaucer's most moving, and it is interesting that Surrey appears to take issue with it.

The complaint of the falcon seems to be answered by a male voice rebutting her accusations in two of Surrey's poems. In poem 25, "Though I regarded not," the speaker denies that he has been inconstant, commenting

> … were my fancy strange,
> And wilfull will to wite,
> If I sought now to change
> A falkon for a kite. (5–8)

The pairing of falcons and kites is not a poetic commonplace; a search of books on EEBO in the date range 1473–1547 (the latter the date of Surrey's death) yields only three hits, all of them from lists of birds deemed unclean in Leviticus and Deuteronomy. Surrey's reference to the exchange of a falcon for a kite therefore seems likely to be a direct response to the falcon's lament in the *Squire's Tale*. This is reinforced by the fact that "wilfull will to wite" also seems to echo Chaucer's falcon's claim "my wyl was his willes instrument;/This is to seyn, my wyl obeyed his wyl" (568–9).

Traces of the falcon's lament can also be discerned in Poem 4, "Such waiward waies hath love," which can be read as another response to the falcon. This poem is a less straightforward response than poem 25, however; indeed it is a play of amazing evasiveness. It begins with a general account of the perversity of love, causing one person to desire and the other to shun. For the first eight lines, the gender of the speaker, the lover, and the beloved are all undetermined. From line 9, the speaker describes how love has caused him to leave a successful situation and turn to a hopeless one:

> From easy ford, where I might wade and passe ful wel,
> He me withdrawes, and doth me drive into a depe dark hel,
> And me withholdes, wher I am cald, and offred place:
> And willes me that my mortall foe I doe beseke of grace.
> He lettes me to pursue a conquest welnere wonne,
> To folow where my paines were lost, ere that my sute begonne. (9–14)

This could easily read as the response of the tercelet, uneasily wriggling to find an excuse for his desertion of the falcon (the "conquest welnere wonne") for the kite. He blames the abstract entity "love" for his change of heart, and argues that it is his experience of his own changing heart which has taught him how to deceive, although he stresses the authenticity of his own love and associated suffering.

Chaucer's falcon dwells on the deceit of the tercelet, expressed through a series of metaphors of concealment: although the tercelet was "ful of treson and falsnesse" (506),

> It was so wrapped under humble cheere,
> And under hewe of trouthe in swich manere,
> Under plesance, and under bisy peyne,
> That no wight koude han wend he koude feyne,
> So depe in greyn he dyed his coloures.
> Right as a serpent hit hym under floures
> Til he may seen his tyme for to byte ... (507–13)

And Surrey's poem picks up on these metaphors. The theme of color and dyeing is common to both texts; the tercelet covers treason "under hewe of trouthe" while Surrey's speaker deliberately displays "painted thoughtes" (20) in his face. Both use the image of the concealed serpent; the tercelet hides his true self "as a serpent hit hym under floures," while Surrey's speaker is familiar with the way "under the grene the serpent how he lurkes" (23).

Both poems use the proverb about a dog being beaten in front of a lion in order to teach the lion to behave (Tilley D443). The application of the proverb is explicit in the *Squire's Tale*: the falcon hopes "for to maken othere be war by me" (490). Surrey's use of the proverb in line 40 seems a deliberate recalling of Chaucer, but in Surrey it is unclear whether the lover is trying to align himself with lion or whelp, and to what end. The most striking aspect of Surrey's use of the proverb is the way it is encased in a declaration that the speaker *knew* "how the Lion chastised is by beating of the whelp." There is a strong emphasis in Surrey's poem on what the speaker knows about love ("I know" occurs 14 times), and what this emphasis reflects is a determined attempt to possess all aspects of the experience of love, to lay claim to it in the most insistent way. The application of the proverb does not matter to the speaker; what matters is his determined attempt to assert himself over the voice of the female falcon, and so to wrest the experience and expression of love and betrayal away from the female.

In many respects, then, *Tottel's Miscellany* has very different interests from Chaucer, and both passively and actively takes issue with his work. In particular, it withstands his sympathetic engagement with women, and his interest in female suffering and women's voices. In this respect, it is characteristic of other early print miscellanies. Elizabeth Heale argues, "[a]s the early Tudor balet moved from manuscript to print, so it became an almost exclusively male-voiced genre with the female-voiced poems of passion and retaliation largely silenced. In moving into print, the role of women as crucial to the culture and the production of courtly verse disappeared from sight."[34] And with this muting of women's voices, some of the most characteristic of Chaucer's interests also faded away.

---

[34]   Heale, "'Desiring Women Writing,'" p. 26.

Chapter 5
Songes and Sonettes, 1557

Peter C. Herman

For reasons that should be obvious, most literary critics treat Richard Tottel's 1557 collection, *Songes and Sonettes, written by the right honorable Lorde Henry Haward late Earle of Surry, and other*, strictly in terms of literary history. William Sessions, for example, proposes that "Tottel inaugurated a new kind of consumerism within early modern print culture and thereby institutionalized the English lyric and a classic English verse form," and Wendy Wall focuses on how this book "makes evident the existence of a real "stigma" at mid-century simply by the fact that it discloses to the public the poems circulating privately that writers had chosen to keep from the realm of print."[1] In this essay, however, I would like to broaden the focus to look at some of the implicit religious and nationalist politics of this collection. I want to explore, in other words, what the *Songes and Sonettes* may have meant at the time of its original publication in the summer of 1557 rather than viewing this text in the light of its subsequent meanings. In printing the *Songes and Sonettes* as well as other texts, I propose that Richard Tottel meant to participate in the creation of a distinctly English, distinctly Catholic culture intended to answer the Protestant nationalism arising in response to Mary I's attempt to bring England back into the Catholic fold. But Tottel's collection also intervenes in the more contested arena of Reformation politics, for in addition to presenting the earl of Surrey as an exemplar of Anglo-Catholic literary achievement (I make no arguments about the earl's actual religion), the *Songes and Sonettes* also contains within it a subtle polemic against Henry VIII, and it is no accident that this volume appears at a time when most historians agree that Mary's attempt at returning England to Catholicism had effectively stalled.[2]

---

[1]   I have throughout this essay adopted the modern usages of u/v, i/j, and vv/w, and silently expanded abbreviations.

[2]   Eamon Duffy, *The Stripping of the Altars: Traditional Religion in England 1400–1580* (New Haven, 1992), pp. 524–64, and his expansion of this chapter, *Fires of Faith: Catholic England under Mary Tudor* (New Haven, 2009), makes the significant point that the historiography of Mary's regime is deeply colored by the religious affiliation of the historian, and he argues that Mary's religious policy was not an exercise in nostalgia that encountered general resistance.

Publishing Catholicism

On the one hand, looking at Richard Tottel's publication record up through 1557 shows that a poetical miscellany seems to be an unusual, if not entirely unprecedented, project. A year after his admission to the Stationers' Company, Edward VI's government granted Tottel a seven-year monopoly on printing "almaner bokes of oure temporall lawe called the Common lawe" (Thomas Norton, part author of *Gorboduc* and translator of Calvin, would later claim that Tottel gained the privilege "at [the] sute of the Judges"),[3] suggesting his close relationship with London's legal community. Certainly, Tottel seems to have taken full advantage of the privilege granted him. According to the British Library's English Short Title Catalogue, Tottel published 67 books between 1553 and 1557 (including reprints), and almost all are legal texts, such as yearbooks and Littleton's *Tenures* (1554). Interspersed, however, among statutes and law reports, we find evidence that Tottel also had a genuine interest in poetry: a book of Psalms from the Sternhold and Hopkins psalter (1554); a revised edition of Lydgate's *Fall of Princes* (1554); and Stephen Hawes *The Pastime of Pleasure* (1555).[4] Yet Tottel's main business focused on legal texts, and his main goal in life seems to have been making as much money as possible, so much so that in 1577, a petition complained that Tottel sold his law books "at excessive prices, to the hinderance of a greate number of pore studentes."[5] In other words, Richard Tottel seems to have been motivated by profits, not ideology. Even so, in addition to a side interest in verse, a closer look at the books he printed suggests a strong subinterest in Catholicism and religious polemics.

From the early 1550s onward, "all of Tottel's associates at this time were Catholics," including an influential group centered at Lincoln's Inn that included William Rastell, William Roper, and Richard Heywood, all three of course being members of the Thomas More circle.[6] Significantly, the first book Tottel published is not a legal text, but Thomas More's *A Dialogue of Comfort against Tribulation*, which appeared on 18 November 1553, a few months after the Protestant Edward

---

[3]   Quoted in Anna Greening, "Tottel, Richard (*b.* in or before 1528, *d.* 1593)," *Oxford Dictionary of National Biography* (Oxford, 2004); online ed., May 2009 [http://www.oxforddnb.com/view/article/27573, accessed 26 April 2011].

[4]   On Richard Tottel's side interest in verse, see Steven May, "Popularizing Courtly Poetry: *Tottel's Miscellany* and its Progeny," in Mike Pincombe and Cathy Shrank (eds.), *The Oxford Handbook of Tudor Literature, 1485–1603* (Oxford: Oxford University Press, 2009), pp. 418–33.

[5]   Quoted in Greening, "Richard Tottel."

[6]   H.J. Byrom, "Richard Tottel—His Life and Works," *The Library*, 8 (1927–28): 204; Louis L. Martz, "Introduction," in Thomas More, *A Dialogue of Comfort against Tribulation*, ed. Louis Martz and Frank Manley (New Haven, 1976), p. xlix. Margaret Trudeau-Clayton, "What is my Nation? Language, Verse, and Politics in Tudor Translations of Virgil's *Aeneid*," in Mike Pincombe and Cathy Shrank (eds.), *Oxford Handbook of Tudor Literature, 1485–1603* (Oxford, 2009), p. 391, also notes Tottel's Catholicism.

VI's death from tuberculosis on 6 July. The young Tottel's inaugural publication is the dialogue Thomas More wrote while awaiting execution in the Tower for maintaining the Pope's supremacy over Henry VIII. While we cannot know for certain, since Tottel does not provide any sort of preface or dedication, it seems fair to assume that by publishing one of the final works by Henry VIII's most famous (but far from only) victim at the very start of the Catholic Mary I's reign, Tottel wanted to align himself with Mary's religious policies and to participate in her attempt at reviving Catholicism by printing a book sure to remind browsers and readers of Henry VIII's tyranny. To be sure, Tottel's primary interest throughout his career remained legal publishing (and making money), but his side interest in promoting Catholicism, and in promoting a Catholic nationalist sensibility, will subtend his non-legal offerings, including the *Songes and Sonettes*.[7]

Mary's accession and marriage to Philip of Spain occasioned a firestorm of opposition that was largely nationalist (as opposed to religious, although obviously the lines were blurred) in origin, and opponents to the match characterized the royal couple as a threat to England itself, not just to Protestantism.[8] In particular, anti-Marian pamphlets often focused on England's conception of itself as a nation of laws rather than men, whose essence lies in the sanctity of private property and the preservation of the subject's liberties. Magna Carta (1215) reaffirmed that "No free man shall be seized or imprisoned, or stripped of his rights or possessions, or outlawed or exiled, or deprived of his standing in any other way, nor will we proceed with force against him, or send others to do so, except by the lawful judgement of his equals or by the law of the land,"[9] and the late fifteenth-century jurist, Sir John Fortescue, in his frequently reprinted, *In Praise of the Laws of England*, regularly describes how in England, very much unlike France, the monarch is subject to the law, not vice versa. The Justinian phrase, "What pleased the prince has the force of law," Fortescue writes, describes France, but "the laws of England do not sanction any such maxim, since the king of that land … is bound by oath at his coronation to the observance of his law."[10] Significantly, Mary's antagonists did not stop at asserting that she only pretended to be English—John Knox wrote that "all her doynges declareth … that under an Englyshe name

---

[7]   On Tottel and the Marian Reformation, see Tom Betteridge's chapter in his *Literature and Politics in the English Reformation* (Manchester, 2004), pp. 130–73.

[8]   D.M. Loades, *The Reign of Mary Tudor: Politics, Government and Religion in England, 1553–1558* (New York, 1974), pp. 159–60; Herbert Grabes, "England or the Queen? Public Conflict of Opinion and National Identity under Mary Tudor," in *Writing the Early Modern English Nation: The Transformation of National Identity in Sixteenth- and Seventeenth Century England* (Atlanta, 2001), pp. 47–88. I am highly indebted to Grabes's analysis and the primary sources he cites. On the connections between Protestantism and English nationalism, see also Liah Greenfeld, *Nationalism: Five Roads to Modernity* (Cambridge, 1992), pp. 54–9.

[9]   http://www.fordham.edu/halsall/source/magnacarta.html. Accessed April 29, 2011.

[10]   Fortescue, *On the Laws and Governance of England*, ed. Shelley Lockwood (Cambridge, 1997), p. 48.

she beareth a Spaniardes herte"[11]—they accused her of undermining England's fundamental values.

Knox, for example, claimed that Mary's marriage plans made her "an open traitoresse to the Imperiall crown of England, [because it is] contrary to the just lawes of the realme, to brynge in a straunger, and make a proude Spaniarde kynge."[12] Indeed, this marriage threatens England's very political structure, as it will lead to "the abaysing of the yomanry, to the slavery of the communaltie, to the overthrowe of Christianitie and Goddess true religion, and finally to the utter subvercion of the hole publice estate and commonwealth of Englande."[13] An anonymous writer warned that the Spanish actions in Naples predict the destruction of the values enshrined in Magna Carta, should Spain gain a foothold in England: "Behold (good reader) in this horrible destruction of the kingdom of Naples/wrought by the king of Spayne and his Spaniardes/the present mysery that hangeth this day over the noble realme of England."[14] There is no rule of law: "the Spaniardes have bene only lordes and maisters over all/byddyng & forbidding what them lusteth"; nor do they respect the sanctity of private property: "No man can kepe hys owne house/ when it once lyketh them. No writinges of landes/or tytell of inheritaunce can serve against their fearfull force/and lawless tyrannie."[15] And another anonymous writer warned that the Spanish marriage would turn the "naturall and fre countre of England/which of all the other contres in Christendome/hath bene the most freyst" into slaves, forced to endure "vyle servitude and bondage."[16]

To be sure, Mary's apologists responded in kind, although as D.M. Loades notes, government sponsored "catholic propaganda and polemic were less, both in quality and quantity, than that of the protestants."[17] Miles Hogarde (sometimes spelled "Huggarde") for example, countered by blaming the economic and political turmoil of Edward's reign (e.g, Kett's Rebellion) on Protestantism, not Catholicism:

---

[11]   Knox, *A faythfull admonition made by John Knox, unto the professours of Gods truthe in England* (Emden, 1554), sig. E5v. These views clearly made an impression on Spain's ambassador to England, Simon Renard, quoted in David Loades, *Mary Tudor: A Life* (London, 1989), p. 231, who reported in 1554 that the English "loudly proclaim that they are going to be enslaved, for the queen is a Spanish woman at heart and thinks nothing of Englishmen, but only of Spaniards and bishops."

[12]   Knox, *A faythfull admonition*, sig. E4v.

[13]   Knox *A faythfull admonition*, sig. E4v-ʳ.

[14]   *A warnyng for Englande conteynyng the horrible practises of the Kyng of Spayne, in the kyngdome of Naples, and the miseries wherunto that noble realme is brought. Wherby all Englishe men may vnderstand the plage that shall light vpo[n] them, yf the Kyng of Spayn obteyne the dominion in Englande* (Emden, 1555), sig. A2r.

[15]   *A warnyng*, sig. A4r.

[16]   Quoted in Grabes, "England," p. 71.

[17]   Loades, *The Reign*, p. 341. For a useful challenge to this generally accepted position, see Jennifer Loach, "The Marian Establishment and the Printing Press," *English Historical Review*, 101 (1986): 135–48.

And so as long as this realme was in unitie thereof undivided, it continewed in inspeakable welth, and prosperitie, in marvelous love & amitie, in true dealing & honest simplicitie, and in al kinde of godliness and pietie. But since it fell from unitie of religion, it hath fallen from the grace of God into al kyndes of wickendness, scarcitie, falshode, deceyt, and other abhominable vices, and from accustomed valiaunce in feates of armes into affeminite myndes contaminate with horrible lecherie. The experiences of vices piteously we dayly fele, as a just rewarde of God, for breache of the unitie of his religion.[18]

Strangely, it largely fell to private individuals to take up the Catholic cause in the propaganda wars, Mary's government preferring to rely on such enforcement mechanisms as replacing Protestant with Catholic clerics, censorship, and burning Protestants at the stake (nearly 30 people died by fire in the months leading up to the publication of the *Songes and Sonettes*). In 1556, a new front opened up when a group of literati started countering Protestant nationalism with their own efforts at defining the English nation, and fascinatingly enough, these efforts focus on culture rather than theology.

Catholic Culture

In 1556, the antiquary, Nicholas Brigham, who also held a variety of important financial offices for Mary, had "at his owne cost and charge" Geoffrey Chaucer's remains reburied in Westminster Abbey "in a traditional Catholic style of tomb" in an attempt to redeem Chaucer "for orthodoxy and at the same time demonstrate the natural and inevitable continuity of that orthodoxy."[19] Thus Chaucer's bones were reinterred in a newly built alter-tomb, and as Derek Pearsall notes, this move carried with it a cultural and religious argument: "Such tombs, providing space for a priest to say private prayers for the soul of the deceased seem to have been particularly in vogue in late fifteenth-century friars' churches. Choosing such a tomb for Chaucer was obviously a way of associating him with a specifically late medieval Catholic practice."[20] Furthermore, the association is as much patriotic as religious: whereas the original epitaph called the deceased "Galfridus Chaucer

---

[18]   Miles Hogarde, *The Displaying of the Protestantes* (London, 1556), sig. L4r-L5v.

[19]   Quoted in Thomas Speght, *The workes of our antient and learned english poet, Geffrey Chaucer, newly printed* (London, 1602), sig. C1v; Derek Pearsall, "Chaucer's Tomb: The Politics of Reburial," *Medium Aevum* 64.1 (1995): 64, 63. See also Joseph A. Dane, *Who is Buried in Chaucer's Tomb? Studies in the Reception of Chaucer's Book* (East Lansing, 1998), pp. 14–15; Thomas Prendergast, *Chaucer's Dead Body: From Corpse to Corpus* (New York, 2004), pp. 47–51, and William A. Sessions, *Henry Howard The Poet Earl of Surrey: A Life* (Oxford, 1999), p. 258. On Brigham, see James P. Carley's entry in the *Oxford Dictionary of National Biography*.

[20]   Pearsall, "Chaucer's," p. 63.

vates," Brigham adds a new term: "*Anglorum* vates"—the *English* poet-prophet (my emphasis).[21]

If Brigham sought to authorize Mary's reign and religious policies by enlisting Geoffrey Chaucer as a cultural ancestor—thus reappropriating him from the Protestants, who claimed Chaucer for their own due to the spurious "Plowman's Tale"[22]—other Marian writers sought to portray her ascension as inaugurating a literal renaissance of English learning and letters. Robert Record, for example, in the dedication to Mary of his astronomical text, *The Castle of Knowledge* (1556), parallels the "longe banishment & tediouse exyle" of both "knowledge" and his queen, and hopes that now that Mary has returned, so "knowledge might bee maintained and revoked from exyle."[23] More precisely, a number of Catholic writers and academics suggest that Mary's reign ushered in a blossoming of the English vernacular.[24]

In 1556, the publisher Thomas Powell (whose Catholic sympathies may be gleaned from his reprinting in 1557 John Gwynne's *A playne demonstration of John Frithes lacke of witte and learnynge in his understandynge of holie scripture and of the olde holy doctours, in the blessed sacrament of the aulter*), brought out John Heywood's extensive pro-Marian allegory, *The Spider and the Fly*, as well as reprinting his *Dialogue Conteinyng the Nomber in effect of all the Proverbes in the Englishe Tongue*, which is designed to recover these lost nuggets of wisdom as well as promote the vernacular:

> Among other things profiting in our tong
> Those which much may profit both old & yong
> Such as on their fruite will feede or take holde
> Are our common playne pithy proverbes olde. (sig. A2ᵛ)

Nicholas Grimald (whose poems will also appear in the *Songes and Sonettes*), in the preface to his 1556 translation of Cicero's *Duties*, will conflate Cicero's virtues with the virtues of English and his translation:

---

[21]   Speght, *The workes*, sig. C1v. Cf., Pearsall, "Chaucer's," p. 66. Thomas Elyot, *The dictionary of Syr Thomas Eliot knyght* (London, 1538), sig. Dd6r, defines "vates" as "a prophete, a poete."

[22]   John N. King, *English Reformation Literature: The Tudor Origins of the Protestant Tradition* (Princeton, 1982), p. 51.

[23]   Record, *The Castle of Knowledge* (London, 1556), sig. A2r. I am grateful to Timothy Duffy for bringing Record's text to my attention. Curiously, the 1596 reprint of this text included the original dedication and preface.

[24]   Richard Foster Jones, *The Triumph of the English Language* (Stanford, 1953), p. 22, therefore, is not exactly right when he writes in his seminal book, that "Distrust in the literary qualities of the vernacular consistently dominated the greater part of the sixteenth century" (p. 22). While he notes, p. 170, Tottel's preface, Jones considers it an exception to the rule, rather than part of a small but concerted attempt at celebrating the vernacular.

These richesse, & trasures of witt, and wisdome, as Cicero transported oute of
Greece into Italie: so have I fetched from thence, & conveied them into England:
and have caused also Marcus Tullius (more, than he could do, when he was
alive) to speake English. Marvailous is the mater, flowing the eloquence, riche
the store of stuff, & full artificiall [artful] the enditing: but how I, in our maner
of Speche, have expressed the same the more the booke bee perused, the better
it may chance to appere.[25]

Granted, Grimald is as much interested in self-promotion as in promoting the
vernacular (the more you read my book, he says, the more you will appreciate
how well I have translated Cicero). But in puffing up his achievement, Grimald
necessarily promotes English, which now equals the virtues of Cicero's Latin.

However, the clearest example of a Catholic writer being promoted as reviving
English culture would be William Rastell's dedicatory preface to the collected
vernacular works of Sir Thomas More, published in 1557 by John Cawod, John
Waly, and not coincidentally, Richard Tottel.[26] As the title of this volume makes
clear—*The Workes of Sir Thomas More Knyght, sometyme Lorde Chancellour
of England, written by him in the Englysh tonge*—this massive tome leaves out
More's voluminous Latin writings, and that is because the purpose of this book is
to not only memorialize a famous martyr, Sir Thomas More, but to create an icon
of specifically English, specifically Catholic achievement:

> When I considered with my self (moost gratious soveraigne) what greate
> eloquence, excellent learninge, and morall vertues, were to be conteyned in the
> workes and bookes, that the wyse and godlie man, Sir Thomas More knighte,
> sometyme lorde Chancellour of England (my dere uncle) wrote in the Englysh
> tonge, so many and so well, as no one Englishman (I suppose) ever wrote the
> like, whereby his workes be worthy to be hadde and redde of everye Englishe
> man, that is studious or desirous to know and learne, not onelye the eloquence
> and propertie of the English tonge, but also the true doctrine of Christes catholike
> fayth … .[27]

Rastell's point is that reading his uncle's works represent a *nationalist* achievement.
His works should be read not by everyone, regardless of origin, but should be
"hadde and redde of everye English man" (just as Chaucer moved from "vates" to
"Anglorum vates"), and his writing not only instructs readers in "the true doctrine
of Christes catholike fayth" (which everybody would understand is opposed to
the "false" doctrines of Protestantism), but the "eloquence and propertie of the
English tonge." The "wider restoration of Catholicism," to use Eamon Duffy's
phrase, goes hand in hand with restoration of the vernacular: More's achievements
in theology being part and parcel of his achievements in English eloquence.[28]

---

[25]   *Marcus Tullius Ciceroes The bokes of duties* (London, 1556), sig. ℭℭ6r.

[26]   Loades, *The Reign*, p. 343, also notes that the "rehabilitation of More was a natural
consequence of the return to catholic policies."

[27]   Sig. ℭ2r.

[28]   Duffy, *Fires of Faith*, p. 179.

Renovating the Vernacular

It is in this context, therefore, that in the summer of 1557 Richard Tottel publishes his two editions of *Songes and Sonettes, written by the right honorable Lorde Henry Haward late Earle of Surrey, and other.*[29] Significantly, Tottel's preface, "To the Reader," repeats some of the rhetoric in Rastell's preface to the More volume as well as Grimald's preface to his translation of Cicero:

> That to have wel written in verse, yea and in small parcelles, deserveth great praise, the woorkes of divers Latines, Italians, & other doe prove sufficiently. That our tong is able in that kinde to do as praise worthelye as the rest, the honorable stile of the noble earle of Surrey, and the weightinesse of the depewitted sir Thomas Wiat the elders verse, with several graces in sundry good English writers, do show abundantly. It resteth now (gentle reder) yf thou thinke it not evil don, to publishe, to the honor of the English tong, and for profit of the studious of English eloquence, those workes which the ungentle horders up of such tresure have heretofore envied thee. (sig. A2ᵛ)[30]

Critics with good reason have often looked at the *Songes and Sonettes* as evidence for a fundamental shift in the publication of lyric verse. Arthur Marotti, for instance, proposes that Tottel "characterizes print as fostering a civilizing process that reaches down to the lowest strata of society," while William A. Sessions sees Tottel as combining profit and altruism, the "higher communal good of publishing the poems" also constituting a major business opportunity.[31] What I would like to suggest, however, is that Sessions is in fact closer to the mark when he writes that what Tottel meant for Surrey's person and poems "will also do the work of Marian *renovatio*," although I would expand the range to include the entirety of the *Songes and Sonettes* (the specific figure of Surrey I will get to below).[32] The contents of this volume, in other words, are meant to present to the world a model of a distinctly English literary achievement. The poems redound "to the honor of the English tong" just as Thomas More's vernacular works demonstrate "the eloquence and propertie of the English tonge," and behind both of them lie the achievements of the now-Catholic Geoffrey Chaucer, "Anglorum vates."

---

[29]   This first version appeared on June 5; the second, much revised, on July 31.

[30]   Unless otherwise noted, all references will be to the second edition of the *Songes and Sonettes*, and will be cited parenthetically. While Rollins's edition is a monument of scholarship, it nonetheless has the unfortunate drawback of erasing the various "marks of historical specificity," as Leah Marcus, *Unediting the Renaissance: Shakespeare, Marlowe, Milton* (New York, 1996), p. 20, puts it. Hyder E. Rollins, ed., *Tottel's Miscellany, 1557–1587* (2 vols., Cambridge, MA, 1966), includes, for example, the poems Tottel dropped from the second edition, and he largely preserves the order of the first edition.

[31]   Marotti, *Manuscript, Print, and the English Renaissance Lyric* (Ithaca, 1995), p. 215; Sessions, *Henry Howard*, p. 274.

[32]   Sessions, *Henry Howard*, p. 273.

Indeed, the *Songes and Sonettes* seems to have formed part of a more general publishing program aimed to renovating the vernacular. On 10 September 1554, Tottel published his version of Lydgate's *The Fall of Princes*, and the difference in the title between Tottel's edition and the one published by John Wayland earlier that year are instructive. The latter calls his book *The tragedies, gathered by Jhon Bochas ... . Translated into Englysh by John Lidgate, monke of Burye*. Tottel, however, gives his product an even more elaborate title, and one that privileges the translation: *A treatise excellent and compe[n]dious, shewing and declaring, in maner of tragedye, the falles of sondry most notable princes and princesses vvith other nobles, ... First compyled in Latin by the excellent clerke Bocatius, an Italian borne. And sence that tyme translated into our English and vulgare tong, by Dan John Lidgate monke of Burye.* Wayland's "*English*" becomes in Tottel a proud assertion of ownership and national identity: "*our English and vulgare tong*". Along with the identification of Boccaccio's nationality—"*an Italian borne*"—, Tottel's title emphasizes not only how this text has moved from one language to another, but like Grimald's preface to his Cicero translation, the equivalence between English and Latin. Tottel performs a similar revision when he brings out in 1557—in between the original and revised editions of the *Songes and Sonettes*—Surrey's translations of the *Aeneid* books 2 and 4. In 1554, William Awen, Thomas Howard's "oratour," published Surrey's translation of Book 4,[33] and in the title he calls Surrey's blank verse "*a straunge metre*," meaning, a *foreign* meter; Tottel, however, has Surrey translating Virgil "*into English meter*," not foreign, but homegrown. The *Songes and Sonettes*, the *Certain Bokes of Virgiles Aenaeis*, and Lydgate's *Fall of Princes* all form part of a nationalist project to revive and revalue the English language.

That project, interestingly enough, extended to Tottel's treatment of the verse itself.[34] While Tottel (to our knowledge) did not alter any of Surrey's blank verse, he most certainly applied his hand to many of the poems in the *Songes and Sonettes,* much to the dismay of various editors who decried Tottel's "regularizing" of English meter in the *Songes* (Hyder Rollins said that "Editorial changes of the kind mentioned were most unfair to Wyatt"[35]), but to my knowledge, only Steven May has noted that Tottel extends the same treatment of Lydgate's verse in the

---

[33]   It might seem strange that the printer for Awen's edition of Surrey's Virgil was the very Protestant John Day. However, Day essentially lost all his business contacts once the Catholic Mary ascended the throne: his royal patents were cancelled, and his ecclesiastical patrons were either in exile or dead (there are some indications that Day himself briefly went into exile). To make ends meet, Day became a freelance printer, although he still retained his status in London's small community of printers; see Bryan P. Davis, "John Day," in James K. Bracken and Joel Silver (eds.), *The British Literary Book Trade, 1475–1700* (Detroit, 1996), p. 83.

[34]   For bibliographic details on the printing of the two editions, see Paul A. Marquis, "Editing and Unediting Richard Tottel's *Songes and Sonnettes*," *The Book Collector*, 56.3 (2007): pp. 356–60.

[35]   Rollins, *Tottel's*, vol. 2, p. 95.

Fall of Princes. In the former, Tottel changed literally "hundreds of readings," and the common denominator is smoothing out the meter: "it is striking how many of the alterations transform [the original's] rhythms from the often irregular beat of Pynson's version into regular iambic pentameter."[36] To give but one example, "Eyther for helpe or encrease of peyne" (sig. A4ʳ) becomes in Tottel "Eyther for helpe or *for* encrease of payne" (sig. A4ʳ; my emphasis), the addition of "for" turning the irregular line into a regular one. As many have noted, Tottel irons out Wyatt in equivalent ways. Again, to give but one example, admittedly chosen at random, "The furious gun in his raging ire"[37] becomes in the *Songes and Sonettes* "The furious goone, in his most raging yre" (sig. O2ʳ). As May notes concerning Tottel's Lydgate edition, and his comment applies equally well to the *Songes and Sonettes*, Tottel "went to a great deal of trouble here," and the question is why.[38] Clearly, Richard Tottel had a vision of what English verse ought to look like, and he wanted, like many of his circle, to promote the English vernacular as the equivalent of Latin and romance languages. In so doing, Tottel anticipates the nationalist fervor for the vernacular that will start in the late 1570s.[39] However, I suggest that Tottel's linguistic nationalism and his aesthetic vision form part of the more general project to forge a new English literary culture, one that is distinctly Catholic.

The polemical, religious orientation of the *Songes and Sonettes* manifests itself in a number of ways. As John N. King pointed out, William Gray's antifeminist "epitaph," probably written during Edward VI's reign (sig. Bb3ᵛ⁻ʳ), which blames his "wicked wife" for "shortnyng" his life, had the last sixteen stanzas expunged, doubtless "because of its vigorous antipapal satire and advocacy of the English Bible as the guide to life."[40] The volume also includes John Heywood's poem in praise of Queen Mary, "A Praise of his Ladye" (sig. R3ᵛ⁻ʳ).[41] More generally, as Stephen Hamrick has persuasively argued, the *Songes and Sonettes* often encodes "a Catholic poetics," incorporating "contemporary Catholic practice and its theology of images" within its Petrarchan verses.[42] Surrey's "Description of

---

[36]   May, "Popularizing Courtly Poetry," p. 426.

[37]   "Epigram XLIII," *Sir Thomas Wyatt: The Complete Poems,* ed. Ronald Rebholz (New Haven, 1978), p. 92.

[38]   May, "Popularizing Courtly Poetry," p. 426.

[39]   Jones, *The Triumph*, pp. 168–79; Richard Helgerson, *Forms of Nationhood: The Elizabethan Writing of England* (Chicago, 1992), pp. 1–4, 25–39; Cathy Shrank, *Writing the Nation in Reformation England 1530-1580* (Oxford, 2004), p. 118.

[40]   King, *English Reformation Literature*, p. 245.

[41]   Rollins, *Tottel's*, vol. 2, p. 3. The first edition of the *Songes and Sonettes* included Nicholas Grimald's translation of Walter Haddon's elegy for Henry Fitzalan, Lord Maltravers, which elaborates the original description of the Queen as "Maria hunc regina Britonum" into "The peerless princesse, Mary queen"; see Rollins, *Tottell's*, vol. 1, p. 114; vol. 2, pp. 3, 246. This poem was omitted for the second edition.

[42]   Hamrick, "*Tottel's Miscellany* and the English Reformation," *Criticism*, 44.4 (2002): 331, 336.

the restless state of the lover," for example, concluding lines—"And now the covert brest I claime,/That worship Cupide secretely,/And nourished his sacred flame:/From whence no blasyng sparkes do flye" (sig. A3ʳ)—evoke the popular practice of "decking" altars and saints or providing money for candles and other material elements of saint construction and adoration.[43] I suggest that Tottel's "emendations" to the poetry fit his vision of metrical correctness and constitute the formal or technical analogue to the kind of Catholic poetics Hamrick describes in two ways.

First, Tottel's smoothing out the verse is, I think, part of the project we have seen in the preface to the collected English works of Thomas More, Grimald's preface to his translation of Cicero, and Tottel's publication of Surrey's translation of Virgil to demonstrate the worth of the English vernacular and to bring English verse up to the standards of Continental and classical verse. In his preface, Tottel asserted "That to have wel written in verse, yea and in small parcelles, deserveth great praise, the [woorkes] of divers Latines, Italians, & other doe prove sufficiently. That our tong is able in that kinde to do as praise worthelye as the rest, the honorable stile of the noble earle of Surrey, and the weightinesse of the depewitted sir Thomas Wiat the elders verse, with several graces in sundry good English writers, do show abundantly" (sig. A2ᵛ). Tottel therefore adjusts the "stile" of the "weighty" Thomas Wyatt (and given the number of adjustments to Wyatt's poetry, it is significant that Tottel praises Surrey's "stile," but not Wyatt's) so that he sounds more like "the honorable stile" preferred by Surrey, and the point is that these poets, as well as the others in this collection, come closer to the mellifluousness found in "the woorkes of divers Latines [and] Italians."[44] English, in other words, is as worthy and as capable a language as its two competitors, and the poets included in the *Songes and Sonettes* can take their place alongside Sir Thomas More and Geoffrey Chaucer as representatives of English, Catholic achievement.

Second, by moving away from the more jagged, less regular meters and the alliteration associated with native lyric traditions, I suggest that Tottel also wanted to differentiate the contents of the *Songes and Sonettes* from the kind of verse one finds in the Protestant literature of this period. As John King has explored, these writers preferred the plain style in prose and rejected "the imported forms" in verse, such as the sonnet, espoused by Surrey and others, while embracing the more rough-hewn metrics of the native traditions. Take, for example, the faux-Chaucerian *The Plowman's Tale*, where one finds such lines as "The Ploweman plucked up his plowe/Whan mydsommer mone was comen in," and "A sterne stryfe is stered newe/In many stedes in a stounde."[45] Or the opening lines to Robert

---

[43] Hamrick, '*Tottel's Miscellany*," 337.

[44] On Tottel's editorial emendations to Wyatt, see Michael Spiller, *The Development of the Sonnet: An Introduction* (London, 1992), pp. 99–101.

[45] *The Plowman's Tale*, ed. James Dean, *TEAMS Middle English Text Series*, http://www.lib.rochester.edu/camelot/Teams/plwtltxt.htm. Accessed 10 May 2011, lines 1–2, 53–4.

Crowley's *Philargyrie*: "Geve eare awhile/And marke my style/You that hath wyt in store/For wyth wordes bare/I wyll declare/Things done long tyme before."[46] By altering Wyatt's and Langland's metrics (possibly others as well, but these two we know were changed), Tottel not only adopts European models of versifying, he implicitly disassociates Surrey and the other poets of the *Songes and Sonettes* from the kinds of native poetics embraced by such Protestant gospellers as the "Plowman Poet" and Crowley. In sum, altering the formal properties in Wyatt signifies a religious as well as an aesthetic argument: Tottel's poets (including Langland) not only represent what the vernacular can achieve, but what Catholic writers can, and have, achieved. They represent, in Sessions's terms, what the Marian *renovatio* means in terms of English literature.

Odious to Many People

There is also, however, a more pointed, more overtly political argument encoded in the *Songes and Sonettes*, one that seeks to endorse the Marian revolution in English religion by reminding readers of Henry VIII's tyranny. By 1557, Mary's attempt to stamp out the Protestant opposition had effectively stalled, at least in good part because the Marian regime's restoration of the heresy laws in 1555 resulted in a procession of martyrs to the Protestant cause. While many, as the Bishop of Worcester and Protestant martyr Hugh Latimer predicted, "went with the world" and accommodated themselves to the restoration of Catholicism, a very significant number maintained their ties to the "new religion," and each attempt at extirpating heresy by fire seemed to create new adherents to the Protestant cause. A report from the Venetian ambassador, Giovanni Michielli, from 1555 exemplifies how Mary's heresy policy had backfired:

> ... two days ago, to the displeasure, as usual of the population here, two Londoners were burned alive, one of them having been public lecturer in Scripture, a person sixty years of age, who was held in great esteem. In a few days the like will be done to four or five more; and thus from time to time to many others who are in prison for this cause and will not recant, although such sudden severity is odious to many people.[47]

As Loades puts it, Mary's government was "afflicted by a sense of failure, of fighting with a hydra which constantly sprouted fresh heads,"[48] as exemplified by how quickly and skillfully Protestant propagandists turned Mary's immolations into the martyrdom narratives that would eventually form the basis for John Foxe's *Acts and Monuments*. Indeed, Hogarde and Bishop John Fisher complained about the "false martyrs" of the Protestants.[49] Which brings us back to Richard Tottel.

---

[46]   Robert Crowley, *Philargyrie of Greate Britayne* (London, 1551), sig. A3r.

[47]   Quoted in Loades, *The Reign*, p. 334.

[48]   Ibid., p. 333; see also John Guy, *Tudor England* (Oxford, 1988), p. 247.

[49]   Loades, *The Reign*, p. 343.

The first complete edition of Thomas More's works in English, which Tottel co-published with John Cawood, the Queen's printer, and one John Waly (the complete More is his only recorded imprint) was an attempt to restore More to his place as a "true" martyr, and I suggest that Tottel tries to do something of the same for Henry Howard, earl of Surrey. The earl, we should remember, was executed by Henry VIII for asserting his right to the throne by altering his coat of arms by moving the arms of Edward the Confessor to the first quarter and using "'three labels silver' to indicate he is the true heir apparent," thereby endangering the accession of Henry VIII's son by Jane Seymour, the future Edward VI.[50] However, Surrey's indictment was based on Henry VIII's 1536 revision of the treason statute to include words, not just deeds, and that allowed Henry Howard to be constructed as Henry VIII's last victim.[51] That is certainly how Mary Tudor thought of him and his father, Thomas Howard, Duke of Norfolk, who had spent most of the last decade clapped in the Tower and who escaped execution only by Henry VIII's timely demise. One of Mary's first acts after entering London in triumph after Northumberland's attempt to place Jane Gray on the throne collapsed was to visit Norfolk, and Mary made a point at her first parliament of repudiating the treason statutes under which Surrey was condemned. According to the eighteenth-century historian John Strype, the Queen "called to her remembrance, that many honourable and noble persons, and others of good reputation, had lately, for words only, suffered shameful deaths, not accustomed to nobles, and therefore, of her clemency, and trusting her loving subjects were contented that such dangerous and painful laws should be abolished[.]"[52] By privileging Henry Howard in the title of his poetic collection, Richard Tottel thus points toward a man known as

---

[50]   Sessions, *Henry Howard,* p. 170.

[51]   On Surrey's indictment (which Henry VIII annotated), trial and execution, see Sessions, *Henry Howard*, pp. 388–409, and Greg Walker, *Writing Under Tyranny: English Literature and the Henrician Reformation* (Oxford, 2005), pp. 383–6.

[52]   John Strype, *Ecclesiastical Memorials, relating chiefly to Religion and its Reformation, under the Reigns of King Henry VIII, King Edward VI, and Queen Mary the First* (London, 1816), vol. 4, p. 59. Sessions, *Henry Howard*, p. 271, mistakes Strype's anti-Catholic rhetoric for Mary's speech to Parliament when he asserts that the Queen "opened her first Parliament with a specific reference to the poet Earl of Surrey and the horror of his death." It is Strype, p. 59, not Mary, who asserts that Surrey for "the poor crime of assuming somewhat into his coat of arms, was actually beheaded." Strype, ibid., goes on to mordantly note that despite Mary's horror at the injustice of this statute, none of the Protestants who "were already taken up and crowded into jails should receive benefit by this wonderful act of clemency." Nor was Mary alone in her revulsion. In a sermon preached before King Edward VI on 22 March 1549, Hugh Latimer, *Sermons by Hugh Latimer*, ed. Geroge Elwes Corrie (Cambridge, 1844), vol. 1, p. 149, recalls that the final period of Henry VIII's reign was "a dangerous world, for it might soon cost a man his life for a word speaking"; see also Alec Ryrie, "The Slow Death of a Tyrant: Learning to Live Without Henry VIII, 1547–1563," in Mark Rankin, Christopher Highley and John King (eds.), *Henry VIII and his Afterlives: Literature, Politics, Art* (Cambridge, 2009), p. 86.

both a victim of Henry VIII's tyranny and someone who Queen Mary likely had considerable sympathy for. Tottel, in other words, constructs Surrey as a Catholic martyr, and he does so by a very simple expedient: including the term "late" in the title.

Martyr Surrey

Now, there are no hard and fast rules as to how long a deceased person should be considered "late," but an examination of the titles of works published between 1473 and 1558 shows that "late" means "recently," as in last year, or maybe the last two or three years. For example, this anonymous poem, *A lamentation of the death of the moost victorious Prynce Henry the eyght late kynge of thys noble royalme of Englande*, was published in 1547, the same year Henry VIII died, and a proclamation also published in 1547 refers to "*the debtes due by his graces father, late kyng of moste famous memory*." Similarly, in 1558 Elizabeth I would issue a proclamation announcing her ascension to the throne because "it hath pleased almighty God by calling to his mercie … our dearest sister of noble memorie, Mary, late queene." Two more examples nearly co-terminus with the *Songes and Sonettes*: Miles Standish in 1556 publishes a defense of the papacy, *The Triall of the Supremacy*, that includes *answeres to the blasphemous objections made agaynste the same in the late miserable yeres now paste*, and from the Protestant side, also in 1556, we have *Certayne godly, learned, and comfortable conferences betwene the two reverende fathers and holye martyres of Christe, D. Nicolas Ridley late byshoppe of London, and M. Hugh Latymer, somtime bishop of Worcester, duryng the tyme of their emprisonmentes* (Ridley was burned at the stake in 1555). The casual browser, therefore, would likely have considered the subclause of Tottel's title for his book, "*written by the right honorable Lorde Henry Haward late Earle of Surrey*" (and the same applies to the browser of Awen's edition of Surrey's translation of the *Aeneid*, Book 4, from which Tottel borrows the phrase), as very strange, since the earl died nearly 10 years before the publication of this volume. According to the conventional use of the term, Surrey was no longer "late."

By inserting this chronologically odd term into the title, Tottel (and Awen) make Surrey's death new again, and remind the reader as to just why and how the earl died. While Henry Howard did not die as a martyr for the faith, as More did (although a rumor circulated on the continent that Howard and his father fell because they had "made a secret attempt to restore the Pope and the monks"[53]), his poems, as Stephen Hamrick has amply demonstrated, evince a Catholic sensibility, and even more importantly, he died because of a terrible bill sponsored by the man who created the split from Rome.[54] At least, that is what Mary believed

---

[53]   Quoted in Sessions, *Henry Howard*, p. 411.

[54]   Surrey's actual religious sympathies seem to lie well within the mainstream of the Henrician church. While some critics have tried to claim him as a Protestant, as Walker, *Writing Against Tyranny*, p. 398, points out, "when he was serving in Boulogne in 1544,

(Howard's attempt to displace Edward VI is left out of this narrative). The *Songes and Sonettes*, therefore, functions as a monument to a victim of Henrician tyranny as the collected English works of Sir Thomas More does for its author, and both volumes mean to counter the proliferation of "false" Protestant martyrs by constructing their authors as genuine ones. In this sense, Henry Howard, "late" earl of Surrey, and Thomas More represent Tottel's answer to, among others, Latimer and Ridley.

Under the shadow of this term, "late," Surrey's love poems take on an especially poignant character. The opening poem, for example, the "Descripcion of the restlesse state of a lover, with sute to his ladie, to rue on his diying hart," may seem like a skillfully done confection of Petrarchan and Chaucerian tropes, but knowing Surrey's actual fate, the poem seems more of an example of "hamartia," or "missing the mark." The speaker may assert that rejected love causes his morbidity: "Strange kinds of death, in life that I do trie" (sig. A2ʳ), but it will be the strangest kind of death of all for an earl that will cause him to be "late"—a judicial execution authorized by an unjust law. Similarly, Surrey's conclusion to his "Complaint of a lover, that defied love, and was by love after the more tormented": "Strive not with love: for if ye do it will ye thus befall" (sig. B1ᵛ), may within the context of the poem refer to his suffering from the pangs of unrequited love, but the sentiment itself applies equally well to striving with monarchs, since the result will be equally unhappy. Similarly, the concluding line to the next poem, "Complaint of a lover rebuked"—"Swete is his death, that takes his end by love" (sig. B1ʳ)—in the context of Surrey's "lateness" takes on an entirely different set of meanings, since the earl's death will be anything but sweet, and not in the least caused "by love." Indeed, every reference to "death" in these poems sets in motion a chain of associations that inevitably lead to just how and why the poet earl met his end.

These associations are, I fully admit, entirely extrinsic to the verse itself. They have to be supplied rather than arise from the words on the page. But a reader alive to the religious and political undertones of the *Songes and Sonettes* would have been pushed in this direction by Tottel's inclusion of poems that "speak of the plight of the beleaguered man of honour, beset by foes, or the solitary prisoner brought down by his enemies, such as 'So crewel prison'" (sig. B3ᵛ-B4ʳ).[55] Tottel also includes some of the poems in which Surrey takes the offensive against Henry VIII, such as the "Praise of certaine psalms of David, translated by sir T. w. the elder," which Surrey pointedly calls a text where "rulers may see in a mirrour clere/The bitter fruite of false concupiscence" (sig. D5v), and "Thassrian king" (sig. E2v), in which Surrey implicitly compares Henry VII to the bloodthirsty and militarily incompetent tyrant, Sardanapulus.[56]

---

the Earl specifically antagonized his more evangelical followers by setting up an altar in a church there in the catholic manner."

[55] Walker, *Writing Against Tyranny*, p. 386.

[56] Ibid, p. 409.

Interestingly, Tottel seems to have had this image of Surrey as a man unjustly killed when he revised the *Songes and Sonettes* for the second edition. As Rollins noted, Tottel "completely changed" the order of the poems, and while he dropped many of Nicholas Grimald's efforts, he moved two of them from their original place to the end of the second edition of the *Songes and Sonettes*. Significantly, these two poems are Grimald's translations of Theodore Beza's two poems on Cicero, "Marcus Tullius Ciceroe's death" (sig. Gg1ʳ-Gg2ᵛ) and "Of M. T. Cicero," which asserts that Cicero does not need a tomb because, as Apollo says, "Tullie lives, and styll alyve shall bee" (sig. Gg2ᵛ), the term "styll" nicely conflating "still" and "style." [57] On the one hand, the two figures are hardly exact mirrors of each other (it is hard to think of the aristocratic Surrey as a "sacred Senate prince" [sig. Gg1v]), but the implied parallels, I think, outweigh the differences. Both Surrey and Cicero are masters of "stile," and both are victims of judicial murder. Mary, we should remember, thought that some (the record does not say that Mary referred to specific persons) had suffered a "shameful" death thanks to "dangerous and painful laws,"[58] and Cicero, in Grimald's translation, also runs to an "undeserved death" (sig. Gg1ʳ). Political murder, therefore, "bookends" the *Songes and Sonettes*, and if "stern Herennius" (the Roman soldier in charge of the squad which killed Cicero) is the instrument of Cicero's death in Grimald's translation, Henry VIII is the architect of Surrey's.

Explicit Polemic

The anti-Henrician polemic becomes explicit in the last poem I want to look at, "Of the troubled comon welth restored to quiet by the mighty power of god," which Tottel added to the second iteration of the *Songes and Sonettes* (sig. Aa2ᵛ-Aa3ʳ). This poem (author unknown) takes the *Aeneid*, Book 2, as its ground for reflecting on a threat to the English commonwealth. After summarizing how Sinon's treason and Trojan credulousness brought about the city's downfall ("They brake the wals, they toke this hors for good,/They demed Grekes gone, they thought al surety then,/ When treason start & set the town on fire,/And stroied Trojans & gave Grekes their desire" [sig. Aa2ʳ]), the anonymous poet explicitly connects these mythical events to a contemporary event: "Like to our time, wherein hath broken out,/The hidden harme that we suspected last,/Wombed within our walles and realme about,/As Grekes in Troy were in the Grekish beast" (sig. Aa2ʳ). As Rollins points out, in all

---

[57]   The presence of Calvin's right-hand man, Theodore Beza, in a volume enlivened by a Catholic poetics might seem anomalous, but I think what is happening here is that Grimald, through his translation, and Tottel, through his editing, are appropriating this very Protestant poet for their own purposes, just as Protestant poets adapted profane love songs (such as "Greensleeves") and other examples of popular art as vehicles for spreading Protestant truths; see King, *English Reformation Literature*, p. 214.

[58]   Strype, *Ecclesiastical Memorials*, vol. 4, p. 59. See above, n. 49.

likelihood the poem's "hidden harme" refers to Wyatt's Rebellion.[59] From the safe perspective of the twentieth and twenty-first centuries, this attempt at unseating Mary posed little to no actual danger to the Queen, but contemporary accounts depict the events in almost apocalyptic terms. The anonymous poet recounts that treason nearly toppled the state:

> Then felt we well the piller of our welth,
> How it sore shoke, then we saw we even at hand,
> Ruin how she rusht to confound our helth,
> Our realme and us with force of mighty band. (sig. Aa2^r)

John Proctor, in his account of Wyatt's Rebellion, uses analogous language: he generally hopes to show "as it were in a glasse, from what calamitie and extreme ruine, by what policie and wisedome their native counties were delivered, besides the great misery and peril they themselves have escaped …" and how Wyatt's "detestable" rebellion in particular is "little inferior to the most dangerous reported in any historie, either for desperate couraghe in the author, or for the monstruous end purported by his rebellion."[60] The poem also follows contemporary discourses in ascribing rebellion's failure to divine intervention. In the poet's account, God, who "secretly beholdes/The state of thinges" (sig. Aa2^r), decides that enough is enough, and so "I, as I have set you all,/In places where your honoures lay and frame:/So now my selfe shall give you eche your fall,/Where eche of you shall have your worthy shame" (sig. AA2^r). Proctor similarly ascribes Mary's success to the Lord, Wyatt's failure demonstrating "howe God always defendethe his chosen and elected vessel, our moost gracious and mercifull princesse, against the malitious and cruell assaultes of her enemies, be they never so craftie, never so stronge."[61]

The final lines of the poem, however, move from thanking God for delivering Mary from Wyatt's rebellion to something considerably broader:

> He is the Lord of man and of his law,
> Praise therefore now his mighty name in this,
> And make accompt that this our ease doth stand:
> An Israell free, from wicked Pharaos hand. (sig. Aa3^v)

The final line significantly alters the conception of England in this poem. Up until this point, England was in a sense the anti-Troy, the country preserved rather than destroyed. But the sudden identification of England with "An Israell Free" shifts the identification from a nation successfully, with God's help, repelling treason to a nation freed from slavery and from the hard yoke of tyranny ("from wicked Pharaos hand"). This image would have been especially striking in 1557 because

---

[59]   Rollins, *Tottel's*, vol. 2, p. 322.

[60]   John Proctor, *The historie of Wyattes rebellion* (London, 1554), sig. A3v, A4v.

[61]   Proctor, *The historie*, sig. L2v.

it appropriates and, in a sense, reverses the common Reformist trope of England as the Hebrew Bible's Israel, the chosen nation. Hence Henry VIII's fondness for Davidic imagery and the many references to Edward VI as "that true Josias [Josiah], that earnest destroyer of false religion, that fervent setter up of Gods true honor[.]"[62] Instead of Protestantism now being identified as a sign of England's special covenant with God, it would be the return to Catholicism. The conflation of England with Israel thus works to confirm Mary and her followers' sense "that her triumph was a miracle, specifically brought about by God to enable her to restore the true church."[63]

The concluding reference, however, to "wicked Pharaos hand" gives this poem a more specific target: Henry VIII, the man who rejected the Pope's authority in England, started the Reformation, and martyred, among others, such Catholic notables as John Fisher and Sir Thomas More. As John N. King has superbly illustrated, early Reformation polemics and iconography often paralleled its leaders with Moses and the Catholic Church with Pharoah. A 1524 broadsheet by Lucas Cranach the Elder casts Luther in the role of Moses and the pope as Pharoah, and closer to home, Catherine Parr replaces Luther with Henry VIII. After thanking God for sending "suche a godly & learned king in these later dayes to reigne over us," Parr makes explicit as possible the comparison indicated by the marginal note "king Henrye the eyght.Moyses":

> But our Moyses, a moste godly, wise governer & kyng hath delivered us out of the pativitie & bondage of Pharao. I mene by this Moyses kyng Henry the eight, my most soverayne favorable lorde & husband, one (If Moyses had figured any mo than Christ) through the excellent grace of god, mete to be an other, expressed veritie of Moyses conqueste over Pharao. And I mene by this Pharao the bishop of Rome, who hath bene, & is a greater persecutor of all true Christians, then ever was Pharao, of the children of Israel.[64]

But Biblical parallels are notoriously labile, and Catholic writers used the story of Moses and Pharaoh to quite different ends. Miles Hogarde, for example, would

---

[62]   Thomas Becon, *A comfortable Epistle, too Goddes faythfull people in Englande* (Strasbourg, 1554), sig. A4v. (EEBO mistakenly gives the publication date as 1542). See also Joy Shakespeare, "Plague and Punishment," in Peter Lake and Maria Dowling (eds.), *Protestantism and the National Church in Sixteenth Century England* (London, 1987), pp. 103–24; John King, *Tudor Royal Iconography* (Princeton, 1989), pp. 75–80, 93, and Christopher Bradshaw, "David or Josiah? Old Testament Kings as Exemplars in Edwardian Religious Polemic," in Bruce Gordon (ed.), *Protestant History and Identity in Sixteenth-Century Europe* (Aldershot and Burlington, VT, 1996), vol. 2, pp. 76–90.

[63]   Loades, *The Reign*, p. 152. For example, this quote from a broadside ballad celebrating Mary's accession and Northumberland's defeat: "god at her great need doth helpe, workynge nothing in vayne/Subdueth to her, her enemies al"; see *An Iinvective against Treason* (London, 1553).

[64]   Catherine Parr, *The lamentacion of a sinner* (London, 1547), sig E1r-E2v; King, *Tudor Iconography*, p. 75.

use the story of Moses turning his staff into a snake as evidence for the efficacy of words, and hence, the mass: "This doth your high reason cleane overthrow/That, hoc est, can not be words to make ought/Much more than no wordes …".[65] As for Henry, Mary's regime, if not Mary herself, were not shy about denouncing the dead king as the source of all evil. John Foxe's notes reveal that court preachers sermonized against both Henry VIII and Edward VI before Mary and her sister, Elizabeth, and in 1554, the Catholic divine, William Chedsay, asked a Protestant his views on the pope, who said "From him and all his detestable enormities good Lord deliver us," which elicited this response: "Mary so may wee saye from King Henry the eighte, and all his detestable enormities, good Lord deliver us."[66] Very significantly, Reginald Pole, "unswerving in his condemnation of his old master," overtly compared Henry VIII to Pharoah in *On the Unity of the Catholic Church.* The Pope, Pole writes, "must lead the people away from a tyrant far more cruel than the Pharao …".[67] "Of the troubled comon welth" concludes, therefore, by pointing directly at Henry VIII, and folds Mary's providential defeat of Wyatt's Rebellion into the larger narrative of England's escape from the Egypt of Henry VIII's reformation.

The fact that Richard Tottel would add such a politically incendiary poem to the second edition of the *Songes and Sonettes*, along with his reordering the poems so that the volume begins and ends with writers destroyed by the political enemies, suggests that Tottel meant for his volume of poems to participate in the culture wars, as it were, of Marian England. As we have seen, Mary's attempt at undoing Protestantism had stalled by the summer of 1557. Her government could not halt the steady stream of anti-Marian pamphlets filtering into England from abroad, and the fires at Smithfield were not as effective as Mary and Cardinal Pole had hoped in weaning the population away from Protestant ideals.[68] Tottel, therefore, decided to enter this fray with a poetic miscellany that countered Protestant nationalism by

---

[65]   Robert Crowley, *The confutation of the mishapen aunswer to the misnamed, wicked ballade, called the Abuse of ye blessed sacrame[n]t of the aultare* (London, 1548), sig. C5r. The original ballad is lost.

[66]   Thomas S. Freeman, "'As True a Subject being Prysoner': John Foxe's Notes on the Imprisonment of Princess Elizabeth, 1554–5', *English Historical Review*, 117 (2002): 105; quoted in Ryrie, "Slow Death," pp. 84–5.

[67]   *Pole's Defense of the Unity of the Church*, trans. Joseph G. Dwyer (Westminster, MD, 1965), 122. I am very grateful to Mark Rankin for supplying me with this reference.

[68]   Duffy, *Fires of Faith*, pp. 160, 155, argues that Protestant historiography has exaggerated the revulsion against the burnings of heretics, and he frequently offers a valuable corrective to received wisdom (e.g., demonstrating that Latimer's ringing embrace of martyrdom—"wee shall this day light such a candle by Gods grace in England, as (I trust) shall never be put out"—was probably invented by the martyrologist, John Foxe. But he also admits that Mary's government recognized that the immolation of Protestants stirred up rather than dispelled sympathy for their cause; e.g., "By the summer of 1558, those managing the burnings in London had recognized that high-profile Smithfield executions were providing the London gospellers with too much of the oxygen of publicity."

providing Catholic models of English literary achievement as well as a Catholic martyr to match the Protestant ones. And at least one poem directly taking aim at King Henry VIII.

On the one hand, Tottel's project was immensely successful. The book became an evergreen of sorts for Tottel (reprinted at least nine times over the course of Elizabeth's reign), and it established Wyatt and Surrey as the foundational poets for Elizabethan literature. Yet at the same time, the book's Catholic polemic seems to have been entirely passed over by Elizabethan readers. George Puttenham, for example, may have been alive to the hidden politics of Virgil's eclogues, where "under the veil of homely persons and in rude speeches to insinuate and glance at greater matters, and such as perchance had not been safe to have been disclosed in any other sort," but he treats Wyatt and Surrey exclusively in terms of their aesthetic qualities: "I repute them (as before) for the two chief lanterns of light to all others that have since employed their pens upon English poesy. Their conceits were lofty, their styles stately, their conveyance cleanly, their terms proper, their meter sweet and well-proportioned, in all imitating very naturally and studiously their master Francis Petrarch."[69] But that does not mean that the religious polemic was not there to begin with, and we can begin to engage the more polemical aspects of the *Songes and Sonettes* by "unediting" this text and reading this book as it appeared in the stalls of Tottel's shop on July 31, 1557.

---

[69]   *The Art of English Poesy: A Critical Edition*, eds. Frank Whigham and Wayne A. Rebhorn (Ithaca, 2007), pp. 128, 150.

Chapter 6
Songes and Sonnettes and Shakespeare's Poetry

Tom MacFaul

In *The Merry Wives of Windsor*, Abraham Slender famously wishes he had his copy of *Songes and Sonnettes* with him; he also longs for a "Book of Riddles" (I.i.198–202). Though *Tottel's Miscellany* may have seemed somewhat outdated at the end of Elizabethan period, a resource for fools like Slender, it seems also to have been a crucial point of nostalgia for Shakespeare and poets of his generation—and perhaps something of a riddle.[1] In the later Elizabethan editions, printers' errors had accumulated to the point where quite a few poems made little sense. Additionally, the avowedly uncertain authorship of many of the poems may have given it a persistent air of mystery or even subversion.[2] The collection remained famous and prestigious enough in late Elizabethan England for poets to nod to its language and atmosphere repeatedly. Shakespeare, in particular, engages in a very various dialogue with the moral and erotic verse of the collection, creating complicated patterns of feeling out of the apparently simpler stances of early Tudor verse. In particular, he uses material from the *Miscellany* to focus his thoughts about poetic memory and immortalization.

One of the better poems by "Uncertain Authors," a sonnet, begins with this powerful octave:

> Lyke as the Larke within the Marlians foote
> With piteous tunes doth chirp her yelden lay:
> So sing I now, seyng none other boote,
> My rendering song, and to your will obey.
> Your vertue mountes above my force so hye.
> And with your beautie seased I am so sure:
> That there avails resistance none in me,
> But paciently your pleasure to endure.[3]

---

[1] Stuart Gillespie, *Shakespeare's Books: A Dictionary of Shakespeare's Sources* (London, 2001), pp. 487–91.

[2] Marcy North, *The Anonymous Renaissance: Cultures of Discretion in Tudor–Stuart England* (Chicago, 2003), p. 178 argues that Tottel's explicit statement of "uncertain" authorship distances the collection from the politics of its authors.

[3] References to *Tottel's Miscellany: Songs and Sonnets of Henry Howard, Earl of Surrey, Sir Thomas Wyatt and Others*, ed. Amanda Holton and Tom MacFaul (Harmondsworth, 2011). Poem 143, lines 1–8.

Several elements of these lines seem to have influenced Shakespeare in the *Sonnets*. In Sonnet 29, the moment at which the poet's despair is redeemed by thinking of the beloved young man comes to him as a springing, lifting emotion which resembles the opening of the Tottel poem: "Like to the lark at break of day arising." The same poem also speaks of the poet's tendency to "Trouble deaf heaven with my bootless cries."[4] The combination of a feeling of bootlessness (helplessness) with the image of the lark rising may well have been suggested by the Tottel poem. Moreover, the stance with which the anonymous poet ends his octave, patiently enduring the pleasure of a superior beloved, is strongly reminiscent of Shakespeare's attitude to the young man of the *Sonnets*. The poet is a mere hanger-on, albeit a hanger-on with a great singing voice; the beloved is an aristocratic falcon to whom the poet must simply abject himself.[5] The poet's song is simply a way of giving oneself up, as it is in Shakespeare: it is a "rendering" song, which returns something due to the beloved even as it indicates surrender. In Sonnet 29, as in most of Shakespeare's *Sonnets*, there is no mutual return; but towards the end of the sonnets to the young man Shakespeare does insist that the relationship between poet and beloved is (or ought to be) one of "mutual render, only me for thee" (125.14), ending with a quiet (sur)rendering of the beloved (126.12), but to whom it is not clear—perhaps to the forces that defy the poet's attempts to immortalize.

Shakespeare's use of this poem is typical of his use of earlier Renaissance poetry, turning the purely lyrical and subjective verse of the past to more dialogic purposes. He treats Tottel's collection as an echo chamber and source for variations, rather as jazz musician might use a songbook of standards. *Tottel's Miscellany* does not deal extensively with the major themes of Shakespeare's nondramatic verse: the collection is not particularly interested in the differences between homosocial and heterosexual love; nor do we get extensive narratives of classical myth or history as we do in *Venus and Adonis* and *Lucrece*; and some of the *Miscellany*'s central subject matter—praising the mean estate, for instance—does not interest Shakespeare. Yet there are many points of contact between Shakespeare's poetic art and the collection first published a few years before his birth. The connections between them are more often matters of technical detail, diction, and tone than of structural or thematic similarities. Above all, the *atmosphere* of the *Miscellany* was a valuable resource for Shakespeare. Its attitudes to the need to reproduce and the immortalization brought by verse may be much simpler than Shakespeare's, but he turns to its modes repeatedly when he wants to reflect on the precariousness of memory and of poetic fame.

This chapter will first consider the limited use Shakespeare makes of the *Miscellany* in the narrative poems and the plays, showing how such uses are consistently focused on matters of memory and fame, before turning to a more

---

[4]   References to Shakespeare's poems are to William Shakespeare, *The Complete Sonnets and Poems*, ed. Colin Burrow (Oxford, 2002).

[5]   For the issue of abjection in later Tudor poetry, see Catherine Bates, *Masculinity, Gender and Identity in the English Renaissance Lyric* (Cambridge, 2007).

extensive treatment of these subjects in the *Sonnets*, where they are the central topic, as they are in *The Phoenix and the Turtle*. In the Renaissance, of course, such subjects were always tied up with issues of social class, and it is clear that the social prestige of Surrey not only helped to sell Tottel's collection, but lent abiding interest to its treatment of literary fame.

Limited Influence

Given the relative paucity of narrative in the *Miscellany*, it is hardly surprising that only limited influence can be seen in the narrative poems. Thirty poems in the *Miscellany* use the *Venus and Adonis* stanza (ABABCC), but most of these are short-line lyrics rather than narrative poems. Poem 220 is a narrative poem (in short lines), but the story is ultimately turned to personal account. The powerful poem 229 is in pentameters as well as being a narrative—describing the fall of Troy—yet again the narrative is used as an *exemplum*, this time of political dangers to the realm, matters which must have seemed urgent during the various crises of the mid-century.

The kind of mythological narratives that Shakespeare uses in his early-1590s poems are not, then, powerfully present in the *Miscellany*. Lucrece, however, does turn up twice, in one case demonstrably influencing Shakespeare's poem about her rape. In poem 212, Lucrece appears as an *exemplum* of the perils of slanderous false friends: "So was the house defilde,/Of Collatine: so was the wife begilde" (19–20). Shakespeare uses the same rhyme in *Lucrece*: "To me came Tarquin armèd, so beguiled/With outward honesty, but yet defiled/With inward vice" (1544–46)— here I follow Malone's reading; the Quarto (followed by Burrow) reads "to beguild." If the *Miscellany* poem did influence Shakespeare, that would count in favor of Malone's "so," yet Shakespeare would then be using beguiled as a kind of intransitive verb, punningly meaning that he is *gilding* himself with honesty in order to beguile her. Such an art, which defiles both Lucrece's husband's family (house) and the artful rapist himself, points to the dangers of artifice, a subject of such general concern to Shakespeare.[6]

Another echo is possible; in the very next *Miscellany* poem, "Maistresse R." is praised by comparison to the Roman rape victim:

> Lo here (quod skill, good people all) is Lucrece left alive,
>> And she shall most excepted be, that least for praise did strive. (213.43–4)

Shakespeare's Lucrece is described in similar terms, but looking forward more to her posthumous fame; she is

---

[6]   See Joel Fineman, *Shakespeare's Perjured Eye: The Invention of Poetic Subjectivity in the Sonnets* (Berkeley, 1986), and A.D. Nuttall, *Shakespeare the Thinker* (New Haven, 2007).

> the Roman dame,
> Within whose face beauty and virtue strived
> Which of them both should underprop her fame. (51–3)

Lucrece is an icon of feminine virtue, a site of competition between abstract principles whose purpose is to be remembered. As in the *Miscellany* poem, the woman herself is not striving for fame, but fame is the result of her virtue. Characteristically, Shakespeare uses material from the *Miscellany* when he wants to touch, however ironically, on the idea of posthumous fame.

There are a few echoes of the *Miscellany*'s language in Shakespeare's plays: for instance, when Cassius grimly jokes about there being "room enough" in Rome (*Julius Caesar*, I.ii.156),[7] Shakespeare may be recalling a similar pun in Grimald's poem 279 ("Marcus Tullius Ciceroes death"), where Cicero says "Now have I lived, O Room, ynough for mee" (49). Cassius, of course, is trying to persuade Brutus at this point to the act that will ensure his fame or infamy, insisting that Rome is an arena for the development of many men's glory, not just Caesar's. For Grimald's Cicero as for Shakespeare's Cassius, Rome is a space for the burgeoning of people's fame, but one must know the limits of how much of this fame one may claim in order to have a proper claim on historical memory. As in the case of Lucrece, a degree of self-effacement is necessary for self-promotion into posthumous fame.

Hamlet's Tottel

The earthly afterlife of individuals need not involve such elevated subjects, however. The sense of memorial remnant is central to probably the most notable use of *Tottel's Miscellany* material in later literature—the garbled version of poem 182 in *Hamlet*'s graveyard scene:

> *1st Clown.* "In youth when I did love, did love,
>   Methought it was very sweet,
>   To contract—O—the time for—a—my behove,
>   O, methought there—a—was nothing—a—meet."
>
> *Hamlet.*   Has this fellow no feeling of his business? 'a sings in grave-making.
>
> *Horatio.* Custom hath made it in him a property of easiness.
>
> *Hamlet.*   'Tis e'en so, the hand of little employment hath the daintier sense.
>
> *1st Clown.* "But age with his stealing steps
>   Hath clawed me in his clutch,
>   And hath shipped me into the land,
>   As if I had never been such."

---

[7]   All references to Shakespeare's works are to *The Riverside Shakespeare*, ed. G. Blakemore Evans et al. (Boston, 1997).

[*Throws up a shovelful of earth with a skull in it*]

Hamlet.   That skull had a tongue in it, and could sing once.
. . . .
Did these bones cost no more the breeding, but to play loggats with them? Mine ache to think on't.

1st Clown. "A pickaxe and a spade, a spade,
                    For and a shrowding sheet:
                    O, a pit of clay for to be made
                    For such a guest is meet."

[*Throws up another skull*] (V. i. 61–97)

The original poem is worth quoting in full, as it has an undeniable power over Shakespeare's imagination. It evokes old age as a time of regrets, not only for youthful love, but for youthful dabbling in poetry;[8] its handling of the passing of time and the changes of the individual have deep significance for *Hamlet* and for Shakespeare's work as a whole, particularly his attitude to poetry. It may remind us, too, of Guiderius's and Arviragus's funeral song in *Cymbeline*, preoccupied as it is with how lusty youth comes "to dust" (IV.ii.258–81).

The *Miscellany*'s poem is a work of decided self-alienation, despising things it once loved and hardly able to believe that there were once objects which could be called sweet. It passively accepts the departure of passion and its associated poetical fancy, knowing that those properties must be handed on to others. Youth is not only a stuff that will not endure, but is merely a badge or a cup that must be passed on to others. Its speaker claims alienation from his own poetic skill even while exhibiting it, and believes that no one will remember him. "*This* youthly idle rime" is self-condemning (18; emphasis added), even self-denying, as Hamlet is. It reads as follows:

> I lothe that I did love,
> In youth that I thought swete:
> As time requires for my behove,
> Me thinkes they are not mete.
>   My lustes they do me leave,   5
> My fansies all be fled:
> And tract of time begins to weave,
> Gray heares upon my hed.
>   For age with steling steps,
> Hath clawed me with his crowch: 10
> And lusty life away she leapes,
> As there had bene none such.
>   My muse doth not delight

---

8   The association of poetry with youth was commonplace—for the classic discussion of this, see Richard Helgerson, *The Elizabethan Prodigals* (Berkeley, 1976).

Me as she did before:
My hand and pen are not in plight,		15
As they have bene of yore.
      For reason me denies,
This youthly idle rime:
And day by day to me she cries,
Leave of these toyes in time.		20
      The wrinkles in my brow,
The furrowes in my face:
Say limping age will hedge him now,
Where youth must geve him place.
      The harbinger of death,		25
To me I see him ride:
The cough, the cold, the gasping breath,
Doth bid me to provide.
      A pikeax and a spade,
And eke a shrowding shete,		30
A house of clay for to be made,
For such a gest most mete.
      Me thinkes I heare the clarke,
That knoles the carefull knell:
And bids me leave my wofull warke,		35
Ere nature me compell.
      My kepers knit the knot,
That youth did laugh to scorne:
Of me that clene shalbe forgot,
As I had not bene borne.		40
      Thus must I youth give up,
Whose badge I long did weare:
To them I yelde the wanton cup
That better may it beare.
      Lo here the bared scull,		45
By whose balde signe I know:
That stouping age away shall pull,
Which youthfull yeres did sow.
      For beauty with her band
These croked cares hath wrought:		50
And shipped me into the land,
From whence I first was brought.
      And ye that bide behinde,
Have ye none other trust:
As ye of claye were cast by kinde,		55
So shall ye waste to dust.

Shakespeare has evidently used the *Miscellany* poem (by Lord Thomas Vaux) not just as a simple *memento mori*, but to call to mind the poetics of an earlier era. Hamlet is in this scene preoccupied with his childhood, apparently 30 years ago; Shakespeare approximates the evocation of a vanished age by parroting the poetry popular in his own youth, and which now perhaps seems rather superseded.[9] Elements of the poem that the Gravedigger does *not* sing are appropriate to Hamlet: he represses the initial idea of loathing his love; the lines "My lustes they do me leave,/My fansies all be fled" (5–6) anticipate Hamlet's rejection of love and his resignation to God's will; like the poetic voice, Hamlet must be prepared to "leave [his] wofull warke" (line 31). It may even be significant that Hamlet, like Vaux's speaker, has just returned to his homeland (in Hamlet's case, from the abortive journey to England), so that the Gravedigger inserts the idea of being shipped into another land (from line 51) into a stanza from much earlier in the poem (based on lines 9–12). These details suggest that Shakespeare was not just using the old poem for effect, then, but was engaging in systematic allusion to it, reflecting on what survives of an individual's life after his death.[10]

Tottel and Shakespeare's *Sonnets*

Such systematic allusion is even more powerfully present in the *Sonnets*, whose chief subject is the poet's ability to immortalize himself and his beloved. Paul Hammond has convincingly demonstrated that Shakespeare's Sonnet 129 was influenced by *Tottel's Miscellany* poem 9, indeed that the poem "might be a rejoinder to it."[11] The poem seems to be by Vaux, though included in the Surrey section of the *Miscellany*. There seems to have been a widespread belief that most, if not all, of the poems in *Tottel's Miscellany* were written by Surrey,[12] and it seems unlikely that the cheerfully unpedantic Shakespeare would have gone into the matter more closely than his contemporaries did. He therefore probably thought that he was responding to the prestigious example of Surrey—the man who, it seems, invented the English sonnet form in which Shakespeare was working.

Sonnet 129 responds to Vaux's attack on beauty as "Jewel of jeopardie that perill doth assaile,/False and untrue, enticed oft to treason" (9–10), but it is clearly a more subjective poem, interested in the internal feeling of "lust in action" (2) rather than the untrustworthy cause of the emotion. Vaux's warning/threat to beauty that "Thou farest as frute that with the frost is taken,/To day redy ripe, to morowe al to shaken" (13–14) may, as Hammond observes, have rhythmic links to Shakespeare's poem, but the sense of beauty's decay is something Shakespeare

---

[9]   See Steven May, "Popularizing Courtly Poetry: *Tottel's Miscellany* and its Progeny," in Mike Pincombe and Cathy Shrank (eds.) *The Oxford Handbook of Tudor Literature 1485–1603* (Oxford, 2009).

[10]   See, further, Seth Lerer's chapter, "Cultivation and Inhumation: Some Thoughts on the Cultural Impact of Tottel's *Songes and Sonettes*," below.

[11]   Paul Hammond, "Sources for Shakespeare's Sonnets 87 and 129 in *Tottel's Miscellany* and Puttenham's *The Arte of English Poesie*," *Notes and Queries*, 50 (2003): 407–10.

[12]   For example, *England's Parnassus* (1600) attributes several passages from Wyatt and the Uncertain Authors to Surrey.

tends to use, with great poignancy, in poems to the young man rather than those to the dark lady.

The *Sonnets'* very first line announces their subject as "increase" (1.1), and though this subject is not common in *Tottel's Miscellany*, there are hints of it. Poem 161, in particular, has one stanza whose subject is very close to that of the generation sonnets (i.e. Sonnets 1–17):

> The poore man ploweth his ground for grain,
> And soweth his seede increase to crave,
> And for thexpence of all his pain,
> Oft holdes it hap his seede to save,
> These pacient paines my part doth show,
> To long for love ere that I know. (161.13–18)

The poor man here is a careful husband, saving his seed and exhibiting patience: in a sense, then, he is very similar to both the niggard young man and the poet who is so patient in his love. Shakespeare takes such examples and gives them greater subjective and interpersonal force and resonance, where the poems of *Tottel's Miscellany* tend only to focus on the one-way effect of one person on another.

Shakespeare is keen on imagery of printing, particularly as a way of expressing the comparison between biological and poetic generativity.[13] Not surprisingly, given that the printing of poetry was still novel in their time, the poets of *Tottel's Miscellany* do not make much use of such language. Interestingly, though, the one poet who does use imagery of printing is Surrey (see 1.51, 4.48, 18.39, 33.13).[14] It is as if in using such imagery, the dead Surrey were licensing in advance the print publication of his poems. It is particularly striking that the *Miscellany*'s first poem makes the demand "Print in your hart some parcell of my tene" (51). The effect of this imagery, as with imagery of increase, is still to emphasize the effect of one person on another rather than the complex dynamic we see unfold in Shakespeare's poetry, in which printing is a mode of exchange between the poet and his friend, a "bounteous gift," but also an obligation to Nature to "print more" (Sonnet 11, lines 12, 14). For Shakespeare, a book can take the "mind's imprint," and its preservation involves an obligation ("offices") to "enrich" one's own legacy (Sonnet 77, lines 3, 13–14). Doing good for oneself involves doing good for others.

The difference in this respect between Wyatt and Shakespeare is perhaps particularly marked: Shakespeare's sense of reciprocality is nicely captured at the end of Sonnet 38, where he writes "The pain be mine, but thine shall be the praise"; Wyatt, by contrast, ends poem 100 of the *Miscellany* (also a sonnet) writing "And yours the losse, and mine the deadly payne." In Wyatt's world, everyone loses; in Shakespeare's the young man can win (though of course there is a subtle,

---

[13]   See my discussion of this in *Poetry and Paternity in Renaissance England: Sidney, Spenser, Shakespeare, Donne and Jonson* (Cambridge, 2010), chapter 5.

[14]   The only other case is poem 154, line 74.

passive-aggressive victory for the poet too).[15] Shakespeare has learned from Wyatt a method of capping a sonnet, but he fights free from the Petrarchan sense of doom. Shakespeare is also preoccupied in the young man sonnets with the idea of him being "you yourself" (e.g., Sonnets 13, 58, 83); indeed, it is almost a verbal tick for Shakespeare to marvel at the beloved being an autonomous self.[16] Wyatt uses the formula much more aggressively, concluding a sonnet with the claim that the addressee is the cause of all error "And you your self the cause therof have been" (43.14). The poem is thrown out *at* its addressee, without a sense of wonder about the other's selfhood. Wyatt's poetry is massively preoccupied with ideas of reward and dessert (see, most famously, "They Flee from Me"— poem 57), but Shakespeare is much quieter about these ideas, not seeing them as part of a system of simple erotic payback. In Sonnet 49, he comforts himself by imagining ensconcing himself in a sense of dessert (9–10), but he never uses the word "reward" as Wyatt does (e.g. poems 44, 53, 130). For Shakespeare, merit is its own reward, for it gathers a kind of posthumous prestige, whereas Wyatt has no such illusion.

Shakespeare's Surrey

Surrey and those Uncertain Authors who were most influenced by him tend to be the poets who have the strongest hold on Shakespeare's imagination, even though he holds their poetry at an ironic distance, using it to give an air of an antique age. Some of Shakespeare's most famous lines in the nondramatic poetry have the open-vowelled, leisurely quality of Surrey's best poems. In his nondramatic verse at least, Shakespeare leans more to the exquisite but understated verbal patterning of Surrey than the sardonic, side-of-the-mouth mumblings of Wyatt. The Surrey mode points up ironies with a certain distance, but allows Shakespeare to short-circuit the consciously aureate patterings of his immediate predecessors Sidney, Spenser, and Lyly. A fresh engagement with nature is crucial to this, treating it as an autonomous realm, alien but consoling to humans because of its permanence, rather than as a treasure chest of Erasmian *exempla*. Surrey gives us powerful, refreshing images of nature, such as these lines from poem 5:

> Nothing more good, than in the spring the aire to fele a space.
>   There shalt thou heare and se all kindes of birdes ywrought,
> Well tune their voice with warble smal, as nature hath them tought. (10–12)

Line 10 enacts the expansiveness of its sense, the trippingly clipped and nasalized [i] sounds of "Nothing," "in," and "spring" subtly acquiring more stress with each

[15]   See my discussion of this in *Male Friendship in Shakespeare and Contemporaries* (Cambridge, 2007), chapter 2.

[16]   See John Kerrigan's comments in his introduction to William Shakespeare, *The Sonnets and A Lover's Complaint* (London, 1986), p. 26.

repetition before giving way to the long and varied open vowels of the line's last three stresses; "the aire" of that line is echoed into the "there" and "their" of the next lines, whose contented stasis needs no sense of purpose. This is nature for nature's sake, the air being felt without the need to specify which sense does the feeling. Shakespeare, meanwhile, criticizes another kind of poet whose verse proceeds by

> Making a couplement of proud compare
> With sun and moon, with earth, and sea's rich gems,
> With April's first-born flowers, and all things rare
> That heaven's air in this huge rondure hems. (21.5–8)

Though there are not particular echoes, the patterning of sound has a similar quality, which Don Paterson aptly describes: "The vowels are fat, which inflates the line, but also carefully varied, which means it's great fun to wrap your mouth around, and enact the distinct shape and sense of each word in turn."[17] As with Surrey, we are taken away from subjectivity and specific forms of feeling into a containing air. In such lines, we have got away from nature as a source for "compare" and find ourselves in the fresh air of things as they are, whose rarity is not a matter of financial value but of simply being themselves in their unique quiddity. Such effects tend to be used by Shakespeare most frequently when he wants to suspend the depredations of time in favour of a cyclical sense of nature's self-contained, unmotivated bounty.

Surrey's approach to his own feelings is habitually made through natural imagery, as in poem 1's *terza rima*:

> The sunne hath twise brought furth his tender grene,
> Twise clad the earth in lively lustinesse:
> Ones have the windes the trees despoiled clene,
> And ones again begins their cruelnesse,
> Sins I have hid under my brest the harm,
> That never shal recover healthfulnesse. (1–6)

Time's despoliations are made worse by their relentless repetitions, the rebeginnings which are so aptly woven into the rhyme scheme, which always seems to be starting a new pattern and is so hard to resolve.[18] Spring and autumn, seasons of change, are primary in such a form, leaving no room for the stability of summer or winter. The speaker's tenderness is attributed to nature, but there is a feeling ("harm") which is fundamentally separate from the processes of nature. Shakespeare makes similar approaches to seasons and the emotions, most famously perhaps in Sonnet 73:

---

[17] Don Paterson, *Reading Shakespeare's Sonnets: A New Commentary* (London, 2010), p. 57.

[18] Shelley uses *terza rima* for purposes in some way similar—at least in relation to the seasons—in "Ode to the West Wind."

That time of year thou mayst in me behold
When yellow leaves, or none, or few, do hang
Upon those boughs which shake against the cold,
Bare ruined choirs, where late the sweet birds sang.
In me thou seest the twilight of such day
As after sunset fadeth in the west. (1–6)

Love, attributed here to the young man (13) is able to rise above such natural
vulnerabilities; it is, like Surrey's "harm," not part of the same world as that
affected by the natural processes of time: it is in it, but not of it. The first poem
of the *Miscellany* is also preoccupied with time: "nothing hath hurt so sore,/
But time in time reduceth a returne" (14–15). The cyclical attitude may be very
different from Shakespeare's ultimately more eschatological attitude to time, but
the sense of time's reflexive agency would be crucial to the *Sonnets*. Also in this
poem Surrey "curse[s] ech sterre as causer of my fate" (26), whereas Shakespeare
more reflexively looks upon himself to "curse my fate" (29.4), before recovering
a better "state" through thinking of the beloved (2, 10). Surrey similarly longs that
he "Of better state could catch a cause to bost" (39): the poets' shared desire for
a state one could be proud of gives them both an ironic, provisional dignity, yet
this dignity is something that both ultimately undermine. Both poets know that
natural dignity cannot be the end of the story: a static *state* is always vulnerable
to natural change; its momentary assertion being a futile if necessary gesture of
human autonomy.

One of the more striking possible uses of a Surrey poem comes in Sonnet 62:

Sin of self-love possesseth all mine eye,
And all my soul, and all my every part;
And for this sin there is no remedy,
It is so grounded inward in my heart.
Me thinks no shape so true, no truth of such account,
And for myself mine own worth do define
As I all other in all worths surmount.
But when my glass shows me myself indeed,
Beated and chopped with tanned antiquity,
Mine own self-love quite contrary I read;
Sin so self-loving were iniquity:
      'Tis thee (my self) that for myself I praise,
      Painting my age with beauty of thy days.

There are echoes here of Surrey's poem 39 (titled "Bonum est mihi quod humiliasti
me" in the *Miscellany*):

The stormes are past these cloudes are overblowne,
And humble chere great rigour hath represt:
For the defaute is set a paine fore knowne,
And pacience graft in a determed brest.
And in the hart wher heapes of griefes were growne,

> The swete revenge hath planted mirth and rest,
> No company so pleasant as mine owne.
> Thraldom at large hath made this prison fre,
> Danger wel past remembred workes delight:
> Of lingring doubtes such hope is sprong pardie,
> That nought I finde displeasaunt in my sight:
> But when my glasse presented unto me
> The curelesse wound that bledeth day and night,
> To think (alas) such hap shoud graunted be
> Unto a wretch that hath no hart to fight,
> To spill that blood that hath so oft bene shed,
> For Britannes sake (alas) and now is ded.

The crucial feature of both poems is that they turn on the reflexive moment of looking in the mirror, but there are other attitudinal similarities or deliberate contrasts. In poem 38, printed immediately before this, Surrey describes "my dented chewes" and "my tothelesse chaps" (15–16), and the collocation of the poems in the *Miscellany* may well have suggested some of the dynamics of Shakespeare's poem. Surrey's mock-arrogant stance that he finds "No company so pleasant as mine owne" anticipates Shakepeare's sense of defining his own worth and the explosion of this solipsistic bubble by reflection (in all senses) on one's relation to the world. The tension between inner and outer worth, which is founded on Surrey's aristocratic blood, is developed in Shakespeare through the contrast between his own self-worth and its apparent validation by the appropriation of the young man's aristocratic status. Where Surrey has noble blood himself, Shakespeare needs the young man; Shakespeare's dialectic with his noble friend virtually constitutes a personification of the tensions in Surrey between his private voice and his familial self-love. Embattled self-reliance is therefore a watchword for both poets. Surrey's attitude that "I know how to content my self in others lust:/ Of litle stuffe unto my self to weave a web of trust" (4.17–18) finds resonances throughout the *Sonnets*. The fragile web of trust is in some ways the structural principle of Shakespeare's collection.

Surrey's touchy pride, though, may inspire other characters in Shakespeare's verse. The attitude of Shakespeare's Adonis may have been inspired by Surrey's response to "a ladie that refused to daunce with him":

> I can devour no yelding pray: you kill where you subdue.
> My kinde is to desire the honour of the field. (29.50–51)

Adonis takes a similarly brusque and aristocratic attitude to the idea of pursuit

> "I know not love," quoth he, "Nor will not know it,
> Unless it be a boar, and then I chase it." (lines 409–10)

The brusque manner, full of short sentences based on simple rules of aristocratic conduct, is common to both Surrey and Adonis, and is based on an attitude that

Shakespeare implicitly projects onto the young man of the *Sonnets*. Surrey was both poet and nobleman, and as such was possessed of two parts of the ideal of the Renaissance self-fashioner: as poet he could make himself, and as nobleman could simply *be*. For the dramatist Shakespeare, the ideal man he made was always alienated from him, forcing him into more dialogic modes.

Other Tottel poems, however, may contribute to a more positive representation of a masculine ideal, albeit a dangerous one. Poems 35–6, lamenting Wyatt, make a startling and blasphemous parallel between the older poet and Christ, a comparison that Shakespeare subtly develops in the poems to the young man. Surrey argues that Wyatt was "sent for our helth, but not received so" (Poem 35, line 36), and that we lost him through our own guilt, a sentiment that might have inspired the near-idolatry of the young man in so many sonnets, and Shakespeare's sense of abjected guilt in relation to him. But Shakespeare may not have known that the poem was about Wyatt. In early editions, the poem simply begins "W. resteth here," and though Q4 restores the name of the poem's subject, printing "Wyat," Q5 and all subsequent editions print "What resteth here," turning the poem (perhaps inadvertently) into a riddle. Shakespeare also makes a mystery of the identity of his godlike W.H.; is it too much to suggest that he got the hint for this from the printed version of Surrey's poem? Shakespeare claims repeatedly that he is preserving the young man's name, but that name is of course famously obscure, rather as Wyatt's name is obscured.

The Surrey section ends with the poet stuck in Boulogne "Against my will, full pleased with my payn" (41.14), an attitude that summarizes many of the involuntary aporias of the *Sonnets* while playing nicely with simple paradox and the suggestive word "will," which Shakespeare would play on so insistently in a poem like Sonnet 135. Surrey's final, defiant stance suggests, however provisionally, that pain is merely ephemeral compared to the poet's ability to will his own connection with the infinite.

Pursuing that connection, Shakespeare is fond of the idea of distillation, as it enables him to get at the essence of the young man (e.g. Sonnets 5, 6, and 54), and that essentialism is something he inherits from Surrey, even if he ironizes it rather more: "My vapord eyes suche drery teares distill" (11.12). More importantly, the *Sonnets* are occupied with the idea of the young man's form transcending his earthly existence. This idea involves several echoes of poem 203 in the *Miscellany*:

> Though in the waxe a perfect picture made,
> Doth shew as faire as in the marble stone,
> Yet do we see it is estemed of none.
> Because that fier or force the forme doth fade.
> Wheras the marble holden is ful dere,
> Since that endures the date of lenger dayes.
> Of Diamondes it is the greatest praise,
> So long to last and alwaies one tappere.
> Then if we do esteme that thing for best,
> Which in perfection lengest time doth last:

> And that most vaine that turnes with every blast
> What jewel then with tong can be exprest?
> Like to that hart wher love hath framed such feth,
> That can not fade but by the force of death.

Love, here, is the preserver of the ideal form, as it is in so many of Shakespeare's sonnets. Line 10's idea of preserving perfection over time may have subtly influenced Shakespeare's Sonnet 15: "When I consider every thing that grows/ Holds in perfection but a little moment" (1–2). The "name of single one" (39.6) is an abiding preoccupation of the young man sonnets: the idea that two become one may be reflected in a slight (and etymologically false) pun on the *di*-amond here. As in lines 2 and 5 here, Sonnet 55 uses marble as an image of permanence. The idea of esteem comes back repeatedly in the *Sonnets* (e.g. 96, 100, 102). Finally, in Sonnet 108, Shakespeare insists that his poems retain the "first conceit" of love, "Where time and outward form would show it dead" (13–14). The *Miscellany* poem, then, is not a case of something Shakespeare had open on his desk (unlike, say, passages he appropriates from North's Plutarch or Golding's Ovid), but one that seems to have haunted and sparked his imagination, particularly when he was thinking about the idea of the permanence or otherwise of human life and its poetic outputs.[19]

This finds poignant focus in perhaps Shakespeare's most powerful reflection of such matters. In poem 216, the dying voice of the Hawthorn tree may anticipate the complex threnody of Shakespeare's "Let the Bird of Loudest Lay" (*alias* "The Phoenix and the Turtle"). The Hawthorn sings thus:

> Dispaired hart the carefull nest,
> Of all the sighes I kept in store:
> Convey my carefull corps to rest,
> That leaves his joy for evermore.
> And when the day of hope is past,
> Geve up thy sprite and sigh the last. (7–12)

---

[19] Surrey's imitators may also inspire Shakespeare. In Sonnet 33, we are told that sunny mornings

> Anon permit the basest clouds to ride
> With ugly rack on his celestial face. (lines 5–6)

It is possible that these lines echo poem 163 of *Tottel's Miscellany*:

> Not alwaies yll though so be now
>   when cloudes ben driven, then rides the racke.
> Phebus the fresh ne shooteth still,
>   somtime he harpes his muse to wake. (lines 37–40)

The Miscellany, then, provides Shakespeare with modes of simplicity—that being a virtue he extols throughout the *Sonnets* even while he comes up with his own version of artistry.

In Shakespeare's poem, the "Threnos" announces that "Death is now the Phoenix' nest" (56), and the word "nest" is made to rhyme, as here, with "rest." This is not decisive influence, of course, but the *Miscellany* poem also concludes:

> And even with my last bequest,
> When I shall from this life depart:
> I geve to her I loved best,
> My just my true and faithfull hart,
> Signed with the hand as cold as stone:
> Of him that living was her owne.
>   And if he here might live agayne,
> As Phenix made by death anew:
> Of this she may assure her plaine,
> That he will still be just and trew.
> Thus farewell she on live my owne.
> And send her joy when I am gone. (67–78)

The dying voice reflecting on the image of the Phoenix at the (continually postponed) point of death may have given Shakespeare the hint he needed for his mysterious compound song, with its "defunctive music" (14). The idea of constancy existing beyond the grave may have stirred Shakespeare's imagination, fascinated as he was by the tension between eternity and mortality. As a kind of eternity is created by verse, but only when it is printed, *Tottel's Miscellany* gave Shakespeare a crucial example of this idea, that there can be joy when one is gone.

A complex nostalgia, then, marks Shakespeare's use of the *Miscellany*. The fragile immortality that printed verse can provide informs his attitude to selfhood and its potential to make connections with the world. Stephen Hamrick has argued that the Petrarchan poetics of Tottel's volume often encode an implicitly Catholic religion of Petrarchan love, despite attempts by the editor(s) to soften or extract this element.[20] That fragile element may have become almost invisible by Shakespeare's time, but the very fragile nature of such poetic processes and their attempts to preserve fleeting essences has an abiding hold on his imagination. At the end of his theatrical career, Shakespeare turned back to the dramatic modes of his youth, with echoes of old plays such as *Mucedorus* and *The Rare Triumphs of Love and Fortune* in the plays Ben Jonson considered mouldy and old-fashioned— *The Winter's Tale* and *The Tempest*; in his poetic career, likewise, Shakespeare never lost touch with an older form of verse and its attitudes. If the *Miscellany* did not sit on Shakespeare's desk throughout his career, he never forgot its presence in his pocket at the start of that career.

---

[20]   Stephen Hamrick, "*Tottel's Miscellany* and the English Reformation," *Criticism*, 44 (2002): 329–61.

Chapter 7
Cultivation and Inhumation:
Some Thoughts on the Cultural Impact
of Tottel's *Songes and Sonettes*

Seth Lerer

Any essay with this title needs to clarify its purview. "Cultural impact" implies many things: it suggests a widespread culture of reading that crossed boundaries of geography, class, and gender; it provokes an inquiry into a range of popular as well as educated audiences; it calls for a reassessment of the ways in which the poems of the book were models for contemporary literary practice; and it invites us to set the *Miscellany* side-by-side the major poets, dramatists, and prose writers of the late sixteenth and early seventeenth centuries (perhaps from Spenser and Shakespeare through Jonson and the Metaphysicals) to find allusions and quotations that enable us to trace the literary imaginations figured over its pages.[1]

Recent scholarship on the *Miscellany* (which, from this point forward, I refer to by the title of its publication, *Songes and Sonettes*), including several chapters in this volume, address many of these concerns.[2] For example, it has become

---

[1]   See, for example, William A. Sessions, "*Tottel's Miscellany* and the Metaphysical Poets," in Sidney Gottlieb (ed.), *Approaches to Teaching the Metaphysical Poets* (New York, 1990), pp. 48–53.

[2]   Modern scholarship on the *Songes and Sonettes* begins with Hyder E. Rollins, *Tottel's Miscellany 1557–1587* (2 vols., Cambridge, 1928–29; rev. ed., 1965). More recent studies that inform my approaches here include the bibliographical studies of Paul A. Marquis, in particular *Richard Tottel's Songes and Sonettes:, The Elizabethan Version* (Tempe, 2007), and his article "Editing and Unediting: Richard Tottel's *Songes and Sonettes*," *The Book Collector*, 56.3 (2007): pp. 353–75; the critical analyses of Stephen Hamrick, "*Tottel's Miscellany* and the English Reformation," *Criticism*, 44.4 (2002), and Stephen May, "Popularizing Courtly Poetry: *Tottel's Miscellany* and its Progeny," in Mike Pincombe and Cathy Shrank (eds.), *The Oxford Handbook of Tudor Literature: 1485–1603* (Oxford, 2010): pp. 418–33; the discussions throughout broader studies of early modern English literary culture, such as Wendy Wall, *The Imprint of Gender: Authorship and Publication in the English Renaissance* (Ithaca, 1993), Arthur Marotti, *Manuscript, Print, and the English Renaissance* (Ithaca, 1995), and Thomas Betteridge, *Literature and Politics in the English Reformation* (Manchester, 2004); the textual materials in such editions of the major poets as Ronald Rebholz, Jr., *Sir Thomas Wyatt: The Complete Poems* (Baltimore, 1978); and the biographical and social materials in such biographies as William A. Sessions, *Henry Howard, the Poet Earl of Surrey: A Life* (Oxford, 1999). I have discussed some aspects of

clear that Richard Tottel was a printer with distinctive commercial aspirations and political alliances. While the great bulk of his publications between 1553 (the date of his first imprint) and 1557 (the year of the first edition of *Songes and Sonettes*) were legal texts, he did reprint some of the most popular poetry of earlier generations. Lydgate's *Fall of Princes* and Stephen Hawes's *Pastime of Pleasure*, for example, represent traditions of post-Chaucerian allegorical and aureate verse that fell out of favor during the decades of Wyatt and Surrey. With their long, limping lines and their elaborate allusions, and with their stanzaic narratives of almost lithic immobility, these poems would have seemed archaic against Surrey's lithe classicism or the Petrarchan compressions of Wyatt.[3] Hawes's poetry in particular—with its quest-romance structures and its profoundly sacramental content—would have also fallen under the purview of the "papist" allegories that Henry VIII's thought machine condemned after the break with Rome. Roger Ascham's criticisms in the *Scolemaster* of 1570 represent the Elizabethan period's refraction of this earlier position: "In our forefathers' time, when papistry as a standing pool covered and overflowed all England, few books were read in our tongue, saving certain books of chivalry, as they said, for pastime and pleasure, which, as some say, were made in monasteries by idle monks or wanton canons."[4] Queen Mary's reign, with its resurgent Catholicism, provided (in retrospect) a narrow window in which these old "books of chivalry" could be reprinted, and Tottel was not alone in his enterprise (*The Pastime of Pleasure*, for example, saw reprinting not just from his press, but from those of John Wayland and John Waley).[5]

---

the *Songes and Sonettes* in my *Courtly Letters in the Age of Henry VIII* (Cambridge, 1997), and in my "Literary Histories," in James Simpson and Brian Cummings (eds.), *Cultural Reformations, From Lollardy to the English Civil War* (Oxford, 2010), pp.75–91. Many of the essays in this volume bear on my chapter, in particular those of Catherine Bates (on the preface to the *Songes and Sonettes*), Tom Macfaul (on Tottel and Shakespeare), and Peter C. Herman (on the cultural and political contexts of the book's first printing).

[3]   See the discussions in my *Chaucer and His Readers: Imagining the Author in Late-Medieval England* (Princeton, 1993), and for a different view, Daniel Wakelin, "Stephen Hawes and Courtly Education," in Pincombe and Shrank (eds.), *Oxford Handbook of Tudor Literature*, pp. 53–68.

[4]   Roger Ascham, *The Schoolmaster*, ed. Lawrence Ryan (Ithaca, 1967), p. 68.

[5]   On the broad contours of Marian literature and its responses to earlier medieval writings, see Eamon Duffy, *The Stripping of the Altars* (New Haven, 1992), pp. 524–64; Brian Cummings, "Reformed Literature and Literature Reformed," in David Wallace (ed.), *The Cambridge History of Medieval English Literature* (Cambridge, 1999), pp.842–7. For the Marian revival of interest in Hawes, in particular, see John King, "The Account Book of a Marian Bookseller, 1553–4," *British Library Journal* 13 (1987): 33–57, especially 39, 49. The Marian reprintings of the *Pastime of Pleasure* are John Wayland's of 1554 (listed in the *Short-Title Catalogue* as 12950), Tottel's of 1555 (*Short-Title Catalogue* 12951), and John Waley's of 1555 (*Short-Title Catalogue* 12952).

This sense of Tottel as a Marian printer has informed recent reassessments of the *Songes and Sonettes*, too. Stephen Hamrick, Steven W. May, Paul A. Marquis, and Peter C. Herman, among others, have come to understand the ways in which the book shared in shaping a distinctively Anglo-Catholic literary achievement for the mid 1550s.[6] Surrey himself, in one view, may have come to emblematize that blend of courtly poetics and pre-Reformation doctrine that Marian readers sought to recall. And while the Petrarchan poetics of Sir Thomas Wyatt looks, to our eyes, presciently modern in its lyric sensitivity, sixteenth-century readers would have found it rife with Catholic idioms drawn from the veneration of the Virgin Mary and the saints, with love seen as a sacrament, and with the sacrifices of desire drawing on the impulses of holy martyrdom. It has even been argued that Tottel's regularization of the prosody of those poets he prints had something of a political, if not religious edge: part of, as Peter Herman has suggested, a "linguistic nationalism" that aspired to refine vernacular versemaking against an alternative ideal of "native poetics" represented by the traditions of *Piers Plowman* and its later Protestant appropriation. "Altering the formal properties in Wyatt," Herman argues in this volume, "signifies a religious as well as an aesthetic argument … . They represent what the Marian renovation means in terms of English literature."[7]

Such arguments may say much about the environment in which the *Songes and Sonettes* first appeared in the summer of 1557. But they say little about the immense popularity of Tottel's book in the post-Marian world. Eleven editions appeared in the 30 years following that summer: editions that did not simply reprint the first but, often, radically rearranged it. Indeed, the second printing appeared only eight weeks after the first, and it was very much a different book. The order of poems changed. Some authors, such as Nicholas Grimald, who were widely represented in the first printing, were truncated in the second. Individual poems, even individual lines and phrasings, were emended. Some of these changes have been attributed to shifts in the religious and political environments of Elizabeth's first decades. Some have been attributed to Tottel's broader, editorial sensibility. The volume, in its publication history, is no fixed artifact of literary culture, but the changing, mobile product of the interplay among the printer and his public: what Paul A. Marquis has defined as the "collaborative activity by a community of professionals and tradesmen."[8]

---

[6]   Hamrick, "*Tottel's Miscellany*"; May, "Popularizing Courtly Poetry"; Marquis, "Editing and Unediting"; Herman, "*Songes and Sonettes*, 1557," pp. 111–130 in this volume.

[7]   Herman, "*Songes and Sonettes*, 1557."

[8]   Marquis, "Editing and Unediting." Marquis acknowledges the two-decade-long critical inheritance of the so-called New Bibliography that reassessed the practices and ideologies of editing and the relationships among authors and audiences in the age of print. Worth noting here are Leah Marcus's *Unediting the Renaissance* (London, 1996), and Steven Zwicker, "Habits of Reading in Early Modern Literary Culture," in David Loewenstein and Janel Mueller (eds.), *The Cambridge History of Early Modern English Literature* (Cambridge, 2002), pp.170–98.

Reviewing these various scholarly assessments of Tottel's career and the reception history of the *Songes and Sonettes* yields no consensus. Steven May sees Tottel himself as the editorial aegis through which the lines of Wyatt, Surrey, and the volume's host of other writers were emended, regularized, and assembled. Peter Herman sees the printer as an engaged participant in the religious politics of his age. Paul Marquis sees him, quite bluntly, "as a hack," whose genius lay in his sensitivity to public taste and temper. How to assess the contemporary cultural impact of this printer's book may be a task, then, far beyond the purview of my chapter.

Whatever the specific take that modern scholars have on the *Songes and Sonettes*, there is, however, a consensus that the book did, somehow, influence the writing and the reading of English verse in the decades that followed its initial publication. There is a general awareness that the book had an impact on verse anthologies, on individual authorial collections, and on an emergent sense of vernacular, literary history. Whether or not, as Steven May has claimed, by the mid-1590s its "poetic style ... was as out of fashion as the codpiece," shards of its verse show up in Shakespeare, and popular anthologies such as John Bodenham's *The Garden of the Muses* and Robert Chester's *Love's Martyr* were hearkening back to it in the early 1600s.[9]

One way of approaching this question of cultural impact, therefore, may be less to try to understand the broad canvas of literary culture than to engage, more pointedly, with the idiom of culture itself. The word "culture" originally connoted plant and animal cultivation. The image of the garden and the farm is central to its uses, and well into the sixteenth and seventeenth centuries, the term evoked far more the tillage of the field than the teachings of the classroom. Only in Tottel's own time does the concept of culture as something intellectual or social broaden into use. *The Oxford English Dictionary* finds its extended uses, "cultivation or development of the mind, faculties, manners, etc.; improvement by education and training," first appearing in the sixteenth and early seventeenth centuries.[10] The *OED*'s first entry for this definition is from Thomas More's translation of a letter of the Italian Humanist Pico della Mirandola from about 1510, rendering the Latin *animi cultum* into the English "to the culture & profit of their myndis." Nearly a century passes until the *OED* records another appearance, from 1608 and another English translation: "necessarie for the culture of good manners." Between these two quotations lies a history of intellectual and social cultivation, a growth of

---

[9]   May, "Popularizing Courtly Poetry."

[10]   *Oxford English Dictionary*, s.v., *culture*, n., accessed online, November 10, 2011, http://dictionary.oed.com. For the broader idioms of cultivation and culture, gardening, and early modern literary practice, see the field-defining studies of A. Bartlett Giamatti, *The Earthly Paradise and the Renaissance Epic* (Princeton, 1966) and Roy Strong, *The Renaissance Garden in England* (London, 1979). See, too, the essays collected in Michael Leslie and Timothy Raylor (eds.), *Culture and Cultivation in Early Modern England: Writing and the Land* (Leicester, 1992); Amy Tigner, "*The Winter's Tale*: Gardens and the Marvels of Transformation," *English Literary Renaissance*, 36 (2006): 114–34.

courtliness, of humanist learning, of travel, of language, or mores, or *sprezzatura*, all out of the medium of Tudor social and political experience.

What I suggest here, therefore, is that the contemporary cultural impact of Tottel's *Songes and Sonettes* lies in its contributions to a new idea of culture itself. The volume's contents and its claims were posited and read—even as those contents changed—as adding to the cultivation and development of mind, faculties, and manners. It is as much a manual of cultivation as any handbook of good manners or guide to disciplinary instruction. The wild vine, quotes the *OED* from Thomas Newton's *Approved Medicine* of 1580, "differeth in nothing from the Gardein vyne, but onely in Culture." One well could argue that this statement of herbaceous observation is as much a commentary on emerging social education as it is an observation about fruit. And one could well argue, too, that what Tottel found in the twisting lines of earlier poetry preserved in manuscripts were akin to the wild vines found in nature. Print cultivated such lines, domesticating them into the regularities of iamb and pentameter.

But what I also would suggest is that against the imagery of cultivation lie the idioms of burial. The garden plot and the graveyard remain the epicenters of the *Songes and Sonettes,* for if many of its poems offer educations in the arts of love and writing, many others offer eulogies of poets and of lovers. The death of Thomas Wyatt, of Lord Mautravers, of Cicero, of Lord Ferres, of Anthony Denny, and of many other patrons, writers, factual and fictional characters—all of these deaths haunt Tottel's collection. If *Songes and Sonettes* taught a generation how to love, it also taught it how to elegize. Thus, to consider the book's cultural impact is to consider how it traces a trajectory along the axes of death and didacticism, and at this chapter's close I find the *Songes and Sonettes* provoking the closing imaginations of the grave in Shakespeare's *Hamlet*.

Small Parcelles

From its first words, the *Songes and Sonettes* brings together writing and cultivation.[11] Such associations, of course, had long been a mainstay of the classical tradition: writing was likened to plowing (the Latin verb for both was *exarare*, to plough up or furrow), and composing verse was seen as similar to tilling fields. "I have a large field to ere," says Chaucer's Knight, anticipating both the length and the complexity of his forthcoming tale.[12] And if writing poetry was tillage, making an anthology was harvesting. The very word *anthology* comes from the Greek meaning a bouquet of flowers, and the Latin *florilegium* is a calque

---

[11]   Unless otherwise noted, all quotations from the prose and poetry of the *Songes and Sonettes* come from the edition of Marquis. For a sensitive reading of Tottel's preface, different but I hope complementary to mine, see Catherine Bates' contribution to this volume, "Profit and pleasure?"

[12]   See my discussion of these terms and their history in my *Children's Literature: A Reader's History from Aesop to Harry Potter* (Chicago, 2008), p. 45.

on that word. Selections from larger works were "flowers" plucked from the plant, and manuscript and early book collections of literature were "gardens of verses" long before Robert Browning used the phrase to title his collection of children's poetry.[13]

So, too, Tottel begins the *Songes and Sonettes* with the images of horticulture. "That to have wel written in verse, yea and in small parcelles, deserveth great praise."[14] Tottel begins by offering a panegyric on the skills of lyric poetry. To write well in verse is praiseworthy, even more so in small forms. And yet, Tottel's word for such forms, *parcelles*, conjures up a range of images far from the writer's study.[15] The word came into English from late medieval Latin and Old French. A parcelle was simply a part of a larger whole, but in later Latin it took on a special form, *parcella*, and a meaning, a piece of land. This sense of a parcel of land was absorbed into Anglo-Norman and Anglo-Latin legal language, as in the 1321 entry in the Rolls of Parliament, cited by the OED, "parceles de terre." By the sixteenth century, the idiom parcel of land or ground filled vernacular English writings, from treatises on husbandry, to guild records, to various translations of the bible.[16]

The preface to the reader continues, making the case that writing well in English is as praiseworthy a possibility as writing in Latin and Italian, and holding up the "honorable stile" of Surrey and the "weightinesse of the depewitted sir Thomas Wiat" as examples. Their work shows the possibility of grace in English verse "abundantly," and there is nothing evil about publishing their works "which the ungentle horders up of such tresure have heretofore envied the[e]." Tottel contrasts their stateliness with the rude skill of common ears, and he exhorts the unlearned to become more skillful by reading rhyme: to "purge that swinelike grosseness that maketh the swete majerome not to smell to their delight."

This is tale of textual recovery and publication told as a narrative of personal cultivation. The imagery here is not just of the page but of the earth. The treasure hoarded by the keepers of the manuscripts (for this is what all have assumed to be the brunt of Tottel's criticism) is an earthen, almost a chthonic image: like characters out of an ancient romance or a legal document, the owners of these manuscripts hoard them against the multitude. And, as if this were not enough, the

---

[13]   See James Hutton, *The Greek Anthology in Italy to the Year 1800* (Ithaca, 1935) and *The Greek Anthology in France and the Latin Writers of the Netherlands to the Year 1800* (Ithaca, 1946); Seth Lerer, "Medieval English Literature and the Idea of the Anthology," *PMLA*, 118 (2003): 1251–67; Leah Price, *The Anthology and the Rise of the Novel* (Cambridge, 2000). For reflections on the nature of the early modern vernacular anthology and the habits of reading as they potentially bear on the reception of the *Songes and Sonettes*, see Marquis, "Editing and Unediting."

[14]   My quotations from texts identified as from the first edition of the *Songes and Sonettes* come from Rollins, *Tottel's Miscellany*; quotations from the subsequent edition are from Marquis, *The Elizabethan Version*.

[15]   For a different interpretation of this portion of the Preface, in particular the word "parcelles," see my *Courtly Letters*, pp. 202–3.

[16]   *Oxford English Dictionary*, s.v., *parcel*, n.

reading of this poetry will purge the audience—from the swinelike grossness of the sty, we move to the sweet marjoram of the field.

The "Preface to the Reader" sets the stage for poems about personal cultivation, and for the associations among land and person that will make the central imagery of culture for the later sixteenth century. This is precisely what Tottel had found in Surrey's verse, and the first poem of the *Songes and Sonettes* brilliantly sustains this imagery.

> The sunne hath twise brought furth his tender grene,
> Twise clad the earth in lively lustinesse.

Surrey begins with the traditional associations among seasonal change and emotional instability. While spring may restore "winters hurt," and while the warmth of summer may bring back the verdancy of nature, the lover's heart remains cold, and his "fresh grene yeres" can never be recovered. The poem oscillates between life-giving nature and anticipated death, between the expectations of renewal and the ruefulness of loss. Tottel's title sets the tone behind these tensions, "Descripcion of the restlesse state of a lover, with sute to his ladie, to rue on his diyng hart," and the choice of leading off the volume with these verses may be not just thematic but textual as well. Surrey's lines brilliantly capture a condition of the early Tudor lover. They also capture the condition of the Tudor printer. Drawing on the imagery of textual production granted by new media of print, and—with its place at the beginning of the *Songes and Sonetts*—echoing Tottel's own language in his Preface, Surrey's poem ends:

> And if I flee, I cary with me still
> The venomd shaft, which doth his force restore
> By haste of flight, and I may plaine my fill
> Unto my self unlesse this carefull song
> Print in your hart some parcell of my tene.
> For I, alas, in silence all to long,
> Of mine old hurt yet fele the wound but grene.

"Print in your hart some parcell of my tene"—the line chimes with Tottel's praise of those who have written well "in small parcelles," and the poet's task becomes akin to that of publisher, printing this text into the heart. The "tender grene" of the poem's first line—an image that resonates with the closing imagery of Tottel's Preface, with its "swete maierome"—now morphs into a wound still fresh from love's arrow.[17]

---

[17] For a different set of approaches to Surrey's first poem in the volume, see Marquis, *The Elizabethan Version*, pp. xxxix–xl, and the discussion in William Sessions, *Henry Howard, Earl of Surrey* (Boston, 1986), who discusses the technical and thematic virtuosity of the poem and concludes, "It is small wonder that this poem is the first in *Tottel's Miscellany*" (p.86; quoted in Marquis, p. xl).

These images of growth and death, of cultivation and inhumation, and of the textuality of desire, interlace throughout the volume's poems. Whether they are the famous verses of Surrey and Wyatt or the lesser known attempts of poetasters now forgotten or anonymous, the parcels of the poetry stand as both little plots of land and little message packets, sent off from the dead.

Nicholas Grimald

Surrey and Wyatt have long been subject to the critical inquiries of scholars in these areas. But what of Nicholas Grimald, the third named poet in the volume, now barely noticed in criticism or the classroom?[18] Grimald offers a fascinating test case for the cultural poetics of the *Songes and Sonettes*. For, while his poetry fills up the middle pages of the volume's first edition (some 40 different poems, ranging from love songs, classical encomia, lyrics on marriage and particular occasions, and a set of epitaphs on historical figures), it serves, in a much briefer selection, as coda to the volume's second printing. Paul Marquis has explored in critical and textual detail the differences between these two printings and, in particular, Grimald's distinctive place in them, and I would not simply repeat his erudition here. What I would note, however, is Marquis's important conclusions: that the shift in Grimald's poetry and its location represents a significant editorial reconception of the volume as a whole; that in its second edition, the *Songes and Sonettes* moves towards a coherent trajectory of artifice and argument. The second printing of the *Songes and Sonettes* works its way, in Marquis's formulation, through a set of verses on virtue and friendship, poetry and power, politics and public life, through verses that provide the reader with "a series of portraits with an educated potential to inspire readers to virtuous action." In their placement at the close of the second edition, then, Grimald's poems "explore the complex nature of virtuous action, its importance to the survival of the human community, and its relationship to martyrdom and immortality."[19] This is the version of the volume, by and large, that would have been reprinted throughout the Elizabethan period. It would have been the version that began with Surrey's pastoral virtuosity and ended with Grimald's verses on the death of Cicero.

It is worth exploring some of these literary differences in order to illustrate the shifting nature of the cultural investment in the classical and literary forms of elegance and elegy throughout the volume. In the first edition, Grimald appears as something of an author on a par with Surrey and Wyatt, and the first poem offered in his section begins, much like Surrey's, with lines on natural renewal and the narrator's distress:

> What sweet releef the showers to thirstie plants we see:
> What dere delite, the blooms to beez: my trueloue is to mee.

---

[18]   My discussion of Grimald is indebted to Marquis, *The Elizabethan Version*, pp. xxxiii, xliii–liv.

[19]   Marquis, *The Elizabethan Version*, p. liii.

Winter comes to this narrator, and his love is so great that, as he concludes, "With her so I may liue, and dye, my weal cannot be tolde." Grimald's poems move through these troped familiarities of nature and emotion. They spin across classical didactic landscapes, paraphrasing Cato and Cicero, praising Virgil; lauding virtue, friendship, and pleasure; addressing individuals within the poet's circle; and presenting elegies on their deaths. To read through Grimald's section in the first edition is to come across a poem such as "The Garden," in which all of the images of human cultivation vie with those of natural efflorescence, in which vines and trees and branches, blooms, and river beds all intertwine together, as if in anticipation of the intricacies of all the artificial gardens that would follow: Spenser's Bower of Bliss and Garden of Adonis from the *Faerie Queene*, and Milton's Eden in Book IV of *Paradise Lost*. Indeed, how can we not hear something of Milton's own verbal *tours de force* in Grimald's final line, a praise of gardens as an inspiration for the poet?

> Seed, leaf, flowr, frute, herb, bee, and tree, & more, then I may sing.

This prosodic technique of having every beat within the line filled by a single word, together with the narrative device of listing all things in the poet's purview, looks ahead to Milton's moment, now not in the Edenic descriptions of life, but in the catalogue of hellish death:

> Rocks, caves, lakes, fens, bogs, dens, and shades of death.[20]

Turn Tottel's page, and from "The Garden" move into a universe of death: epitaphs on knights and ladies, courtiers and cognoscenti. Now, Tottel's titles read like tombstones:

> An Epitaph of the Ladye Margart Lee 1555
> Upon the tomb of A. w.

The dozen poems that follow "The Garden" are all elegies, including the extended classical meditation on "The death of Zoroas, an Egiptian Astronomer, in the first fight, that Alexander had with the Persians." Opening with rattling sounds of "clattering arms" and "ragyng broyls of warr," the poem strives for epic histrionics, as the war against the Persians rings with onomatopoetic phrases and alliterations: "taratantars"; "shrowded with shafts"; "Whose greedy gutts the gnawing hoonger pricks." Amid this welter, Zoroas speaks, condemning Alexander, while the conqueror replies:

> O monstrous man (quod he) whatso thou art,
> I praye thee, lyue: ne do not, with thy death,
> This lodge of lore, the Muses mansion marr.

---

[20]   John Milton, *Paradise Lost*, in *The Complete Poetry of John Milton*, ed. John T. Shawcross (New York, 1967), Book II, line 621.

> That treasure house his hand shall neuer spoyl:
> My sword shall neuer bruze that skylfull brayn,
> Longgatherd heapes of science soon to spyll.

Overwrought words to a modern reader, perhaps, but to one coming, again, from Tottel's own Preface, there would be resonances with the notions that the legacy of English verse was a "treasure," ungently hoarded up, and that the publishing of these treasures remains an act in need of "learned" readers "to defend their learned frendes."

These images and idioms are all, of course, conventions ossifying into clichés. Little is truly new here. But what is distinctive, as I am suggesting, is the compilation of this body of verse prefaced by a message to the reader that offers a map to this imagery. If Tottel had a hand in reshaping the lines of iambic pentameter, he also had a hand in putting them together to build, by accretion, bodies of imagery that center on the tensions between cultivation and decay, elegance and elegy. And it is to this end that he (or his editors) radically relocated Grimald's work in the second edition. Fewer than a dozen poems come together at the book's end. They are "Songes written by N.G.," and the authorial identity established in the first edition (together with the many local and occasional references) is effaced in favor of a set of more abstract and absolute, classically inspired works on virtue. They close a volume, in Paul Marquis's words, that now traces "the plight of the personae from the private world of courtly love to the public world of politics and religion."[21] The *Songes and Sonettes* thus becomes much less a handbook of desire than guide to the perplexed, and it is as that kind of guide that, I believe, its post-Elizabethan cultural impact may lie.

Tottel's Graveyard, Hamlet's Grave

Years ago, I had argued for an understanding of the *Songes and Sonettes* as a book of the dead: a resting place for letters, loves, and lives that populated Henry VIII's court. I had worked through the poetics of dying in Surrey and Wyatt, and I had argued, too, that in Tottel's preface the language of inhumation opens from the start. "It resteth now … to publish," Tottel had written, and what rests here in the book are the words and wills of those long dead. As Surrey wrote, in the opening of his eulogy on Thomas Wyatt,

> W. resteth here, that quick could never rest:
> Whose heavenly giftes encreased by disdain,
> And vertue sank the deper in his brest.
> Such profit he by enuy could obtain.

The verbal parallels to Tottel's Preface are striking: rest, profit, envy. These are the terms of eulogy, and I suggested once (and raise again the thought) of reading the

---

[21]   Marquis, *The Elizabethan Version*, p.lxii.

entire *Songes and Sonettes* as place in which the early Tudor literary corpse and corpus may now rest in peace.[22]

I turn, now, to what I believe to be the afterlife of these poetic inhumations. Was Tottel's *Songes and Sonettes*, to recall Stephen May's words, as outdated as the codpiece by the sixteenth century's end? Certainly, as May himself implies, Justice Slender's avowal in Shakespeare's *Merry Wives of Windsor* that he would rather have his "book of Songes and Sonnets here" than 40 shillings strongly suggests that Shakespeare's character is something of an out-of-date lover. Slender longs for Tottel's book, as Deanne Williams has pointed out, "as for a dish of stewed prunes," and the "hopelessly derivative Slender" can only conjure up what Williams calls a set of "polysyllabic terms [that] are unthinkingly mimetic and evacuated of all signification."[23]

But the book's cultural significance may be more finely textured than marking nostalgia. The publication of its two editions in 1585 and 1587 does suggest that the book retained some commercial potential well into the age of Sidney. And even if the *Songes and Sonettes* was serving as something of a handbook for the creatively disabled, it may have served as well as script for the servile. The courtiers of the late Elizabethan and the early Jacobean courts may have found in Tottel's books archaisms, fit for a provincial like Slender. Perhaps they would have found its poems fit for provincial actors and voluble clowns, as well.

Act 2, scene 2 of *A Midsummer Night's Dream* begins with the rustics assembly around their plan for a play. Pyramus and Thisbe, that mainstay of post-Chaucerian amorous classicism, is their topic, and Nick Bottom, the Weaver, blows in with a question about Pyramus himself. "A lover, or a tyrant?" Peter Quince answers: "A lover that kills himself, most gallant, for love," and Bottom unwinds the stem of his wit to offer this now famous oration:

> The raging rocks
> And shivering shocks
> Shall break the locks
> Of Prison gates,
> And Phibbus' car
> Shall shine from far
> And make and mar
> The foolish Fates.[24]

---

[22] These few sentences recast remarks in my *Courtly Letters*, pp. 202–3.

[23] Deanne Williams, *The French Fetish From Chaucer to Shakespeare* (Cambridge, 2004), p. 224.

[24] All Shakespeare quotations are from Stephen Orgel and A.R. Braunmuller, *The Complete Pelican Shakespeare* (New York, 2002). Tom Macfaul's contribution to this volume enhances many of my observations here, especially his brief, suggestive section on *Hamlet*.

Long derided for its mispronunciation and its meter, its clanging rhymes and awkward alliterations, Bottom's speech has been seen as both ludicrously bombastic and yet literary, and I think what makes it both is its resonance precisely to the kind of verse that Shakespeare would have found in Tottel's selection from Nicholas Grimald.[25] Bottom's alliterations and his rhymes, his aching onomatopoeia, could come straight from Grimald's poem on the death of Zoroas (and now I quote from Marquis's edition of the Elizabethan version of the book).

> Now clattering armes, now ragyng broyls of warre,
> Gan passé the noyes of dredfull trompets clang:
> Shrowded with shafts, the heven: with clowd of darts,
> Covered the ayre: against full fatted bulls,
> As forceth kindled yre the Lyons keen:
> Whose greedy gutts the gnawyng honger pricks:

Such lines—with their bombast transmuted into rustic parody in Bottom's mouth—would have seemed to a reader of the 1590s as overdone and archaic as the lines of the players in *Hamlet*, whose classical exaggerations stand as verbal foil to Shakespeare's own lithe idiom. Indeed, it may well be a commonplace of Shakespeare criticism to note that the playwright's presentation of plays-within-plays often devolves to critiques of generational distance. Shakespeare's players evoke idioms of earlier performance, whether they be the intricacies of the interludes at Inns of Court, or the rusticities of cycle drama or itinerant mummings.

In this mix, I would suggest, Tottel's *Songes and Sonettes* represents an earlier generation of literary performance: one held up as fodder for tired clowns, rather than for aspirant kings. And yet, as Shakespeare knew, the line between the clown and king was very vague. His plays often invite the audience to see through the lunacy of fools and lovers to find pathos underneath. Bottom may oversee some of the best/worst theater ever, but Hippolyta does say (perceptively and touchingly), "Beshrew my heart, but I do pity the man."[26]

And so, too, perhaps with Hamlet. Paul Marquis saw the *Songes and Sonettes* as tracing "the plight of the personae from the private world of courtly love to the public world of politics and religion." Bottom does not quite make that leap, but Hamlet tries, and in his tragic failure he provides a provocation for a final look at Tottel's book at court or columbarium.

"What do you read, my lord?" asks Polonius when the prince enters, self-absorbed, in Act 2, scene 2, and Hamlet replies simply, "Words words words." What book does he bear? The text itself gives no explicit clue, but there are many implications. Hamlet offers a digest of its "matter":

> Slanders, sir, for the satirical rogue says here that old men have gray beards, that
> their faces are wrinkled, their eyes purging thick amber and plum-tree gum, and
> that they have a plentiful lack of wit, together with most weak hams.

---

[25] The associations of bombast and literature go back, at least, to G.K. Chesterton; see "A Midsummer Night's Dream," *Good Words*, 45 (1904): 621–26.

[26] I am indebted to Peter C. Herman for these provocations.

To Polonius, this is madness, but when he asks the prince if he "will walk out of the air," Hamlet blithely replies: "Into my grave."

Old men do have gray beards and wrinkled faces, much in life as in verse, and Hamlet would have found such clichés easily in Tottel's *Songes and Sonettes*:

> My lustes they do me leave,
> My fansies all be fled:
> And tract of time begins to weave,
> Gray heares upon my head.
>
> The wrinkles in my brow
> The furrowes in my face;
> Say limping age will hedge him now,
> Where youth must geve him place.

These lines come from the poem titled, "The aged lover renounceth love," and they chime with another, anonymous poem from the book, this one titled "The lover lamenteth that he would forget love, and can not." In lines immediately preceding the final section of Grimald's songs in second and all subsequent editions of the *Songes and Sonettes*, the poet remarks:

> The reason runnes about,
> To seke forgetfull water:
> To quench and clene put out,
> The cause of all this matter.
> And saith dead flesh must nedes,
> Be cut out of the core.
> For rotten withered wedes,
> Can heale no grievous sore.

And in its final stanza, the poet avers, "Let dead care for the dead," lamenting that all this pain and strife "Will bring me to my grave."

There's more of grave than gravy in the funeral baked meats at Elsinore, and Hamlet's conversation with Polonius, as well as his frequent asides throughout the play ("an unweeded garden": "rotten in the state of Denmark") evoke verses embedded in Tottel's book. Taken together, they build to the impression that *Hamlet*, like *Songes and Sonettes* (to return to Marquis's phrasing) traces the plight of the persona from the private world of courtly love to the public world of politics and religion. Both the play and book of poems hover on the knife edge of graciousness and the grave. These are narratives that ask us to reflect on generational change, the power of speech, and the conflicts of the courtier. Where else, then, should we expect to find the *Songes and Sonettes* but in the burial plot itself.

On the last page of that volume, Cicero's tomb is prepared. "Such maner things becoom the ded." What things become the dead at *Hamlet*'s close? What small parcels of land become the stages for its courtiership? In Act V, when the clowns come in to dig Ophelia's grave, when Hamlet enters and engages one of them in a reflection on the ways of inhumation, we hear the Gravedigger singing something that he would have learned, as Shakespeare would have learned it too, from Tottel.

> In youth when I did love, did love
>   Methought it was very sweet
> To contract—O—the time for—a—my behove,
>   O, methoutht there—a—was nothing—a—meet.

These garbled, halting lines, as generations of Shakespeareans have known, draw on "The aged lover renounceth love" from *Songes and Sonettes*, and the Gravedigger's two subsequent forays into song come from the same:

> But age with his stealing steps
>   Hath clawed me in his clutch,
> And hath shipped me into the land,
>   As if I had never been such.
>
> A pickax and a spade, a spade,
>   For and a shrouding sheet.
> O, a pit of clay for to be made
>   For such a guest is meet.

Scholars have long identified the differences between Shakespeare's version of the text and that printed in Tottel, and the poem itself (attributed to Lord Thomas Vaux) circulated in at least two other versions in late sixteenth-century collections.[27] But there is more to this association than source-mongering. The scene beside the grave in *Hamlet* is an episode of understanding the relationships between the courtly and the moral life. It draws distinctions between the show of flattery and flair, on the one hand, and the realities of mere decay, on the other. With each verse, we imagine, Shakespeare's Gravedigger throws up another skull, until, of course, he gets to Yorick's. And when Hamlet picks up the skull, reflecting on the passage of time and the loss of youth, he shows us all that time has passed—that the gambols and gibes, the songs and flashes of merriment are not just buried in the ground with Yorick but past purpose in the present. Taken in all its parts—the allusions to Tottel's *Songes and Sonettes*, the reflections on the courtly life, the understanding that a generation has now passed—this episode distances the present world of the play of Hamlet from the past world of earlier Tudor performance. It is not enough to aver, with Stephen May, that Tottel's book may have been as old-fashioned as the codpiece. Here, at this moment at the close of *Hamlet*, we see that the culture of courtly song has now been buried with the courtier's skull, only to be exhumed for sad nostalgia.

The poem that the Gravedigger excerpts takes us to the world of the bared skull. It generates the play's entire scene—an allusion to a story of disinterment

---

[27] See the summary review in Ross Duffin, *Shakespeare's Songbook* (New York, 2004), pp. 211–14.

and remembrance. If, as I had suggested once, that Tottel's is a book of the dead, then this allusion in Act V of *Hamlet* confirms its cultural impact: that it is a book of elegies and elocutions, a guide not only to the making of new poetry but to the inhumation of a past. Tottel has dug up those treasures hoarded by others. It is left for Shakespeare to hold up the skull of courtiership before him, to ask where its songs and gambols may remain, and then toss it back into the grave. No marjoram grows sweetly here. The songs and sonnets that once graced a Tudor court are fit now only for madmen and menials.

From its first printing, Tottel's *Songes and Sonettes* was an unfixed thing: a book of poems written by the courtly dead that would be altered, edited, and recast in successive issues. We should not think of it as a single, iconic book. Rather, it is testimony to the changing tastes and pressures of the printing house, a witness to the ways in which collaboration among publishers and readers shape the printed text. To understand its cultural impact, I think, is to attend less to the many minor poetic anthologies that may have followed in its wake than to explore how it had come to represent a literary past continuously changing for its many readerships. The book enables the *memento mori* moments of Hamlet precisely because it is such a mutable object: a changing sequence of editions whose contents reflect on cultivation and decay.

Chapter 8
"Their Gods in Verses":
The Popular Reception of
Songes and Sonettes 1557–1674

Stephen Hamrick

Almost without exception, scholarship published prior to the present collection has focused on *Songes and Sonettes* as primarlily distorting Henrician verse or simply as marking a milestone in the material history of publishing. These perspectives have been fruitful in many ways, yet such studies often ahistorically limit the longevity and broad impact of Tottel's anthology. Although scholars recognize the long-term impact of texts such as *The Geneva Bible* and *The Book of Common Prayer*, *Songes and Sonettes* tends to be analyzed as a static text published and frozen in 1557, rather than a hugely popular text published at least 11 times before the end of the sixteenth century; a reasonable estimate would suggest some four to six thousand copies in circulation by 1600. Although originating in the early Tudor period, the so-called "drab" age, the text remained in circulation throughout the sixteenth and into the seventeenth centuries. As such, consumers read the text alongside the so-called "Golden age" texts written by Sidney, Spenser, and Shakespeare. Read broadly and used extensively, the landmark text remained influential throughout the century.

Songes and Sonettes contributed to the formation of a protean English vernacular tradition quickly used and contested by a broad range of individuals. Conveying both a language of interiority and a lexicon of coded political commentary, Tottel's anthology foregrounded the possibilities of economic, erotic, and political agency within the English language: forms of agency presented (at times) as accessible and imitable through study of the text. Much of the text's popularity, then, resides in its purported practicality and applicability to different needs. Critical comments on *Songes and Sonettes* written in the first century after its initial publication assert such a utility, yet they remain largely unstudied. To begin to understand Tottel's great popularity, a history of its reception in the period 1557 to 1674 follows. Tottel's own influence on this tradition manifests in repeated interpretations of the anthology as characteristically English, transformatively foundational, and accessibly powerful.

"To the Reder"

In addition to offering Horatian profit and pleasure to his customers, Richard Tottel's prefatory epistle "To the reder" established an influential interpretive lens that continues to inform readings of his collection. Such a strong hermeneutic perspective ameliorates the ostensibly derivative nature of English poetry revealed by the epistle. Relying upon and exploiting the fraught and overlapping discourses of class, Renaissance humanism, and nationalistic sentiment, Tottel positions his commodity at the center of contemporary concerns over agency, linguistic and otherwise.

Aware of the reputation of verse imported from France, Italy, and elsewhere, Tottel refuses to subordinate the English vernacular to contemporary or classical languages. Initially setting English on a par with other languages, Tottel conceives of those languages as largely preparing the way for the English writers gathered in his collection. Tottel's "To the reder" begins, declaring

> That to have wel written in verse, yea and in small parcelles,
> deserveth great praise, the workes of divers Latines, Italians,
> and other, doe prove sufficiently. That our tong is able in that
> kinde to do as praise worthelye as the rest, the honorable stile
> of the noble earle of Surrey, and the weightinesse of the
> depewitted sir Thomas Wiat the elders verse, with several graces
> in sondry good Englishe writers, do show abundantly. (1–7)[1]

Syntactically beginning *in medias res* with the subordinating conjunction, "*That* to have wel written in verse," Tottel strategically shifts immediate attention away from the nominal subject, "Latines, Italians,/and other" and onto English verse. In appropriate humanist fashion, Tottel acknowledges the Latin and Italian precedents for English verse, yet his syntactical arrangement strategically begins the text with a *fait accompli*: "to have wel written." The construction, "to have wel written," thus asserts that poets wrote excellent verse in the past but, as the present perfect verb tense indicates, other poets *continue to* or *will* write excellent verse. The second sentence of "To the reder" replicates this syntax, again focusing attention on an accomplished fact, namely, "our tong is able" to produce excellent short poetry. Shifting attention through syntax, Tottel subtly fashions the excellence of English, engaging in vernacular apologetics, as Peter Herman examines in chapter 5.

Tottel's syntactical manipulations participate in an ongoing Renaissance process of elevating vernacular languages and using those "purified" languages to reform culture. Scholars, courtiers, and monarchs increasingly recognized that possession of an august vernacular literature created a positive ethos, establishing the credibility of their texts, their abilities, and their empires, respectively; poets,

---

[1]   Throughout this chapter, *Songes and Sonettes* refers to the second edition of the text; *Richard Tottel's Songes and Sonettes: The Elizabethan Version*, ed. Paul Marquis (Tempe, 2007), and will be cited paranthetically.

like Sir Thomas Wyatt and Henry Howard, earl of Surrey, moreover, also recognized that such a purified language could be used to critique contemporary politics.[2] As Richard Helgerson adroitly demonstrates, during the sixteenth and seventeenth centuries, a range of institutions and individuals worked assiduously at

> Gaining for the English language a degree of eloquence, perspicuity, regularity, fixity, and accomplishment that would make it a fit rival to the great ancient and modern languages of political and cultural rule. But it also meant pushing to the side not only foreign imports like liturgical Latin and law French but various debased and unreformed versions of itself as well. Absolute sovereignty of the sort England was now claiming made the English language both an instrument and an object of rule.[3]

More immediately concerned with economic gain than with ethnolinguistic imperialism, Tottel subordinates the "foreign imports" of continental verse in order to sell *Songes and Sonettes*. Not only syntactically "pushing to the side" "divers Latines, Italians, and other," but also filling their rooms with Surrey's "honorable stile," "the weightinesse" of Wyatt's deep wit, and the "several graces" of "sundry good Englysh writers," Tottel's "To the reder" replaces previous writers and foreign poetry with English poets and English verse. Through this tripartite parallelism, Tottel further undermines the value of foreign tongues, implying that the "Latines" may lack an honorable style, that the Italians produce lightweight, witless verse, and that "other" countries only generate "sundry bad" poets. The inclusive "our tong," moreover, balances linguistic pride with the fact that individuals must nevertheless learn other languages, "the rest" (Latin, Italian, French, etc.), in order to maintain legal, cultural, religious, and/or social agency. Even as the text elevates the English language in this fashion, it refuses to cede linguistic authority to elite writers.

Tottel's text undermines class-based concepts of honor, hoping to replace essentialist identities based on birth with performative identities based on learned skill or style. As Jason Powell writes, "early modern humanists sought to create or recover a value system independent from either the whims of an individual monarch or the reputation upon which honour depended."[4] With the increasing centralization of political power accelerated by the Tudors, a range of individuals and groups sought alternative forms of agency and used language *per se* to pursue

---

[2]   Avoiding the anachronistic concept of "the nation," I follow William Kennedy, *The Site of Petrarchism: Early Modern National Sentiment in Italy, France, and England* (Baltimore, 2003), in recognizing the "national sentiments socially and culturally articulated" in the period.

[3]   Helgerson, "Language Lessons: Linguistic Colonialism, Linguistic Postcolonialism, and the Early Modern English Nation," *The Yale Journal of Criticism*, 11.1 (1998): 292.

[4]   Jason Powell, "Thomas Wyatt and Francis Bryan: Plainness and Disimulation," in Mike Pincombe and Cathy Shrank (eds.), *The Oxford Hanbook of Tudor Literature, 1485–1603* (Oxford, 2009), pp. 192–3.

this end. The yoking of "honorable" and "stile," then, allows Tottel to relocate honor within the "stile," i.e., the poetry, of Surrey and *Songes and Sonettes*, rather than within the individual. As Marotti establishes, Tottel "exploited the hierarchical social structure that the more democratic environment of print helped to undermine" and therein advanced his own economic agency by presenting "himself as a class mediator taking advantage of print technology's ability to open the closed communication of an elite to a wider audience."[5] As the erstwhile custodians of dominant discourse, "elite" communicators struggled to maintain cultural authority against the aggressive centralization of authority by the Tudor dynasty and the more "democratic" impulses made available in and through print and humanism. Tottel dramatically expands such a traditionally class-based linguistic (and thus cultural) authority in "To the reder" to include anyone who reads and appreciates his collected verse.[6] As Catherine Bates establishes in chapter 2, however, such linguistic authority also granted knowledge of a depressed economy in which love and honor functioned as debased commodities.

Where the first two sentences of the prefatorial "To the reder" manipulated syntactical structure and tense to distinguish English verse as an ostensibly desirable intellectual and political commodity for all classes of readers, the next two sentences use a supposed social transgression to attract readers. Subtly mimicking the style of forensic argument common to the law books he published extensively, as Paul Marquis examines in chapter one, Tottel asserts that

> It resteth now (gentle reder) that thou thinke it not evil don, to publishe, to the honor of the english tong, and for profit of the studious of Englishe eloquence, those workes which the ungentle horders up of such tresure have heretofore envied the. And for this point (good reder) thine own profite and pleasure, in these presentlye, and in moe hereafter, shal answer for my defence. (8–14)

Poetically criminalizing the publication of *Songes and Sonettes*, "To the reder" thereby capitalizes upon the apparent social *faux pas* of printing private coterie verse for public consumption; perhaps this represents a Tudor example of creating scandal to sell texts. In any case, the epistle further excuses such a purported social gaff by personifying language itself and placing it within the context of early modern honor culture, hoping thereby to increase the "honor of the english tong." Tottel, nevertheless, distorts the makeup of the poems' first coteries, which included a broader range of participants than he indicates.[7] Increasing the appeal of

---

[5]   Arthur Marotti, *Manuscript, Print, and The English Renaissance Lyric* (Ithaca, 1995), pp. 295–96.

[6]   Waller, Gary, *English Poetry of the Sixteenth Century* (New York, 1986), pp. 56–9, argues that Tottel knew that the rhetorical models offered in the collection might serve as one means of ideological control of the populace. Tottel seems to possess a more emancipatory sense of poetry.

[7]   On the coterie, see Greg Walker, *Writing Under Tyranny: English Literature and the Henrician Reformation* (Oxford, 2005), p. 432.

his literary commodity through such distortion, Tottel accentuates a transgressive and thus tantalizing access to "such tresure" by subsuming a range of sins or ethical ambiguities entailed in the production, purchase, and consumption of the text, including "evil" actions, selfishness, and covetousness or "envie."

The "gentle" and "good reder," however, remains free of ethical taint through Tottel's strategies of misdirection. The metaphoric "it resteth now … that thou thinke" simultaneously posits the readers' agency to judge the (publication of the) text—"thou thinke"—and elides the printer's role in publishing private verse—the strategically passive "it resteth." Replacing feudal honor with the "honor of the english tong," "To the reder" deploys synecdoche to tie ideal concepts, here honor and language, *per se*, to readers' material experiences. Where Surrey and, to a lesser degree, Wyatt, redefined the role of the poet and the English language to provide an alternative to the authority of the Tudor dynasty, Tottel further locates moral and intellectual authority within language itself and thus initially fashions a commodity that promises profit through study.[8] Tottel also strategically distances himself from inappropriate behavior through the use of passive voice, writing, "it [is] not evil don," therein removing any actor (namely himself) from evil action; the text further distances Tottel by placing him in a passive position needing to ensure his own "defence." Also deftly addressing individuals, Tottel's prefatory letter contrasts the plural "ungentle horders" to the lone "reder" (used twice). Such a contrast helps create Tottel's appeal by structurally categorizing readers as exemplary and honorable and *not* as selfish hoarders.

Recognizing the need to create and instruct consumer tastes, moreover, Tottel emphasizes patriotism even while he encourages readers to enjoy *Songes and Sonettes* in order to distinguish "real" English men and women from uncouth and barbaric animals. With the repetitious "our tong," "Englishe writers," "english tong," and "Englishe eloquence," Tottel further accentuates a distinctly English discourse. Conveniently ignoring (or using, for Peter Herman above) the fact that, by 1557, many of the authors included in the miscellany were dead, Tottel ends his didactic preface aligning readers with the authors of the text. Completing his forensic argument, the editor addresses possible objections to his case, asking

> If parhappes some mislike the statelinesse of stile removed from the rude skil of common eares: I aske help of the learned to defende their lerned frendes, the authors of this woork: And I exhort the unlearned, by reding to learne to bee more skilfull, and to purge that swinelike grossenesse that maketh the swete majerome not to smell to their delight.

---

[8]   Walker, *Writing Under*, chs. 8–10; W.A. Sessions, "Surrey's Wyatt: Autumn 1542 and the New Poet," in Peter Herman (ed.), *Rethinking the Henrician Era: Essays on Early Tudor Texts and Contexts* (Urbana, 1994), pp. 168–92; and Tom Betteridge, *Literature and Politics in the English Reformation* (Manchester, 2004), pp. 44–86.

Hopefully mitigating potential problems with two conditionals, "if" and "parhappes," the text nevertheless must address the inevitable negative responses to the new style of poetry. Engaging *argumentum ad verecundiam* by aligning the authoritative "lerned frendes" with "the authors of this/woork," Tottel simultaneously defines the function of the critic (and criticism), i.e., "to defende their lerned frendes" and, perhaps to a lesser degree, identifies readers as middle and/or working class through the term "woork." Later Tudor writers, in fact, developed Tottel's understanding of poetic "work" even presenting such work as the true form of nobility and authority.[9] By blurring the distinction between poetry conceived of as noble effervescence and poetry conceived of as skilled labor, Tottel works to define verse in a way that appeals to all classes of consumer.

In sum, Tottel's "To the reder," positions *Songes and Sonettes* within an international milieu that centralizes the English language as a guarantor of personal, economic, and ethnic identity. Humanist in orientation, Tottel's prefatory verse ostensibly transforms consumers into "gentle" readers who, through reading the text, enable themselves to transcend the limitations of birth and class. Both economic and social, the "profit" offered (if not delivered) by Tottel taps into the increased social mobility made possible by the very humanism embodied in and by the text. Marketing the collection in such a fashion, Richard Tottel's "To the reder" dramatically shaped published responses to the text in the next hundred years.

"Trim Songes of Love"

In response to the highly popular but now incomplete courtly and Petrarchan text, *The Court of Venus*, poet and surgeon John Hall wrote and published *The Court of Virtue: containing many holy songs, sonnets, psalms and ballettes* (1565), a text which obliquely comments on the popularity of *Songes and Sonettes*. A surgeon and prolific writer, Hall published *The Court of Virtue* in order to combat the popularity of what he thought of as illicit and sinful poetry. A compendium of moral and religious verse, including psalm paraphrases, biblical sententiae, extended biblical quotations, and dream vision, Hall's text strategically parodies or, more accurately, co-opts popular Petrarchan forms, including Wyatt's "My lute awake," and "My pen, take pain."

Aptly dubbed a "Christian miscellany," *The Court of Virtue* overtly attacks the kind of poetry published in *Songes and Sonettes*.[10] Bemoaning an immoral age of dissolution and disorder, Hall writes,

---

[9]   On George Pettie's development of Tottel and the nobility of work, see Wendy Wall, *The Imprint of Gender: Authorship and Publication in the English Renaissance* (Ithaca, 1993), pp. 28–9.

[10]   See Lily Campbell, *Divine Poetry and Drama in the Sixteenth Century* (Cambridge, 1959/1961), pp. 47–8. All references are to *The Court of Virtue*, ed. Russell Fraser (New Brunswick, NJ, 1961) and will be cited parenthetically in the text.

Suche as in carnall love rejoice,
Trim songes of love they wyll compile,
And sinfully with tune and voyce
They syng their songes in pleasant stile,
To Venus that same strompet vile:
And make of her a goddes dere,
In lechrie that had no pere. (19–25)

Hall's lines attack contemporary Petrarchan verse as sinful, dedicated to the false idol "Venus that same strompet vile." Hall decries the fact that "a booke also of songes they have,/And Venus court they doe it name" (26–7). As the first text to print musical settings with many of the songs, *The Court of Virtue* also asserts that Christians must have "godly songes to synge" (12) and provides a "boke of songes holy," to which later writers or "godly men may adde" (18). In this, Hall enunciates a sense of the openness with which writers and, as we will see with *Songes and Sonettes*, readers treat even the printed text, welcoming additions to be written directly into the purchased texts.

Described as "an anti-Tottel endeavor," Halls *The Court of Virtue* rejects Petrarchan poetry as sinful and destructive of Christian values.[11] Rather than simply rejecting the poetry printed in *Songes and Sonettes*, Hall revises that poetry to reflect Christian values. Tottel, for example, records Wyatt, asserting

My lute awake performe the last
Labour that thou and I shal wast:
And end that I have now begonne:
And when this song is song and past:
My lute be stil for I have done. (91.1–5)

By way of sacred parody, Hall revises the poems, writing

My lute and I sythe truth we tell,
(Meaning no good man to offende)
Me thinke of right none should refell
The godlines that we intend:
But much rather if they have grace,
They will our good counsell imbrace,
Then blame my lute. (165–166.1–7)

Hall provides a headnote to his revision, describing it as "a ditie named blame not my lute." Although other readers will provide explicit reference to *Songes and Sonettes*, Hall's publication highlights the fact that Tottel's groundbreaking anthology had achieved enough popularity within eight years that some readers felt required to combat or contest that popularity—here through revision.

---

[11] Elizabeth Bellamy, "The Sixteenth Century," in Frank Magill (ed.), *Critical Survey of Poetry. Revised Edition* (8 vols.; Pasadena, 1992), vol. 8, p. 3808.

"In Prayse of Surreys Skill"

Seemingly ubiquitous in the second half of the sixteenth century, *Songes and Sonettes* quickly evolved into a valued cultural commodity deployed by a wide range of writers, scholars, churchmen, a monarch, and, as Tom MacFaul establishes in chapter 6, the modern age's most vaunted Tudor writer, William Shakespeare. Throughout the period 1557–1567, for example, printers repeatedly extracted individual poems from Tottel's collection and published them as broadside ballads, serving all classes of readers well into the next two centuries.[12] Although such selective textual dismemberment and the circulation of particular poems divorced those verses from the informing context of the anthology, the practice itself nevertheless suggests the great utility *Songes and Sonettes* quickly developed.

In his *Epitaphes, Epigrams, Songs, and Sonets* (1567), humanist poet George Turbervile accentuates such utility and provides an extended analysis of the groundbreaking anthology. Printed two years after *The Court of Virtue*, Turbervile's long text ignores or rejects Hall's reforming text. In addition to extensively paraphrasing Tottel's collection, Turbervile asserts that *Songes and Sonettes* transformed English poetry.[13] Translator of Ovid and Mantuan, secretary to Thomas Randolph on his embassy to Russia's Ivan the Terrible, and briefly popular as a poet in the mid-1560s, Turbervile largely ceased publishing by 1580. Part of an Inns of Court coterie including George Gascoigne and Barnabe Googe, Turbervile received a pardon for killing an assailant on 26 September 1573.[14] Turbervile's highly qualified poetic response to Tottel usefully outlines a number of critical concerns expressed by readers thereafter.

In his "Verse in prayse of Lorde Henrye Howarde Earle of Surrey," Turbervile echoes Tottel's prefatory assertions while also asserting that Surrey's verse, available in published form only in Tottel's text, transforms English language and literature. Engaging early in what W.A. Sessions defines as a cult of the poet earl,[15] Turbervile deploys a rhetorical question and its corresponding answer, hyperbolically writing

> What should I speake in prayse of Surreys skill
> Unlesse I had a thousand tongues at will;
> No one is able to depaint at full,
> The flowing fountaine of his sacred Skull. (9ᵛ)

Strategically lowering readers' expectations by elevating the earl's poetic abilities far above his own, Turbervile praises "Surreys skill" (9ᵛ) and paints him as the life-

---

[12]   Rollins, *Tottel's Miscellany*, vol. 2, p. 107–9.

[13]   On Turbervile, see Rollins, *Tottel's Miscellany*, vol 2, p. 110.

[14]   On Turbervile, see Raphael Lyne, "George Turbervile," *Oxford Dictionary of National Biography* (Oxford, 2004).

[15]   On the cult, see W.A. Sessions, *Henry Howard, The Poet Earl of Surrey: A Life* (Oxford, 1999), pp. 4–6.

giving and sacred source of a new English poetic tradition. Here and elsewhere throughout the period, "Surrey" serves as shorthand or a synecdoche for *Songes and Sonettes*: most readers knew his poetry only through Tottel's text, and only his name appears in the title.[16] A single volume of Surrey's poetry, moreover, failed to find a publisher until the nineteenth century.

As the reference to the life-giving "fountaine" suggests, Turbervile interprets the publication of *Songes and Sonettes* as inaugurating a new kind of English poetry. Painting Surrey as a later-day British Hippocrene fountain sacred to the Muses on Mt. Helicon, Turbervile extols "the flowing fountaine of his sacred Skull" (9ᵛ). With the life-giving qualities of the metaphoric "fountain," Turbervile also suggests that Surrey redefines the vocation of poet. As Peter Herman demonstrates, Wyatt and Surrey "transform the medieval concept of the poet as a craftsman into the Renaissance notion of the poet as an orphic voice of communal honor and nobility."[17] Placing *Songes and Sonettes* in the context of orphic and prophetic discourse through the terms "fountain" and "sacred," Turbervile connects the text, and the English language, to classical and biblical traditions of inspired poets like Homer, Virgil, King David, the prophet Daniel, and others.

Prompting or preempting George Puttenham's familiar adulation of the "courtly makers" in *The Arte of English Poesie* (1589), Turbervile also extols the earl as a maker of decorous verse that achieves formal excellence and rhetorical balance. Turbervile accentuates the formal strengths of Surrey's work through the use of tactile metaphors, writing that

> Where such a *skill in making* Sonets grue
> Eche worde in place with such a sleight is couch,
> Eche thing whereof he treates so firmely toucht,
> As Pallas seemde within his Noble breast. (10ʳ; my emphasis)

Turbervile's focus on "making Sonets" draws attention to *Songes and Sonettes* and to the skill of using the English language well. The constructions "Eche worde," "Eche thing," "couch," and "toucht," moreover, fashion the poetry, through repeated designation of the term "eche," in staunchly material terms, thereby implying the solidity of Surrey's verse; aptly, period meanings of "couch" imply layering stones and building edifices (*OED*, 1–4). Solid yet balanced, Surrey's culturally and discursively constructive English words remain, for Turbervile, "in place" and his poetic skill or "sleight" (*OED*, 3–5) establishes *Songes and Sonettes* as a foundational text for modern English. As this building metaphor indicates, within 10 years of its first publication, then, Turbervile recognized that Tottel's runaway bestseller had inaugurated "modern" English.

---

[16] Wall, *Imprint of Gender*, pp. 97–8. For an alternate reading, see Marotti, *Manuscript, Print*, pp. 215–16.

[17] Peter Herman, ed., *Rethinking the Henrician Era: Essays on Early Tudor Texts and Contexts* (Urbana, 1994), p. 9.

With the construction "Pallas seemde within" Surrey's "Noble breast," Turbervile also deploys the contemporary mythography of Pallas Athena, stressing therein, the earl's balanced verse. The paragon of the *vita theorica* or contemplative life, the mythopoeic figure of Pallas Athena traditionally combines earthly and heavenly wisdom, therein further representing Surrey's poetry in humanist-prophetic terms.[18] In his highly influential *Book of Emblems* (1546), Andrea Alciato encapsulates a traditional understanding of Pallas in Emblem 23, "that foresight is improved by wine," which depicts Athena and Bacchus together on a plinth. The poetic motto ends indicating "justly are they joined; for if an abstemious man hates wine, he'll have no help from the goddess."[19] As Turbervile places Pallas within Surrey, he implies that *Songes and Sonettes* embodies precisely this balance of Bacchanalian excess (equivalent to the *furor poeticus* offered by the divine fountain) and Aristotelian restraint—the later represented in Pallas' chaste life.

Further echoing Tottel's paratextual "To the reder," Turbervile praises *Songes and Sonettes* as a distinctly English text. Where "To the reder" refashions the worth of "our tong" (1) and the "honor of the english tong" (9), Turbervile echoes such ethnolinguistic pride, writing

> Our mother tongue by him got such light,
> As ruder speach thereby is banisht quight.
> Reprove him not for fansies that he wrought,
> For fame thereby and nothing else he sought.
> What though his verse with pleasant toyes are fright;
> Yet was his honours life a Lampe of light.
> A Mirrour he the simple sort to traine,
> That ever beate his brayne for Britans gaine. (10ʳ)

Invoking the "mirror for magistrates" tradition, Turbervile asserts that Surrey's exemplary life, a highly visible "Lampe of light," excuses any "toyes" or immature sentiments expressed within the poetry. Reinforcing the claim that sacred wisdom emerges from *Songes and Sonettes*, Turbervile uses the visual metaphors of "a Lampe" and "such light," therein recalling Tottel's assertion that the poetry would "show abundantly" that English verse is "as praise worthelye [sic] as the rest"; this also looks forward to George Puttenham's use of the same lamp imagery. Turbervile's "ruder speach" and "the simple sort to traine" also replicate Tottel's humanist desire that the anthology "purge that swinelike grossenesse" of "the unlearned" who prefer "the rude skil of common eares" (15–19). The political

---

[18]   On Pallas, see Jane Chance, *Medieval Mythography: From Roman North Africa to the School of Chartres, A.D. 433–1177* (Gainesville, 1994), pp. 404–6.

[19]   http://www.mun.ca/alciato/e023.html; accessed 6/6/2011. See also, Stephen Batman, *The Golden Booke of the Leaden Goddes* (1577), 5ʳ–5ᵛ, writing on Pallas: "wisdome joined to force, to qualifie extremities. It concerneth a wise man to be fenced, as well against frowarde affections, as the outward enemie."

metaphor "banisht," paired with the inclusive "Britans gaine," moreover, positions *Songes and Sonettes* within the humanist and political movements that stressed the centrality of a noble vernacular to one's ethos. Turbervile thus reifies *Songes and Sonettes* as the premiere reformer of English eloquence and, by extension, culture or empire.

At least within the first decade of its popularity, then, Tottel's prefatory manifesto, "To the reder," directed readers like Turbervile to the poetry's didactic, moral, and ethnolinguistic themes. Turbervile's repeated focus on the *English* nature of this poetry recalls the fact that Tottel published his miscellany within a period of religious turmoil, a period wherein the English language played a central role in religious conflict. Throughout the English reformations, polemicists defined both Protestantism and Catholicism as "foreign" imports. Significantly (if frustratingly) both Catholic and Protestant interest in the vernacular during this period suggests Tottel's Anglo-centric emphasis may transcend simple religious affiliation.[20] If Tottel's editorial project seeks to embrace or celebrate Catholicism (and not simply carnal idolatry as Hall suggested), some readers rejected such an interpretation or, at the very least, rejected what they interpreted as Catholic effects within *Songes and Sonettes*.

"Gothes in Ryming"

In *The Scholemaster* (1570), Roger Ascham rejects the kind of poetry included in *Songes and Sonettes* and states that such poetry embraces sin and damnation— not unlike Hall in *The Court of Virtue*. Although *Scholemaster* first circulated at Elizabeth's court in 1563, it only achieved a broad readership after its publication, and after multiple editions of Tottel's miscellany appeared.[21] Famed educator, gifted prose writer, and tutor to Queen Elizabeth, Ascham staunchly forwarded English vernacular writing and served the last three Tudor monarchs as Latin secretary. Widely traveled as an ambassadorial secretary, Ascham forwards an apocalyptic Tudor humanism that rejects works of Italian, i.e., Catholic, origin, as well as Tottel's anthology.[22]

The Scholemaster recognizes, among other things, the central role of the vernacular in educating the English populace. Embracing the humanist credo that

---

[20]   On this period, see Eamon Duffy, *The Stripping of the Altars: Traditional Religion in England, 1400–1580* (New Haven, 1992), chapter 11. Although the Marian return to the Latin Mass undermines his claim, Tom Betteridge, *Literature and Politics in the English Reformation* (Manchester, 2004), p. 139, writes that "the valorization of native English writing" in *Songes and Sonettes* "is a common polemical trope of Mary Tudor's reign."

[21]   On dating *Scholemaster*, see Ryan Stark, "Protestant Theology and Apocalyptic Rhetoric in Roger Ascham's *The Schoolmaster*," *Journal of the History of Ideas*, 69.4 (2008): 527.

[22]   *DNB*, vol. 1, pp. 622–31. On Ascham as an apocalyptic humanist, see Stark, "Protestant Theology."

the educated individual must work for a better world (to expand the number of saved souls prior to the impending apocalypse), the Latin secretary emphasizes the central role of the poet in refining and manipulating the vernacular. Ascham decries that fact that, despite knowing better, English poets

> Follow rather the Gothes in ryming, than the Greeks in trew versifying, were even to eat ackornes with swyne, when may freely eate wheate bread emonges men. In deede, Chauser [*sic*], Th. Norton, of Bristow, my L. of Surrey, M. Wiat, Th. Phaer, and other Jentlemen, in translating Ovide, Palingenius, and Seneca, have gone as farre to their great praise, as the copie they followed could cary them. (60ʳ)

Yoked as both translators and poetic founders—"trew versifying"—in this passage, Chaucer, Thomas Norton, Surrey, Wyatt (all included in Tottel's anthology), and others nevertheless achieve as much or have "gone as farre" as their source materials allowed. For Ascham, however, the translators' source material fails to produce excellent English translations because of its origin: "the Gothes." Representing the ancient Germanic tribes that invaded and establish kingdoms in Italy, Spain, and France (*OED*, 1), the term "Gothes" serves as an euphemism for Catholic writing, culture, and religion, which, in Ascham's lifetime, largely or completely dominated those countries. Not mentioned by name, Tottel's *Songes and Sonettes* and its influence nevertheless operate within this passage.

In addition to impeccable credentials for publishing law texts, Richard Tottel also possessed a reputation for publishing the classics. Inadvertently bridging Tottel's legal and lyric publications, Ascham includes four translators whose poetry also appeared in *Songes and Sonettes*.[23] Although Ascham here and elsewhere speaks somewhat positively of contemporary English *translations* of classical authors, he nevertheless judges Wyatt and Surrey less kindly because they engage in "barborous and rude ryming," likening that practice to eating acorns with swine, which again recalls Tottel's "To the reder." Where Tottel wished to educate the "unlearned" commoners and purge them of their "swinelike grossenesse," Ascham's rejection of Gothic or Catholic verse originates in religious sentiment rather than class conflict or cultural ignorance.[24]

In *The Scholemaster*, Ascham's guarded approval of Surrey and Wyatt's translations corresponds to his expressed attitudes towards popular verse. Reporting a contemporary craze for poetry, which *Songes and Sonettes* initiated, Ascham feels troubled that

> Rash ignorant heads, which now can easely recken up fourten sillabes, and easelie stumble on every Ryme, either durst not, for lacke of such learnyng: or

---

[23]   O.B. Hardison, Jr., *Prosody and Purpose in the English Renaissance* (Baltimore, 1989), p. 151.

[24]   On Ascham's nationalist sentiments, see Liah Greenfield, *Nationalism: Five Roads to Modernity* (Cambridge, 1992), pp. 42–4.

else would not, in avoyding such labor, be so busie, as everie where they be: and shoppes in London should not be so full of lewd and rude rymes, as commonlie they are. (61ʳ)

Although Ascham focuses primarily upon the lack of classical "learnyng" in such poetry, *The Scholemaster* also notes that the majority of verse that fills the "shoppes in London" consists of both "rude" and "lewd" or salacious texts. When we recall that "fourteeners," poems alternating 12- and 14-syllable verse lines, remained a favorite of Surrey's, Ascham's rejection of that kind of verse seems suggestive.[25]

Nevertheless, as he continues, Ascham's comments increasingly apply to *Songes and Sonettes*. Immediately after belittling "lewd" rhymes, Ascham delineates specific kinds of poetry that he finds objectionable:

> But now, the ripest of tong, be readiest to write: And many dayly in seeting out bookes and balettes make great shew of blossomes and buddes, in whom is neither, roote of learnyng, nor frute of wisedome at all. Some that make Chaucer in English and Petrarch in Italian, their Gods in verses, and yet be not able to make trew difference, what is a fault, and what is a just prayse. (60ᵛ)

One of the central influences in Tottel's collection, Petrarch might seem like the "God in verse" of that text. Nevertheless, Ascham criticizes "the folowers of Chaucer and Petrarke" (61ʳ) not, perhaps, primarily for the salacious nature of their poetry, but because they naively or uncritically read all such poetry as beautiful— i.e, "blossomes and buddes"—without determining "what is a fault, and what is just prayse." Such an ignorant reception of poetry, for Ascham, corresponds to the ignorance with which readers consume the Catholic worldviews subsumed within text such as *Songes and Sonettes*.

Ascham provides a clear indication that *Songes and Sonettes* provoked negative reaction, even as it achieved such early and dramatic success. Aligned with Ascham's own vernacularism, Tottel's anthology nevertheless fails, from his more general perspective, because it imports and, through translation, recreates fallen attitudes and religions. As a weapon of mass destruction, he argues, the kind of poetry printed in *Songes and Sonettes* serves as a tool for a Catholic fifth column. Unable to convert pious Englishmen through their "contentious bookes," these hidden agents, "the sutle and secrete Papistes at home, procured bawdie bookes to be translated out of the Italian tonge" and thereafter "do now boldy contemne all severe books that sounde to honestie and godlines" (27ᵛ). Although Ascham betrays a distinct ignorance concerning Italian culture, his comments publically attack the kind of literature included in Tottel's anthology.[26]

---

[25]   On Surrey, Wyatt, and "fourteeners," see Harold Child, "The New English Poetry," *Cambridge History of English Literature: Renascence and Reformation*, ed. A. Ward (15 vols., New York, 1932), vol. 3, p. 177.

[26]   Michael Wyatt, *The Italian Encounter with Tudor England: A Cultural Politics of Translation* (Cambridge, 2005), pp. 159–63, establishes Ascham's ignorance concerning Italy.

Ascham's concern that "bawdie bookes," i.e., eros-centered texts like *Songes and Sonettes*, alter reading practices originates in religiously motivated xenophobia. Like Tottel, Ascham understands that popular literature profoundly influences English culture. Seen as conveying a Catholic worldview by Ascham, such powerful verse produces heresy. "Mo[re] Papistes," he states, "be made, by your mery bookes of Italie than by your earnest bookes of Louvain" (26ᵛ). While Ascham clearly represents a hostile opinion, his anti-Catholic reaction to the kind of poetry at the heart of Tottel's text oddly anticipates Herman's assertion that *Songes and Sonettes* serves as part of a Catholic project. With multiple editions circulating in early modern England (and beyond), Ascham's ostensibly alarmist cultural critique may represent more than a rhetorical scarecrow or whipping boy. Whether or not individuals actually converted to Catholicism as a result of reading Petrarchan verse, Ascham suggests that some readers might have received Tottel's anthology with a disdain generated by religious discourse.

"Trim Verses"

In *Hundreth good Pointes of Husbandry* (1570), also published by Richard Tottel, Thomas Tusser invokes *Songes and Sonettes* as a standard of excellence—even for practical writers such as himself.[27] Educated as a chorister at St. Paul's school at Eton under Protestant Nicholas Udall, and at King's College, Cambridge, Tusser served for a decade as a musician to William, first baron Paget. As a farmer thereafter, Tusser introduced barley culture to Suffolk and wrote *Hundreth good Pointes of Husbandry*, which he published again in 1571 and expanded to five hundred "good Pointes" in 1573; the expanded treatise was published at least 12 times before the end of the seventeenth century. Tusser died while in Poultry Compter imprisoned for debt.[28] With such a long publishing life, Tusser's critical comments on *Songes and Sonettes* reached a very broad audience.

By 1570, Henry Howard, the poet earl of Surrey, represented by *Songes and Sonettes,* served as a literary touchstone—even for those who fell far short of his poetic abilities. Provocatively addressing readers' expectations at the very beginning of his text, Tusser asks in "The Preface,"

> What lookest thou here for to have?
> Trim verses, thy fansie to please?
> Of Surry (so famous) that crave,
> Looke nothing but rudeness in these. (1–4)

Strategically addressing readers' expectations and noting the earl's "trim verses," Tusser shares Turbervile's affirmation of the balanced nature of *Songes and Sonettes*, as well as valuing the pleasure, "fansie to please," that Tottel promised

---

[27]   On Surrey as the standard of excellence in the period, see Douglas Peterson, *The English Lyric from Wyatt to Donne: A History of the Plain and Eloquent Styles* (Princeton, 1967), p. 48.

[28]   *DNB*, vol. 19, pp. 1306–8.

in "To the reder." Tusser informs readers that if they seek "grave sentences," then "Chaucer hath twentie and ten,/Ye thousandes to pleasure thy minde" (6–8). Eschewing "Tearmes painted with rethorike fine" in his own work, he directs readers to "makers of Englishe." "Makers of Englishe" may recall Turbervile's "making Sonets," yet Tusser's "what lookest," "so famous," and "crave" nevertheless elevate Surrey's poetry and Tottel's *Songes and Sonettes*, not only defining that text as the standard used to judge *all* writing but also asserting that readers have come to expect, and, as the repeated visual metaphors (again reminiscent of Turbervile) indicate, to seek such excellent verse.

Although Tusser's invocation of readerly desire might originate in unabashed self-interest, the multiple editions of *Songes and Sonettes* (at least seven by 1570) suggests that Tusser recognized the popular demand for the anthology and attempted to harness it to his own needs. In part, such contemporary opinions of the excellence of the anthology contribute to the kind of reaction offered by Ascham. Simultaneously elevating the passions and the individual, Petrarchan poetry merits vilification for Protestants such as Ascham because it draws attention away from God and hierarchical relationships. For writers like Tusser, however, Tottel's collection serves as an aesthetic *axis mundi* around which other texts congregate and receive judgment. As the collection immediately achieved immense popularity, and served as *the* English Petrarchan urtext, attacks perhaps remained inevitable.

"We Have Gotten our Songs and Sonets"

Within 15 years, *Songes and Sonettes* had achieved such a high cultural profile, in fact, that Edward Dering and John More apparently felt required to comment on it in their highly popular English catechism, *A Briefe and Necessarie Catechisme or Instruction* (1572). Hailing from Kent and a graduate of Christ's College, Cambridge, reforming Protestant Edward Dering achieved some contemporary fame for preaching and wrote on behalf of the Privy Council against Catholicism. On one infamous occasion, Dering preached directly to Queen Elizabeth, urging her to rectify the sinful and ailing English clergy. A scholar of languages, Dering died young in 1576, regularly hauled before the authorities, including Star Chamber, yet remained an unapologetically outspoken enemy of episcopacy and bishops in particular.[29] Originally from Westmorland, also a graduate of Christ's College, Cambridge, and dubbed the controversial "Apostle of Norwich," John More remained an influential reforming Protestant and avid preacher until his death in 1592.[30]

---

[29]   On Dering, see *DNB*, vol. 5. See also Neal Enssle, "Patterns of Godly Life: The Ideal Parish Minister in Sixteenth- and Seventeenth-Century English Thought," *Sixteenth Century Journal*, 18.1 (1997) 3–28.

[30]   On More, see *DNB*, vol. 13 and Matthew Reynolds, *Godly Reformers and their Opponents in Early Modern England: Religion in Norwich 1563–1643* (Woodbridge, 2005), ch. 4.

Recovering the patristic tradition of catechism, continental reformers (Calvin, in particular) strongly influenced the content of English catechistical texts in the reigns of Henry VIII, Edward VI, and Elizabeth I, including the Dering/More catechism. Written by both the influential and the less well known, these didactic texts outlined statements of faith and instructions for practice for communicants of all ages. Used by the clergy in confirmation instruction, such texts influenced private individuals who also used them for self-improvement, teaching, and/ or reading to others.[31] A highly popular and frequently published text, *A Briefe* introduced many readers to Tottel's equally popular collection.

As an instrument of government, the official catechism allowed Henry VIII, Edward VI, Mary I, and Elizabeth I (slowly) to fashion a semblance of unity through religious practice and doctrine. Stressing the need for obedience to superiors, *Brief* thus produced scholars, churchmen, and citizens attuned to the doctrine of the Elizabethan church and to the Queen's authority over both Church and State. With 42 editions, Dering and More aimed their catechism at adults, inculcating a decidedly Calvinistic Reformed piety. Next to multiple editions of the Bible, both Protestant and Catholic catechisms greatly influenced contemporary understanding of religious belief and practice, including reading strategies. With over 280 catechistical texts published between 1549 and 1646, these texts remained a key component in the simultaneous protestantization and increasing literacy of Elizabethan Britain.[32]

The Dering/More catechism devotes considerable type to arming readers against what the text interprets as profane and profaning literatures, including, by name, *Songes and Sonettes*. After castigating the continued popularity of classical tales of eros, medieval romance, tales of Robin Hood and Robin Goodfellow, and

---

[31]   On catechism, see Mary Patterson, *Domesticating the Reformation: Protestant Bestsellers, Private Devotion, and the Revolution of English Piety* (Cranbury, 2007); Scott Wenig, *Straightening the Altars: The Ecclesiastical Vision and Pastoral Achievements of the Progressive Bishops Under Elizabeth, 1559–1579* (New York, 2000); Ian Green, *The Christian's ABC: Catechisms and Catechizing in England, c. 1530–1740* (Oxford, 1996); Malcolm Hardman, *A Kingdom in Two Parishes: Lancashire Religious Writers and the English Monarchy, 1521–1689* (Cranbury, 1989); John Booty, *The Book of Common Prayer 1559: The Elizabethan Prayer Book* (Charlottesville, 1976); Alexander Nowell, *A Catechisme : or, First Instruction and Learning of Christian Religion (1570)*, intro. Frank V. Occhiogrosso (Delmar, 1975); Edward Dering, *Workes. The English Experience: Its Record in Early Printed Books* (New York, 1972); T. Baldwin, *William Shakespere's Petty School* (Urbana, 1943); Laurence Vaux, *A Chatechism or Christian Doctrine* (Menston, 1969); George Corrie, *A Catechism Written in Latin by Alexander Nowell, Dean of St. Paul's: Together With the Same Catechism Translated into English by Thomas Norton* (Cambridge, 1853).

[32]   According to Green, *The Christian's*, p. 425, the most popular catechisms include Laurence Vaux's Catholic *A Chatechism or Christian Doctrine* (1568), Alexander Nowell's *Catechisme, or first Instruction in Christian Religion* (1563/1570), and Dering and More's catechism.

the highly popular hagiographic text, *The Golden Legend*, Dering and More attack the bestsellers of their day. Although ignorant and sinful consumers, according to *A Brief*, run after "new delights," these erotic and adventure texts "justifie the idolatrous superstition of the elder world" and, moreover, "to this purpose we have gotten our Songs and Sonets, our Pallaces of Pleasure, our unchast Fables & Tragedies, and such like sorceries, more then any man may reckon" (A1ᵛ). Writing from a hostile perspective, this statement nevertheless corroborates the central place of Tottel's collection for aspiring poets, courtiers, and even "hotter" Protestants. The representations of interiority shared by Protestant and Petrarchan discourse fails to arrest Dering/More's distrust of Tottel's collection and other "unchast[e]" texts.[33]

Rather than a prudish moralism uncomfortable with courtly and Petrarchan sexuality, Dering/More and others identified *Songes and Sonettes* as maintaining, and even celebrating, a Catholic worldview—"superstitions of the elder world"— within their narratives. The phrase "such like sorceries" metahorically fashions the almost magical effect of Petrarchan English verse, which accentuated the individual's emotions and personal conscience in the midst of a rapidly changing culture. Dering/More joins a group of Protestant churchmen and writers, like Ascham, the martyrologist John Fox, and poet Barnabe Googe, who identify specific texts within popular culture as destructive of "true religion."[34] At the end of Elizabeth's first decade of rule, this group of writers, and others, published a range of texts that engaged Reformation beyond churches, catechisms, and cathedrals. Ironically, the one text that arguably popularized the vernacular more than any other secular text, now achieved such a presence in Tudor society that cultural critics felt the need to attack it directly, as well as its type of verse more generally.

Such attacks emerged because the text served as more than a repository of poetic forms or didactic morals. As Seth Lerer establishes in Chapter 7, *Songes and Sonettes* was "as much a manual of cultivation as any handbook of good manners." Baldesar Castiglione urged, in *The Book of the Courtier*, that the consummate courtier must "be versed in the poets as well as in the orators and historians, and let him be practiced also in writing verse and prose, especially in our own vernacular ... in this way he will never want for pleasant entertainment with the ladies."[35] Even as many readers interpreted *Songes and Sonettes* as a broadly didactic social and cultural text in the manner outlined by Castiglione, for some readers

---

[33]   Elizabeth Heale, *Wyatt, Surrey,and Early Tudor Poetry* (London, 1988), p. 192, identifies part of the success of *Songes and Sonettes* as the fact that "it made courtly culture more palatable to growing Protestant suspicions of insincerity and verbal manipulation by constructing little narratives in which the poems play an apparently self-expressive role."

[34]   On Googe, see Stephen Hamrick, *The Catholic Imaginary and the Cults of Elizabeth, 1558–1582* (Aldershot, 2009), ch. 2.

[35]   Baldisare Castiglione, *The Book of the Courtier*, trans. Charles Singelton (New York, 1959), p. 70.

the anthology embodied nonbiblical or irreligous models of thinking, acting, and communicating.[36] For aspiring humanists, however, the poetic anthology served as an alternative to religious texts used in the process of fashioning the self.

Perhaps following in the tradition of an English linguistic pride initiated by Tottel's "To the reder," critics, editors, and readers have, in part, diminished the Italian strains in *Songes and Sonettes* in order, in effect, to fashion an originary myth for modern English. To recognize and approve of the presence of an unreformed Italian Petrarch in the founding document of modern English would dilute English distinctiveness. Rejections of Petrarchan discourse, then, find some original motivation in (a perhaps unrecognized) xenophobic and religious bigotry, coded solely or dominantly in ethical (*caritas* over *cupiditas*), classical (*logos* over *pathos*), and/or formal (decorum over excess) critical terms.

"Honoryng in Harte the Erle of Surrie"

Contributor to *Songes and Sonettes*, erstwhile servant to Henry Howard, the earl of Surrey, soldier, prisoner of war, performer before Queen Elizabeth, royal pensioner, agent to the Prince of Orange, international messenger, and oppressor of the Irish, the amazingly prolific writer Thomas Churchyard provides a unique analysis of Tottel's collection. Like Dering/More, Churchyard bemoans the state of the English book market, but, unlike the catechists, his complaints derive from economic rather than religious or moral concerns.

Churchyard dedicates his text, *A Light Bondell of Livly Discourses Called Churchyardes Charge* (1581) to Philip Howard, earl of Surrey, and the grandson of Tottel's poet earl. Evoking an honorable ethos of his own, Churchyard proceeds to

> Enter into the cause of this my boldnesse, the troth is in callying to remembrance a promes that I made, touching some verses. And honoryng in harte the Erle of Surrie, your Lordshipps grandfather, & my master (who was a noble warriour, an eloquent Oratour, and a second Petrarke) I could doe no lesse but publishe to the worlde somewhat that should shewe, I had lost no time in his service ... I thought I might dedicate a booke to your Lordshippe. (ii[v])

Churchyard participates actively in the posthumous fashioning of his former "master" within "the extraordinary cult of the Earl of Surrey."[37] Sharpening Turbervile's interpretation, Churchyard defines Surrey's nobility in terms of his martial masculinity, humanist rhetorical abilities, and poetic brilliance. Churchyard may have begun his military service with Surrey in France, providing warrant for

---

[36] On *Songes and Sonettes* as a model for the aspiring courtier, see Elizabeth Pomeroy, *Elizabethan Miscellanies: Their Development and Conventions* (Berkeley, 1973), chapter 3; Waller, *English Poetry*, pp. 21, 52; Stephen Foley, *Sir Thomas Wyatt* (Boston, 1990), pp. 106–7; Heale, *Wyatt, Surrey*, pp. 191–2; and Walker, *Writing Under*, p. 424.

[37] W.A. Sessions, "'Enough Survives': The Earl of Surrey and European Court Culture," *History Today* (June 1991): 50.

his judgment of the "warriour" earl.[38] More significantly, however, Churchyard provides a strange reaction to (the success of) *Songes and Sonettes.*

Churchyard worries over changing literary tastes that, for the working writer, ostensibly threaten the marketability of works like *Songes and Sonettes.* Praising the living earl, Churchyard compliments him "who hath taste and feelyng in the good giftes of nature, and noble vertues of his auncestours" (2ᵛ), including his grandfather's superior oratory and his verse. With these sensuous metaphors, Churchyard connects the dedicatee's aesthetic sense or literary "taste and feelyng in the good gifts of nature" to "the noble vertues of" the poet earl. The middle class Churchyard extends the democratization of honor by depicting nature as the source of nobility and not class. Enjoyment of the poet earl's poetry, i.e., *Songes and Sonettes,* thus constitutes good taste and aesthetic sensitivity, which recalls not only Tusser's assertion that Tottel's collection serves as a universal standard of good writing but also Tottel's democratization of honor in "To the reder." Much to the poet's chagrin, however, current literary trends marginalize the kind of art represented in the anthology.

> But now, right noble Earle, the worlde lovyng change and varietie of matter, waxeth awearie of frevoulous verses (because so many are writers of Mieter) and looketh for some learned discourse, by which meanes my barrain bookes maie remaine unred, or misliked, and so lye on the Stationers stall, as a sillie signe of a newe nothyng, neither worthe the buying, nor the regardyng. (2ᵛ)

Churchyard fashions readers, "the worlde," as addicted to or "lovyng change," which recognizes that the popular book market thrives on "change and varietie of matter." Readers' tastes, in other words, vacillate over time, altering more in response to literary fads than to poetic excellence. That which previously held value, now seems "frevoulous" and "maie remaine unred" or unliked. Rather than celebrating the free play of cultural signs and material texts, Churchyard's image of (his) unpopular books, which "lye on the Stationers stall," bemoans the fact that, as he claims with crocodile tears, his poetry represents "a sillie signe of a newe nothyng," producing neither monetary, "the buying," nor cultural capital, "the regarding." Ostensibly glutted with poetry, readers, for Churchyard, desire "some learned discourse" rather than poetry.

Having identified himself with Surrey and his poetry with the possessive "my master," Churchyard's suggestion—that good English verse suffers from changing tastes and the flood of poetic texts—serves perhaps as the genesis of the critical assertion that the poetry published between *Songes and Sonettes* and Edmund Spenser was drab and largely unpopular.[39] Motivated, however, more by money

---

[38] On Churchyard's military career, see Elizabeth Heale, "The Fruits of War: The Voice of the Soldier in Gascoigne, Rich, and Churchyard," *Early Modern Literary Studies,* 14.1 (2008): 5.139.

[39] C.S. Lewis, *English Literature in the Sixteenth Century Excluding Drama* (Oxford, 1954), pp. 222–71.

than by aesthetic considerations, Churchyard's assertion deserves closer scrutiny. Churchyard's complaint that "so many are writers of mieter," in fact, accurately speaks to the competition faced by Tottel's collection and his own works, including texts such as Barnabe Googe's *Eglogs, Epytaphes, and Sonnettes* (1563), the now lost edition of *A Handful of Pleasant Delights* (1566), George Turbervile's *Epitaphs. Epigrams. Songs and Sonets* (1567), and his *Epitaphes and Sonnettes* (1576), Thomas Howell's *The Arbor of Amitie* (1568) and *Newe Sonets, and Pretie Pamphlets* (ca. 1568), George Gascoigne's, *A hundreth sundrie flowres bounde up in one small poesie* (1573), and his *The posies of George Gascoigne Esquire* (1575), Richard Edwards' *The Paradise of Dainty Devices* (1576), the most popular anthology of the period, and another edition in 1578, Timothy Kendall's *Flower of Epigrammes* (1577), Thomas Proctor's, *A Gorgeous Gallery of Gallant Inventions* (1578), and Humfrey Gifford's *A Posie of Gillowflowers* (1580). At least five of these collections lifted poems directly from Tottel, including *A Handful, Arbor, Paradise, Gorgeous Gallery*, and *Flower.*

With these 12 poetic collections in circulation in 1580, and with more than 30 separate publications to his name by that date, then, Churchyard's claim that his (and other poets') works fail to find an audience seems, if not simply wrong, overstated.[40] An examination of the *English Short Title Catalogue* confirms this suspicion, listing Churchyard's multiple single-sheet publications, including one on an earthquake, as well as multiple copies of all of his major works surviving in British and American libraries. Churchyard's assertion, moreover, that his own poetry (and Surrey's) quickly went out of style fails to account for the 11 editions of *Songes and Sonettes* published during the Elizabethan period.

Perhaps Churchyard suggests the lack of popularity of his and the poet earl's work as a marketing strategy: his writing might appeal to the current earl's sense of tradition; his excellent poetry outstrips the public's intellectual abilities but not the current earl's; perhaps the current earl will feel pity for his plight and reward him. Alternately, because Tottel omitted Churchyard's name from the anthology, he may feel little attachment to it as a source of his own reputation as a writer; in *Churchyard's Challenge* (1593), however, he claims that "many things in the booke of songs and Sonets, printed then, were of my making." An air of disappointment and/or jealousy seems to attend his comment that, "an infinite number of other Songes and Sonets, given where they cannot be recovered, nor purchase any favour when they are craved."[41] Churchyard's celebration of Surrey, moreover, might negatively impact Churchyard or the current earl's reputation as Englishmen. If a large number of readers identified *Songes and Sonettes* with Catholicism, then association with the text or its authors might tarnish one's

---

[40]   On the influence of Tottel, see Rollins (ed.), *Tottel's Miscellany, 1557–1587* (2 vols., Cambridge, 1928–29; rev. ed., 1965) p. 107 ff. For an annotated list of Churchyard's works, see William Adnitt, *Thomas Churchyard 1520–1604* (Oswestry, 1880).

[41]   W.C. Hazlitt, ed., *Prefaces, Dedications, Epistles Selected from Early English Books, 1540–1701* (privately printed, 1874), pp. 145, 147.

religious and thus political reputation. Nevertheless, eliciting reactions positive, negative, and, apparently, indifferent, Tottel's anthology functions as a protean and contested cultural signifier within 25 years of its first publication.

"Tasting of a Noble Birth"

In *An Apology for Poetry* (1580–81), Philip Sidney famously mentions only four English poetic texts, including Surrey's "lyrics," offering, therein, a positive review of *Songes and Sonettes* by the Elizabethan period's preeminent poet and poetic theorist.[42] Not unlike Ascham, Sidney asserts in Horatian mode that poetry and poets must both delight and teach readers to live a moral, Protestant life. As Sidney creates an august English literary tradition that he inherits and extends, he asserts that "in the Earl of Surrey's lyrics" readers find "many things tasting of a noble birth, and worthy of a noble mind" (113). As W.A. Sessions demonstrates, Sidney focuses on Surrey's "noble birth" and "noble mind" in order to place himself within the tradition of English writers who fashioned poetry (and poets) as an independent authoritative discourse. Like Surrey, Sidney represented the Tudor court as a dissolute, ineffectual, and religiously lukewarm environment detrimental to Protestant wayfaring and warfaring in the world.

Very much as Richard Tottel projected in his prefatory epistle, then, Tudor readers of *Songes and Sonettes* asserted the foundational nature of that collection, therein establishing both its cultural dominance and, by association, their own. Sidney's own political Petrarchanism may owe more to Wyatt than to Surrey, yet his use of Surrey, and thus *Songes and Sonettes*, attests to the broader cultural presence of the text within the first century of its reception. Engaging political, religious, and erotic discourses in their original contexts, the poems collected by Tottel would go on to serve other readers and writers including Sidney and his coterie.

Penna Gloria Perennis

Songes and Sonettes, in fact, remained a valuable commodity throughout the 1580s, meeting the needs of a very broad range of readers. In *Philotimus* (1583), for example, Brian Malbancke lifted whole passages "*verbatim* from the miscellany and printed them as prose to help carry on his narrative."[43] Henry Petowe engaged the same process of lifting poems directly from the anthology, yet retained the verse form to complete Christopher Marlowe's *The Second Part of Hero and Leander* (1598); he would also lift lines from *Songes and Sonettes* and place

---

[42] Sir Philip Sidney's *An Apology for poetry and Astrophil and Stella: Texts and Contexts*, ed. Peter Herman (Glen Allen, 2001). Chaucer's *Troilus and Cressida*, *A Mirror for Magistrates*, and *Spenser's Shepherd's Calendar* each receive Sidney's imprimatur.

[43] Rollins, *Tottel's Miscellany*, vol. 2, p. 112.

them in *Philochasander and Elanira the Faire Lady of Britaine* (1599).[44] Such "borrowings" indicate the cultural saturation of Tottel's text and, to some degree, its economic value for writers and publishers—if not readers or purchasers.

In addition to the mercantile value of the poems, *Songes and Sonettes* also served both political and emotional needs. In 1586–87, Mary, Queen of Scots, for example, used a diamond to inscribe two lines from *Songes and Sonettes* into a window during her imprisonment in Fotheringhay castle; the last known early modern edition of S*onges and Sonettes* appeared in 1587, as well. Engaging her own fall from power, she inscribed, "And from the toppe of all my trust,/Myshap hath throwen me in the dust" (145.5–6). Tottel's thus apparently provides quite an appropriate verse for Mary's situation as the deposed Queen of Scotland, one-time hopeful queen of England, and convicted prisoner destined for the chopping block. Clearly not influenced by Tottel's Petrarchan title as scholars have contended of readers, the Scottish Mary deploys the text as comment on her own political position and not as an erotic commonplace.

John Harington, the elder, in fact, wrote Tottel's 145, "The lover that once disdained love is now become subject, being caught in his snare," while imprisoned with Princess Elizabeth when Queen Mary I came to the throne.[45] A poet himself, Harington wrote two anti-Catholic poems that "inaugurate a significant Protestant appropriation of Petrarch."[46] Imprisoned in the Tower of London by Queen Mary for his loyalty to Elizabeth, the later made his heir, Sir John Harington, her godson. John Harrington's religious politics notwithstanding, individual poems, as well as the anthology *per se*, served a very broad range of individuals—Catholic and Protestant—ensuring, therein, its popularity throughout the period.

In *A Choice of Emblems* (1586), Protestant Geffrey Whitney engages *Songes and Sonettes* as part of a plea for patronage from, first, Philip Sidney, and then Edward Dyer, the acclaimed poet, courtier, and diplomat. The ambitious and religiously committed Whitney studied at Cambridge, Oxford, and Leyden, where he presented a manuscript copy of *A Choice* to the Earl of Leicester in support of Anglo-Dutch action against Catholic Spain during the Dutch Revolt.[47] Contributing

---

[44]   See Rollins, *Tottel's Miscellany*, vol. 1, pp. 112–19.

[45]   On these events, see *DNB*, vol. 8, 1269–73, and Charles Crawford, "Tottel's 'Miscellany,' Sir Antony St. Leger, and John Harington, the elder," *Notes and Queries*, 11.3 (1911): pp. 423–4.

[46]   Anthony Mortimer, ed., 'Introduction', *Petrarch's Canzoniere in the English Renaissance* (Amsterdam, 2005), p. 17.

[47]   On Whitney, Dyer, and *A Choice of Emblems*, see Bart Westerweel, "On the European Dimension of European Emblem Production," in Alison Adams and Marleen van der Weij (eds.), *Emblems of the Low Countries: A Book Historical Perspective*, Glasgow Emblem Studies, vol. 8 (Glasgow, 2003): pp. 1–16; John Manning, *The Emblem* (London, 2003), pp. 275–7; H.R. Woudhuysen, *Sir Philip Sidney and the Circulation of Manuscripts, 1558–1640* (Oxford, 1996), pp. 94, 252; Martin Garrett (ed.), *Sidney: the Critical Heritage* (London, 1996), pp. 102–3; *The Spenser Encyclopedia*, ed. A.C. Hamilton (Toronto, 1990); and Henry Green (ed.), *Whitney's Choice of Emblemes* (London, 1866).

dedicatory verse to Spenser's *Amoretti*, Whitney dedicated his emblem book to Dyer only after Sidney declined the honor. As a poetic mythographer, Whitney recalls the deaths of classical heroes who often founded cities—Orestes, Theseus, and others—and imagines a mythopoeic death for Surrey.

Following several of his critical predecessors, Whitney characterizes Surrey as a founder of modern English, a fallen hero mourned by the gods, and a celebrated artist lauded by English poets. As the primary textual conduit for this cultural influence, *Songes and Sonettes* again surfaces as the foundational text of modern English language and culture. On page 196 of his emblem-book (see the image on the cover of this book), Whitney presents the motto *Penna gloria perennis*, "The glory of the pen is everlasting," over an emblem of Victory armed with a swordlike pen; she blows a horn above a classical landscape. In the (extended) epigram, Surrey's death saddens even the gods:

> When frowning fatal dame, that stoppes our course in fine,
> The thred of noble SURREYS life, made hast for to untwine.
> APOLLO chang'd his cheare, and lay'd awaie his lute,
> And PALLAS, and the Muses sad, did were a mourninge sute,
> And then, the goulden pen, in case of sables cladde,
> Was lock'd in chiste of Ebonie, and to Parnassus had.

With these mythopoeic lines, Whitney engages the legendary founder Surrey in order to immortalize Sidney and Dyer. As the god of inspiration, prophecy, and poetry, Apollo embodies the traits ascribed to Surrey by later poets. Apollo's unhappiness and abrogation of his beloved lute playing establishes the great magnitude of the loss of the poet earl.

During the Renaissance, classical gods like Apollo often served as complex symbols of absolute reality—a reality wherein Christian truths were contained in pre-Christian forms. As Edward Panofsky and others demonstrate, the rise of Renaissance neoplatonism denotes a desire to justify human action on ontological, religious, and/or metaphysical grounds.[48] As such, the representation of divine beings and their approval, like Apollo and Diana, provides a symbolic representation of poetry as sacred or prophetic. As the gods represent higher ideals or Christian truth, their mourning Surrey's death establishes his role as sacred precedent, which Turbervile established in 1567.

Even as the text canonizes Surrey, Sidney, and Dyer, *Songes and Sonettes* again emerges as the foundational English text that makes such poetic deification possible. Exalted as the instrument of Surrey's foundational achievements, "the goulden pen" receives its own burial in a "chiste of Ebonie" and internment on Mt. Parnassus, the *axis mundi* sacred to the muses, including the muse of poetry,

---

[48] Erwin Panofsky, *Idea: A Concept in Art Theory*, trans. Joseph Peake (New York, 1968). See also Ronald Levao, "Sidney's Feigned Apology," *PMLA*, 94.2 (1979): 223–33. See also Jean Seznec, *The Survival of the Pagan Gods: The Mythological Tradition and Its Place in Renaissance Humanism and Art*, trans. Barbara Sessions (New York, 1972).

Calliope. Whitney provides a side note (see the cover of this book) that defines the epigrammatic reference to "SURREYS," clarifying for readers that he means "the Erle of Surrey that wrat the booke of Songs and Sonettes." Significantly, Whitney defines Surrey not as the noble lover, heroic soldier, or wronged martyr of his legendary cult, but rather as the author of the foundational English text. Surrey's ostensible treason, his honorable military service, and/or his munificent patronage remain absent, represented only in the vague "life." Whitney thus defines the text as a validating talisman that ensures the reputation of the poet earl. In this fashion, *Songes and Sonettes* serves as the defining achievement of the earl, even though his verse totals less than 20 percent of the collection.[49]

Although Surrey's life continued to inspire admiration throughout the period, Whitney's focus on the pen and Surrey's authorship contribute to the ongoing process of locating poetic ability within individual skill and in the English language itself, not in noble birth. Not unlike Churchyard, Whitney adapts the cultural capital of *Songes and Sonettes* to his own needs: glorification of Sidney, Dyer, and the Anglo-Dutch Protestant cause. Regardless of any particular meanings of any particular poem, *Songes and Sonettes* thus serves as a cipher for excellence used to characterize other works. In the case of Churchyard, Ascham, and Tusser, the collection and its verse become foils against which they define themselves, their work, or the English language, variously. As such, Richard Tottel's text serves as an early modern touchstone for writers—Petrarchans, anti-Petrarchans, and others—regardless of their class, religion, or goals.

"Poeticall Workmanship"

Educated at Cambridge, translator of Virgil's *Georgics*, and friend of Edmund Spenser and Gabriel Harvey, William Webbe wrote *A Discourse of English Poetrie* (1586) which engages *Songes and Sonettes* as a powerful reforming text—in contrast to Dering/More, who rejected the text as corruptively Catholic. Protestant Webbe worked for a number of gentry families, including the brother of Lady Jane Grey, and attended the performance before Queen Elizabeth of the tragedy of *Tancred and Gismund* at the Inner Temple in 1568.[50] Webbe's subtitle, *Together with the Authors Judgment Touching the Reformation of our English Verse*, and preface, "to the noble poets of England," presents *Songes and Sonettes* from a Protestant humanist perspective that locates nobility in religious orthodoxy and vernacular linguistic excellence. Proper contextualization of Tottel's anthology requires a more extended analysis of *A Discourse*, because Webbe contributes significantly to the ongoing formation of both an English poetic cannon and of the poet's political role in society.

Webbe, not unlike Ascham and Churchyard before him, provides a negative assessment of the contemporary book trade, deriding both verse and prose writers.

---

[49]   On Surrey as consummate patron, see Sessions, *Henry Howard*, p. 177.

[50]   On Webbe, see *DNB*, vol. 60, pp. 111–12.

Decidedly of the "middling sort" and disregarding the so-called "stigma of print," Webbe informs readers that he decided "to make a draught of English Poetry … but indeede more like to a learner then one through grounded in Poeticall workmanship" (A3ᵛ). Rather than a courtly maker, then, Webbe's "draught" offers an image of the poet as one who provides an imperfect or preliminary version of poetry. With this journeyman's expertise, Webbe castigates the "innumerable sortes of Englyshe Bookes, and infinite fardles of printed pamplets, wherewith thys Countrey is pestered, all shopes stuffed, and every study furnished." "Innumerable" and "infinite" in number, these "Englyshe Bookes," from Webbe's hyperbolic position, threaten to clog the arteries of the body politic as a pestering disease or plague. Webbe interprets this legion of publications as some kind of threat, because "the greatest part," he writes, consist of works "either meere Poeticall, or which tend in some respect … to Poetry" (A4ʳ). The adjective "meere" or "mere" means pure and unmixed in the early modern period (*OED* 1), which sense Webbe uses throughout *A Discourse of English Poetrie*.

Webbe writes his text to encourage others to produce good poetry, but forwards a distinctly normative pedagogy. Assuming a Protestant humanist readership, he asserts that "wee may not onelie get the meanes which wee yet want, to discerne betweene good writers and badde, but perhaps also challenge from the rude multitude of rusticall Rymers, who will be called Poets, the right practice and orderly course of true Poetry" (A4ʳ). Ascham, as noted above, conceived of profane poetry like *Songes and Sonettes* as dulling the aesthetic and moral senses, yet Webbe offers readers a critical tool that will allow them to recognize "true Poetry" and "Poets" and to "discerne betweene good writers and badde." Where Tottel implicitly defined criticism as defense of a poet, here Webbe defines criticism as a practice of aesthetic judgment. Although, he argues, the great English poets, including Surrey, succeeded in purging English poetry "from faultes, weeded of errours, & … barbarousnes" (A4ʳ), Webbe follows Tottel and asserts that poetic workers must continue to "labour to adorne their Countrey" with "true Poetry" (A4ᵛ). Quoting "Master Ascham's" rejection of the poetry of "Hunnes and Gothians" (C2ᵛ), Webbe asserts that future "true" and not "barbarous" poetry must forward Protestant English values rather than foreign and/or Catholic concerns.

In tracing poetry from the Greek and Roman comic, tragic, and epic writers through the medieval English poets, including Gower, Chaucer, Lydgate, and Skelton, Webbe further defines "true Poetry" as both spiritually inspired and superior to common ballads. Addressing "the famous and learned Lawreat Masters of Englande, that they would but consult one halfe howre with their heavenly Muse," Webbe asserts that such poets will honor their "native speeche" and that "they might wipe out" "enormities" from vernacular verse. Seemingly influenced by a manuscript copy of Sidney's *An Apology for Poetry*, which was published posthumously in 1595, Webbe recalls Sidney's use of the Roman "*vates*" or inspired poets who brought sacred knowledge to their cultures. Webbe pleads with contemporary poets "to looke so lowe from your divine cogitations, when your Muse mounteth to the starres, and ransacketh the Spheres of heaven" to "take compassion of noble Poetry, pittifullie mangled and defaced" (B1ʳ). Presaging writers such as Milton and the English Romantics as well as citing Edmund Spenser, Webbe asserts that "true poetry" must come from "celestiall instinction" (B3ʳ), which neatly combines innate powers or instinct and divine or "celestiall" inspiration (*OED*, 1–2). English poets, however, have "mangled and defaced" verse and therefore require instruction in "true" poetry, which, borrowing Spenser's language, must come from the "Heavenly Muse" or someone with divine inspiration. His earlier definition of himself as a poetic "draughtsman" ostensibly undermines his ability to determine good poetry from bad and thus, by extension, he must call upon his own muse.

For Webbe, the urge to deface vernacular poetry, and thus the English language, originates in lower class culture, as well as in heretical circles. These wannabe climbers, he charges, work very hard or "make meanes to be promoted to Lawrell" (D1ʳ), i.e., poetic authority. Further reinforcing the authority of "high culture" forms and guardians, the poetic theorist vilifies the "uncountable rabble of ryming Ballet makers, and compylers of sencelesse sonets, who be most buy to stuffe every stall full of grosse devises and unlearend Pamphlets ... Alehouse song[s] ... Northen Jigge[s] or Robyn hoode [tales]" (D1ʳ). Excessive in its grossness, uneducated in its opinions, and uncontrolled in its drunken habits, the rabble here celebrate a Northern, and, for many, a Catholic, worldview that praises robbery and the redistribution of wealth.[51] Rather than conflating Catholicism and poetic meter or style, this analysis recognizes that some contemporary readers identified romance, Petrarchan, and medieval discourses as conveying Catholic worldviews and sensibilities.

Although the popular tales of Robin Hood offered religious critique of Catholicism, Protestant writers, like Dering/More, for example, understood these popular romance and adventure tales as promoting and sustaining Catholic religion and culture; arguably, Webbe joins their ranks. Both covertly and overtly Webbe uses (and quotes) Ascham's barbaric and Gothic trope, which references and rejects poetry written by Catholics. He also extensively praises Edmund Spenser as the best poet in England who deserves to be made poet laureate. Repeatedly referencing and quoting *The Shepherds Calendar*, he informs readers that Spenser's exemplary text provides "warning to other young men, who being intangled in love and youthful vanities, may learne to looke to themselves in time." In addition to warning against such erotic pursuits, he claims that "many good Morall lessons are therein contained." The poetic theorist includes "the reverence which young men owe to the aged in the second Eglogue," "the commendation of good Pastors, and shame and disprayse of idle & ambitious Goteheardes in the seaventh, and loose and retchlesse lyving of Popish Prelates in the ninth" (E4ᵛ).

---

[51]   On Robin Hood and wealth, see Christine Chism, "Robin Hood: Thinking Globally, Acting Locally in Fifteenth-Century Ballads," in Emily Steiner and Candace Barrington (eds.), *The Letter of the Law; Legal Practice and Literary Production in Medieval England* (Ithaca, 2002), pp. 12–39.

Attached to both patriarchal and Protestant values, Webbe's standards of "true poetry" include the religious bigotry of anti-Catholicism forwarded by Spenser, Dering/More, and others.

Seemingly interpreting the medieval author's anticlerical satire as proto-Protestantism, Webbe's English literary cannon nevertheless substantially begins with Chaucer, and builds itself predominantly of writers in Tottel. Carefully avoiding his own poetic idolatry, Webbe reports that "Chawcer, who for that excellent fame which hee obtayned in his Poetry, was alwayes accounted the God of English Poets (such a tytle for honours sake hath beene given him)." For the sixteenth century theorist, Chaucer's style rings a bit harshly in his "modern" ears, yet nevertheless he presents "a true picture or perfect shape of a right Poet" (C3^r). Intriguingly sensual for an iconophobic poetic theorist, these visual and tactile metaphors seek to materialize or embody the qualities that constitute the "true" English poet.

Writers included in *Songes and Sonettes* dominate Webbe's approved cannon of religiously and politically acceptable English poets. Although Wyatt disappears from the list, the poetic theorist praises

> The dyvers workes of the olde Earle of Surrey: of the L. Vaux, of Norton, of Bristow, Edwardes, Tusser, Churchyard. Wyll: Hunnis: Haiwood: Sand: Hyll: S.Y. M.D. and many others but to speake of their several gifts, and aboundant skill shewed forth by them in many pretty and learned workes, woulde make my discourse much more tedious. (C4^r)

Tottel's collection looms large in this list of poets. Surrey, Vaux, Norton, Churchyard, Heywood, and Sand each contributed verse to *Songes and Sonettes*.

Accomplished in multiple genres—"dyvers workes"—Surrey receives the honorable epithet "olde," as well as heading the nonchronological list of verse writers. For Webbe, the work represented by Tottel's anthology, moreover, plays a central role in the ongoing process of locating social and cultural excellence within English as a modern language constituted by "several gifts, and aboundant skill." Much as Turbervile dubbed Surrey's work as "sacred," Webbe praises the poets included in Tottel's collection who, he implies, also turned to their heavenly muse. Although literary historians normally avoid such a metaphysical claim, the sacralization of the text for Protestant use contradicts earlier Protestant rejections of the text, suggesting that, regardless of its poetic content, a broad range of readers deployed *Songes and Sonettes* as a type of influential cultural icon seemingly guaranteed to impress consumers.

"Such Honour"

Although modern editors recognize that George Puttenham's oft-cited *The Arte of English Poesie* (1589) offered nothing new in terms of poetic theory, they praise the text for its comprehensiveness and connection to its historical moment. Although a favorite for modern critics, Puttenham's text offers little new in its analysis of

Songes and Sonettes. Interestingly middle class it its orientation, Puttenham begins Book 1, chapter 31, "who in any age have bene the most commended writers in our english Poesie, and *the* Authors censure given upon them," praising his many "coutreymen [who] have painfully travelled" (73) or suffered to create excellent English verse. Seemingly with Tottel's anthology in front of him, Puttenham wishes to restore

> Such honour as seemeth due to them for having by their thankefull studies so much beautified our English tong, as at this day it will be found our nation is in nothing inferiour to the French or Italian for copie of language, subtiltie of device, good method and proporation in any forme of poeme. (73)[52]

Although French replaces Tottel's Latin poetry, Puttenham joins Tottel's "To the reader," engaging the same ethnolinguistic sentiment that recognizes the vernacular as a source of pride for "our nation."

Reaffirming the poetic cannon established by earlier critics, *The Arte* cites Chaucer, Gower, Lydgate, Harding, and Skelton prior to addressing *Songes and Sonettes*:

> In the latter end of the same kings raigne sprong up a new company of courtly makers, of whom Sir Thomas Wyat th'elder and Henry Earle of Surrey were the two chieftaines, who having travailed into Italie, and there tasted the sweete and stately measures and stile of the Italian Poesie as novices newly crept out of the schooles of Dante Arioste and Petrarch, they greatly polished our rude and homely maner of vulgar Poesie, from that it had bene before, and for that cuase may justly be say the first reformers of our English meetre and stile. (74)

Puttenham, following in Turbervile's footsteps, asserts that Wyatt and Surrey constituted a "new company of courtly makers" who polished "rude and homely" poetry as "reformers." Again following critical tradition, Puttenham reinscribes the leadership role played by Wyatt and Surrey. Fashioned as under the leadership of such "chieftains," meaning both war leaders and heads of highland clans (*OED*, 2, 3), Puttenham represents the reformation of the English language as requiring a fight. The terms "sprong up" and "crept," however, define the courtly makers as close to the ground and thus childish and/or animalistic: less advanced than Puttenham's peers. With the foil "novices," moreover, Puttenham suggests that his contemporary poets have achieved a kind of mastery, surpassing those earlier poets.

Largely replicating a poetic cannon previously constituted by the writers examined above, Puttenham follows Turbervile (who he also commends) in his further assessment of Wyatt and Surrey:

52   George Puttenham, *The Arte of English Poesie: A Facsimile Production*, ed. Edward Arber (Kent, 1970).

Henry Earle of Surrey and Sir Thomas Wyat, betweene whom I finde very litle difference, I repute them (as before) for the two chief lanternes of light to all others that have since employed their pennes upon English Poesie, their conceits were loftie, their stiles stately, their conveyance cleanely, their termes proper, their meetre sweete and well proportioned, in all imitating very natrually and studiously their Master Francis Petrarcha. (76)

Although he criticizes the "two chief lanternes of light" for imperfect rhymes, clearly here his focus remains on Surrey and Wyatt—combined as a composite author, ignoring important differences between the two poets. Asserting that they imitated "their Master," Petrarch, "in all," however, Puttenham largely reduces Wyatt and Surrey to slavish copyists who simply illuminated the correct path for later writers to follow. If critics failed previously to denigrate Wyatt and Surrey's poetry successfully, Puttenham's evolutionary model of literary history clearly and negatively influenced generations of critics, including, perhaps, C.S. Lewis, among others.

"The Erle of Surries Sonnets"

By the 1590s, *Songes and Sonettes* sat on the literary landscape as a monument to English poetic excellence, but—perhaps in response to Puttenham's evolutionary analysis—it no longer garnered the attention it had received in previous decades. After the final sixteenth-century edition on record arrived in 1587, the reading public apparently no longer sought the text with the same fervor. Nevertheless, a range of readers continued to engage the text.

If *Songes and Sonettes* could serve as solace to an imprisoned Catholic monarch, it could also create problems for Protestant merchants. In *A Briefe Discourse of the Spanish State* (1590), Edward Daunce reports that Spanish authorities had arrested English merchants for possessing contraband English books. Englishmen abroad suffered imprisonment for possessing "the Psalmes of David, or some treatise of Scripture in the vulgar; the same being either the Erle of Surries sonnets, or some other like matter."[53] Made up of verse, *Songes and Sonettes* might be confused with *Psalms* by a non-English reader quickly scanning the text, yet, more significantly, the purported presence of Tottel's anthology in Spain speaks to its continued cultural cache, otherwise Daunce could not expect his readers to understand the allusion and the implied insult to the Spanish who (apparently) failed to distinguish sacred and profane literature.[54]

---

[53] David Hale, "'The Erle of Surries Sonnets': Another Reference," *Notes and Queries*, 50.4 (2003): 394.

[54] Although the text once again serves the needs of someone other than Richard Tottel, Daunce connects Surrey's name to (part of) the collection title, once more suggesting that "Surrey" serves as synecdoche for the entire collection.

Published two years after the Spanish Armada failed to conquer England, Daunce's text participates in the contemporary vogue of travel literature written by and about merchants, English corsairs, and other travelers. Reports of shipboard reading identify the voyages of Marco Polo and others as highly popular.[55] *Songes and Sonettes* thus disursively circulates among a broad range of English texts. Significantly, moreover, seventeenth century readers, including a clergyman, imported *Songes and Sonettes* into New England, again accentuating its wide effect on English language and letters.[56]

In his translation of Ariosto's *Orlando Furioso* (1591), to which he appended, "A Preface, or Rather a Briefe Apologie of Poetrie," Sir John Harrington, whose grandfather contributed to Tottel's, praises "the Earle of Surrey, and Sir Thomas Wiat that are yet called the first refiners of the English tong, were both translators out of the Italian." Evidently an "Italianated Englishman," Harington reads the text as a courtier, rather than a cultural or religious critic. Godson to Queen Elizabeth and educated at Cambridge and Lincoln's Inn, Harington never achieved the courtly rewards he sought; he translated the whole of *Orlando*, in fact, as Elizabeth's punishment for earlier translations that offended the Queen's sensibilities.[57]

While critics and editors writing and publishing in the 1590s most often only briefly noted *Songes and Sonettes* in the fashion of Harington or published its poems within their own collections, their comments form a pattern. As evidence of the collection's continued influence in the last decade of the century, *Brittons Bowere of Delights* (1591, 1597) used poems from *Songes and Sonettes* as did *The Arbor of Amorous Devises* (1594, 1597).[58] In his *Pierce's Supererogation* (1593), omnivorous critic and *littérateur* Gabriel Harvey included the poetry of Tottel's collection in his purview. Fashioning his own literary cannon, Harvey asks "and how few may wage comparison with Reinolds, Stubbes, Mulcaster, Norton, Lambert, and the Lord Henry Howard whose severall writings the silver file of the workeman recommendeth to the plausible interteinment of the daintiest Censure" (291ʳ). Like Tusser before him, Harvey more democratically conceives of poetry as the product of a "workeman," but, unlike Ascham and Tusser, sees no harm in reading such erotic texts—even though he includes "hotter" Protestant Phillip Stubbes in his cannon.

---

[55] On merchant travel, reading, and writing practices, see Donald Beecher, "John Frampton of Bristol, Trader and Translator," in Carmine Di Biase (ed.), *Travel and Translation in the Early Modern Period* (New York, 2006), pp. 102–22. See also Peter Womack, "The Writing of Travel," in Michael Hattaway (ed.), *A Companion to English Renaissance Literature and Culture* (Malden, 2000), pp. 148–61.

[56] On Tottel's imported to New England, see C.A. Herrick, "The Early New Englanders: What Did They Read?", *The Library*, 33.9 (1918): 1–17.

[57] On Harrington, see Rudolf Gottfried, *Ariosto's Orlando Furioso: Selections from the Translation of Sir John Harrington* (Bloomington, 1966), introduction.

[58] Rollins, *Tottel's Miscellany*, vol 1, p. 109.

At the end of the century, Francis Mere includes the writers of Tottel's anthology in his *Palladis Tamia* (1598) as part of "a comparative discourse of our English Poets, with the Greeke, Latine, and Italian Poets." Much like Tottel's "To the reder" before him, for Mere

> These are the most passionate among us to bewaile and bemoane the perplexities of Love, Henrie Howard Earle of Surrey, sir Thomas Wyat the elder, sir Francis Brian, sir Philip Sidney, sir Walter Rawley, sir Edward Dyer, Spencer, Daniel, Drayton, Shakespeare, Whetstone, Gascoyne, Samuell Page ... Churchyard, Bretton. (284ʳ)

Without the benefit of the centuries-old public relations machine that produced "the Bard," Shakespeare rubs shoulders here with the likes of Surrey, Wyatt, Brian, and Churchyard—all contributors to *Songes and Sonettes.* Although critics describe Surrey as largely uninterested in Petrarchan worldviews, here Mere reduces the progenitors of the first phase of English Petrarchanism to "passionate" writers who best "bewaile and bemonate the perplexities of Love." Attention to the complexity of Tottel's verse, which many critics had observed, all but disappears from public view.

"Lustrous English"

Although new commentary on Tottel's disappears in the first two decades of the seventeenth century, a range of texts in the 1620s, including Shakespeare's, returned to *Songes and Sonettes*, asserting again that it had established modern English. Edmund Bolton's *Hypercrtica* (1621), for example, commends the text by name, writing "in Noble, Courtly, and Lustrous English, is that of the Songs and Sonnets of Henry Howard, Earl of Surrey ... written chiefly by him, and by Sr Tho. Wiat." Bolton may blithely combine class, social context, and linguistic reformation in "Noble," "Courtly," and "Lustrous," yet he then demotes amorous verse. Bolton, in fact, asserts that readers commend *Songes and Sonettes* as "exercises of honourable Wit" but that actually they must understand such verse collections as simple "Foils and Sportives" compared to the poet earl's translations of the *Aeneid* (251).[59]

Further distancing the anthology from its original elite contexts, Henry Peacham, *Compleat Gentleman* (1622), identifies skill as the foremost quality that distinguishes the poetry in Tottel's *Songes and Sonettes.* He praises these poetic progenitors, "for their excellent facultie in Poesie were famous, the right noble Henrie Earle of Surrey (whose Songs and Sonnets yet extant, are of sweetre

---

[59] Edmund Bolton, *Hypercritica* (1621), in *Ancient Critical Essays Upon English Poesy,* ed. Joseph Haslewood (2 vols.; London, 1815), vol. 2, pp. 221–54. On the dating of *Hypercritica*, see Thomas Blackburn, "The Date and Evolution of Edmund Bolton's *Hypercritica,*" *Studies in Philology*, 63.2 (1966): 196–202.

conceipt:) and the learned, but unfortunate, Sir Thomas Wyat." Setting aside Peacham's historical gaff (taking the poet of Tottel's as the executed rebel and not his father), his focus on poetic skill or "facultie" balances "right noble", leaving ability as the marker of excellence in "Poesie." His "yet extant," meaning in the period: "existing so as to be publicly seen, found, or got at," "prominent," and "still existing" represents a contemporary respect for the text (*OED*).

In an elegy appended to *The Battaile of Agincourt* (1627), Michael Drayton returns to many of the themes set by Richard Tottel's "To the reder." Drayton commends fulsomely,

> That Princely Surrey, early in time
> Of the Eight Henry, who was then the prime
> Of Englands noble youth; with him there came
> Wyat; with reverence whom we still do name
> Amongst our Poets, Brian had a share
> With the two former, which acompted are
> That times best makers, and the authors were
> Of those small poems, which the title beare,
> Of songs and sonnets, wherein oft they hit
> On many dainty passages of wit
> Gascoine and Churchyard after them againe.

Drayton's focus on youth and poetic ability, as the "best makers," helps to solidify the transition of poetic excellence from noble birth exclusively to poet skill. As such, although "we still do name" these individuals as "Poets," they no longer stand apart. The repeated stress on the past, "early in time," "was then," "still," "That times," and "authors were," distinctly ages the text even as it pays it a clear "reverence." Drayton subtly critiques "songs and sonnets" by asserting that "oft they hit/On many dainty passages of wit." The term "oft," combined with "many," carefully delimits the text as producing some excellent "passages" but not whole poems. Damning Tottel's text with such faint praise, his use of "hit on" or "hit upon" implies that they simply found this poetry, as if by accident (*OED*, 11). If these terms fail to denigrate, at least to some degree, *Songes and Sonettes*, then the terms "small poems" clearly diminish the impact and importance of the text, therein recalling but negatively charging Tottel's "smal parcels."

In addition to referring to *Songes and Sonettes* by name, Shakespeare made use of the text: he owned a copy and gave it to Reginald Brome of Woodlow, Warwickshire, as a gift.[60] Some scholars suggest that Shakespeare disliked the anthology, yet in addition to providing it as a gift, he deploys the text within the First Folio (1623) version of *The Merry Wives of Windsor* (1597–1601); as Hyder Rollins indicates, Tottel's poem achieved greater fame because, after its inclusion in *Hamlet*, Goethe "included a version of it in *Faust*." Shakespeare extended the

---

[60]   John Fleming, "A Book from Shakespeare's Library Discovered by William Van Lennep," *Shakespeare Quarterly*, 15.2 (1964): 25–7.

impact of *Songes and Sonettes* by deploying verbal echoes in his poems (and plays), as Tom MacFaul explores in chapter six.[61]

Complexly deploying the anthology, Shakespeare refers directly to *Songes and Sonettes* in *Merry Wives*, his only play set in contemporary England. Act 1.1 introduces Mistress Anne Page and her father, around whom three suitors, including Slender, congregate. Mr. Page invites Slender (his preferred son-in-law) and others to dine with the family. In response, Slender exclaims, "I had rather then forty shillings I had my booke of Songs and Sonnets heere: How now *Simple*, where have you been? I must wait on my selfe, must I? you have not the booke of Riddles about you, have you" (1.1; p. 40)?[62] In response, the servant Simple wonders, "Booke of Riddles? why did you not lend it to *Alice Short-cake* upon Allhallowmas last, a fortnight afore Micahaelmas" (ibid.).

Scholars often deride Slender here and interpret his desire to have his copy of Tottel's as part of a negative characterization. As Adam Zucker writes, "he looks to old books for the scripts of seduction, hoping the canned sentiments of Wyatt and Howard or popular jests of a riddle book might provide him with the social fluency he so obviously lacks."[63] The appellation "old books," however, assumes that early modern readers judged poetry based on age. Repeated publications of Homer, Ovid, and Chaucer, etc., suggest that the age of a text failed to deter readers. Edmund Spenser's neomedieval pose in *The Faerie Queene,* moreover, sought to paint itself as an "old" romance, apparently with little negative effect.[64] In a period that still used the term "new" pejoratively and looked to the classics for instruction in life, the phrase "old books" deserves closer scrutiny.

Sixteenth-century readers besides the imaginary Slender possessed 36-year-old books, which represents the number of years between the last known edition of *Songes and Sonettes* (1587) and Slender's reference to the text in *The Merry Wives of Windsor* (1623). Francis Russel, second earl of Bedford, for example, possessed a library of at least 221 books, 162 of them not duplicates. With 11 literary, 12 political, 12 Italian, and 161 religious books, Bedford's library aptly reflects the contemporary distribution of types of books printed in the sixteenth century. Germaine to *Merry Wives*, Bedford possessed four copies of the same 33-year-old book, owned two 34-year-old books, one 36-year-old book, and one

---

[61]   Rollins, *Tottel's Miscellany*, vol. 2, p. 121. On Shakespeare's verbal echoes to Tottel, see Stuart Gillespie, *Shakespeare's Books*: *A Dictionary of Shakespeare Sources* (London, 2001), pp. 490–91.

[62]   Unless otherwise noted, all quotes from Shakespeare come from the First Folio, *Mr. VVilliam Shakespeares comedies, histories, & tragedies. Published according to the true originall copies* (London, 1623), and will be cited parenthetically in the text.

[63]   Adam Zucker, *The Places of Wit in Early Modern English Comedy* (Cambridge, 2011), p. 47. By way of contrast, Mortimer, *Petrarch's Canzoniere*, pp. 18–19, asserts that Shakespeare "was familiar with *Tottel* and pays it good-natured tribute" in *Merry Wives*.

[64]   On Spenser's neomedievalism, see Hamilton, *The Spenser*, p. 194.

37-year-old book.[65] Although not conclusive, these numbers suggest that care should be taken in interpreting the representations of books and readers' attitudes in Tudor England—Slender may represent the average book owner. Rather than representing the anthology as an "old book" or simply a "script for seduction," moreover, Shakespeare's play provides a more complex sense of *Songes and Sonettes.*

Examining *Merry Wives* 1.1 closely, Shakespeare places Slender's comments in the context of an imminent dinner party at which he plans to fast. Slender might read from the Petrarchan verse to "seduce" Anne Page, but in the communal context of a meal, this seems unlikely. When he asks the tardy Simple for his "booke of Riddles," he further establishes why he wants the named books: entertainment. Although no copy of "Riddles" survives, Robert Laneham included it in a long list of heterogeneous texts within his *Letter Describing the Magnificent Pageants Presented Before Queen Elizabeth, at Kenilworth Castle, in 1575* (1575; rpt. 1585). *Riddles* comes in a paragraph describing an individual's library of books labeled "moral and natural" philosophy, including "*The Shepherds Kalendar; The Ship of Fools ... Julian of Brentford's Testament; The Castle of Love; The Budget of Demands; The Hundred Merry Tales; The Book of Riddles; the Seven Sorrows of Women; The Proud Wives Pater-Noster*" and others.[66] Included in such a heterogeneous list, Slender's "Riddles" may or may not have been seen in the early modern period as suitable for seduction, but in the context of *Merry Wives* 1.1, Slender's request for the second text further suggests a desire to entertain. *Songes and Sonettes* and *Riddles* arguably offered different forms of social agency, yet Slender promptly requests the second book from his servant. Planning not to eat, and hoping to wed Anne, Slender wishes to read from either text in order to entertain the parents of his beloved. Lending *Riddles*, moreover, on "Allhallowmas" or All Saints Day, the legal holiday of 1 November, again suggests the reading of "Riddles" for pleasurable edification, as, on a holiday, Alice Shortcake would be free from work and thus possess time to read.[67]

Few question the interpretation of Slender as a fumbling suitor doomed to fail in his pursuit of Anne Page; however, classifying that text as "old," and, therefore, old fashioned and without cultural capital, seems overstated. Wendy Wall argues, moreover, that Slender's use of "my" *Songes and* Sonettes—without the use of Surrey's name in the reference—indicates that "the book is free to become the 'property' of the reader" and therefore that it functions as "a text open to

---

[65]   The age and number of these texts was tabulated using the list provided by M. St. Clare Byrne and Gladys Scott Thomson, "'My Lord's Books': The Library of Francis, Second Earl of Bedford, in 1584," *The Review of English Studies*, 7.28 (1931): 385–405.

[66]   *Laneham's Letter Describing the Magnificent Pageants Presented Before Queen Elizabeth, at Kenilworth Castle in 1575* (London, 1821), pp. 36–7.

[67]   For a more positive interpretation of Slender and his touching humanity, see E.J. West, "On Master Slender," *College English* 8.5 (1947): 228–30; see also Waller, *English Poetry*, p. 52.

identification within multiple sites of production."[68] In the context of the critical reception of *Songes and Sonettes* analyzed heretofore, and in the context of Wall's findings, Shakespeare's reading of Tottel's collection and Slender's reference demonstrate that the text, regardless of its age, retained the ability to produce meaning—including comic meaning—and continued to serve multiple "owners."

The fact that Slender wishes to entertain the whole dinner party rather than woo Anne might serve as part of his larger characterization as a confused and confusing lover; perhaps a case, to quote Demetrius in *A Midsummer Night's Dream*, of Slender ensuring that he will continue to "have her fathers love" (146). In this case, Slender's use of *Songes and Sonettes* might better be understood within its actual dramatic context and, thereby, understood as more than simply seduction. Given, moreover, the contemporary opinion of Tottel's anthology, Slender's risible actions (as "lover") may consist more in wishing to read from an ostensibly courtly book rather than recite verse from memory and therein display his courtly *sprezaturra*.[69] Someone edited the Folio *Merry Wives*, moreover, to stress the "'high' presence of the royal court" in the play world, as Leah Marcus establishes.[70] As such, the inclusion of *Songes and Sonettes* in the Folio *Merry Wives of Windsor*, a text consistently critical of the court, may serve more to characterize Slender as an aspiring upper-class twit pursuing the good will of the parents of an heiress rather than as an out-of-date lover.[71]

That Shakespeare's editors and/or his company would include Slender's comment in the 1623 First Folio edition of his works, and not in the 1602 first quarto, which would be closer in time to the last edition of the collection printed in 1587, presents a critical and historical problem of determining the longevity of cultural or popular memory. Would semiliterate audiences more readily recall Tottel's in 1602, some 15 years after its last recorded publication? Several possibilities suggest themselves. The 1623 version of *Merry Wives* might be dated closer to 1602 when Tottel's still had some name recognition. Alternately, a meaningful and recognized reference to *Songes and Sonettes* in the 1623 play suggests that the collection emerged from the press again sometime during the first two decades of the seventeenth century. In any case, as MacFaul establishes above, Shakespeare knew *Songes and Sonettes* well, using it in multiple ways for multiple audiences.

---

[68]   Wall, *Imprint of Gender*, p. 98.

[69]   Castiglione, *The Booke*, p. 43, writes, "to practice in all things a certain *sprezzatura,* so as to conceal all art and make whatever is done or said appear to be without effort and almost without any thought about it … nor must one be more careful of anything than of concealing it, because if it is discovered, this robs a man of all credit and causes him to be held in slight esteem."

[70]   Leah Marcus, *Unediting the Renaissance: Shakespeare, Marlowe, Milton* (London, 1996), p. 88.

[71]   On the court critical nature of the Folio *Merry Wives*, see Arthur Kinney, "Textual Signs in *The Merry Wives of Windsor*," *Yearbook of English Studies*, 23 (1993): 206–34.

"Sufficiently Famous"

Within the space of 60 years, Richard Tottel's *Songes and Sonettes* rose to great fame and, having made its mark on the culture, subsided into obscurity. Some 117 years after the publication of the first edition of the text, Edward Phillips, John Milton's nephew, asserted the excellence of the anthology, but indicated that the text had disappeared from public view. In *Theatrum Poetarum: or a Compleat Collection of the Poets* (1674), Phillips partially buoys the cult of Surrey at the expense of Tottel's collection, praising

> Henry Howard, the most Noble Earl of Surry, who Flourishing in the time of King Henry the 8th, as his Name is sufficiently famous for the Martial Exploits of that Family for many Generations, so deserves he, had he his due, the particular Fame of Learning, Wit, and Poetic Fancy, which he was thought once have made sufficiently appear in his publish'd Poems.

For Phillips, Surrey's name remains "sufficiently famous," indicating that a more general appreciation has diminished. Phillips asserts that Surrey still "deserves" such a reputation "had he his due," but apparently does not. Nevertheless, the critic's focus on Surrey's "Learning, Wit, and Poetic Fancy" recalls and recuperates many of the earlier critical opinions examined in this chapter. Phillips's omission of the title of Tottel's collection, referring instead to "his publish'd Poems," i.e., *Songes and Sonettes,* seems indicative of its disappearance from public view.

Recognized immediately as a distinctly new kind of poetry, *Songes and Sonettes* enjoyed a publishing career far in excess of the minimal impact defined by modern criticism. On the contrary, in its first decade, readers conceived of the text as both foundational for modern English verse, and, in the same moment, chastised it as destructive of "true religion." By the 1580s, Tottel's collection served as a touchstone for both verse and prose, suggesting that the text's cultural saturation had reached its zenith. In the 1590s, the writers collected in Tottel's formed the center of an explicit tradition defined by a range of writers as on a par with the best of classical and modern foreign verse. At the turn of the century, *Songes and Sonettes* largely disappears from critical view, although Ben Jonson, following Puttenham, includes Wyatt, Surrey, and other Tottel's writers collected as the center of the group that "began Eloquence with us."[72] By the Restoration, however, the text had all but been forgotten.

That disappearance, however, occurred long after the publication of poems written by Spenser, Sidney, and Shakespeare—the stars of the so-called "Golden Age" of Renaissance literature as conceived of by twentieth- and twenty-first century critics. Popular throughout this period, the text undermines attempts to relegate it to obscurity and dismiss its influence on culture. More than its ubiquity, *Songes and Sonettes* achieved great popularity precisely because it introduced

---

[72]   J. Spingarn, ed. *Critical Essays of the Seventeenth Century* (3 vols., Bloomington, 1957), vol 1., p. 26.

powerful modes of discourse readily usable by a broad range of readers and writers. Strikingly, the text achieved such a status that writers from all walks of life, not just would-be courtiers and love poets, relied upon and used the text in many different and differing ways. As such, future scholars and literary critics will need to continue to reconfigure our understanding of early modern literary history, placing Tottel's anthology alongside writers of the period, rather than relegating them to an earlier and purportedly less sophisticated period. Richard Tottel's *Songes and Sonettes* thus provides a useful and complex site at which multiple cultural conflicts and discourses meet, surely offering readers a wealth of texts and contexts for further study.

Bibliography

Manuscript Sources

Bodleian Library, University of Oxford MS. Rawl. poet. 32.

Printed Primary Sources

An invective against Treason (London, 1553).
Allott, Robert, *England's Parnassus* (London, 1600).
A New Ballad Against Unthrifts (London, 1562).
Ascham, Roger, *The Schoolmaster*, ed. Lawrence V. Ryan (Ithaca: Cornell Univeristy Press, 1967).
A Warnyng for Englande conteynyng the horrible practises of the Kyng of Spayne, in the kyngdome of Naples, and the miseries wherunto that noble realme is brought. Wherby all Englishe men may vnderstand the plage that shall light vpo[n] them, yf the Kyng of Spayn obteyne the dominion in Englande (Emden, 1555).
Batman, Stephen, *The Golden Booke of the Leaden Goddes* (1577).
Becon, Thomas, *A comfortable Epistle, too Goddes faythfull people in Englande* (Strasbourg, 1554).
Bolton, Edmund, *Hypercritica* (1621), in Joseph Haslewood (ed.), *Ancient Critical Essays Upon English Poesy* (2 vols.; London: T. Bensley, 1815), vol. 2: 221–54.
Castiglione, Baldisare, *The Book of the Courtier*, trans. Charles Singelton (New York: Anchor, 1959).
Chaucer, Geoffrey, *Plowman's Tale*, ed. James Dean, *TEAMS Middle English Text Series*, http://www.lib.rochester.edu/camelot/Teams/plwtltxt.htm.
———, *The Riverside Chaucer*, gen. ed. Larry D. Benson (Oxford: Oxford University Press, 1987).
———, *Troilus and Cressida*, ed. David Bevington (Walton-on-Thames: Thomas Nelson and Sons, 1998).
———, *The Workes of Geffray Chaucer Newly Printed* (London, 1532).
———, *The Workes of our Antient and Learned English Poet, Geffrey Chaucer, newly printed* (London, 1602).
Cicero, Marcus Tullius, *Tullius Ciceroes thre bokes of duties*, trans. Nicolas Grimald and ed. Gerald O'Gorman (London: Associated University Presses, 1990).
Crowley, Robert, *Philargyrie of Greate Britayne* (London, 1551).

————, *The confutation of the mishapen aunswer to the misnamed, wicked ballade, called the Abuse of ye blessed sacrame[n]t of the aultare* (London, 1548).

Daniel, Samuel, *A Defence of Ryme* (1603), in *Poems and A Defence of Ryme*. ed. Arthur Colby Sprague (Chicago: University of Chicago Press, 1930).

Dering, Edward, *A briefe and necessarie catechisme or instruction* (London, 1572).

————, *Workes. The English Experience: Its Record in Early Printed Books* (New York: De Capo Press, 1972).

Douglas, Gavin, *The Poetical Works of Gavin Douglas*, ed. John Small (4 vols., Edinburgh, 1874).

Edwards, Richard, *The Works of Richard Edwards: Politics, Poetry and Performance in Sixteenth Century England*, ed. Ros King (Manchester and New York: Manchester University Press, 2001).

Eliot, Thomas, *The dictionary of Syr Thomas Eliot knyght* (London, 1538).

Fortescue, John, *On The Laws and Governance of England*, ed. Shelley Lockwood (Cambridge: Cambridge University Press, 1997).

Gascoigne, George. "Certayne Notes of Instruction," in G. Smith (ed.) *Elizabethan Critical Essays*, (2 vols., Oxford: Clarendon Press, 1904), vol. 2.

Gottfried, Rudolf, ed., *Ariosto's Orlando Furioso: Selections from the Translation of Sir John Harrington* (Bloomington: University of Indiana Press, 1966).

Hall, John, *The Court of Virtue (1565)*, ed. Russell Fraser (New Brunswick: Rutgers University Press, 1961).

Harington, John, *The Epigrams of Sir John Harington*, ed. Gerard Kilroy (Farnham:Ashgate, 2009).

Hazlitt, W.C., ed., *Prefaces, Dedications, Epistles Selected from Early English Books, 1540–1701* (privately printed, 1874).

Hogarde, Miles, *The Displaying of the Protestantes* (London, 1556).

Horace, The Odes and Epodes, ed. and trans. C.E. Bennett (London: Heinemann, 1929).

Howard, Henry, Earl of Surrey, *Certaine Bokes of Virgiles Aenaeis turned into English meter by the right honorable lorde, Henry Earle of Surrey* (London, 1557).

————, *Poems*, ed. Emrys Maldwyn Jones (Oxford: Clarendon Press, 1964).

————, *Richard Tottel's Songes and Sonettes: The Elizabethan Version*, ed. Paul A. Marquis (Tempe, AZ: ACMRS, 2007).

————, *Tottel's Miscellany, 1557–1587*, ed. Hyder Rollins (2 vols., Cambridge: Harvard University Press, 1928–29; rev. ed., 1965).

————, *Tottel's Miscellany: Songs and Sonnets of Henry Howard, Earl of Surrey, Sir Thomas Wyatt and Others*, eds. Amanda Holton and Tom MacFaul (London: Penguin Books, 2011).

Hughey, Ruth (ed.), *The Arundel Harington Manuscript of Tudor Poetry* (2 vols., Columbus: Ohio State University Press, 1960).

Jones, Richard, *A handefull of pleasant delites containing sudrie new sonets and delectable histories* (London, 1584).

Knox, John, *A faythfull admonition made by John Knox, unto the professours of Gods truthe in England* (Emden, 1554).

Laneham's Letter Describing the Magnificent Pageants Presented Before Queen Elizabeth, at Kenilworth Castle in 1575 (London: J.H. Burn, 1821).

Milton, John, *Paradise Lost*, in *The Complete Poetry of John Milton*, ed. John T. Shawcross (New York: Anchor Books, 1967).

Nashe, Thomas, *The Works*, ed. Ronald McKerrow (5 vols., Oxford: Blackwell, 1958).

Nowell, Alexander, *A Catechisme: or, First Instruction and Learning of Christian Religion (1570)*, intro. Frank V. Occhiogrosso (Delmar: Scholars' Facsimiles & Reprints, 1975).

———. *A Catechism Written in Latin by Alexander Nowell, Dean of St. Paul's: Together With the Same Catechism Translated into English by Thomas Norton*, ed. G. Corrie (Cambridge: Cambridge Unviersity Press, 1853).

Ovid, *Heroides; and Amores*, ed. G.P. Goold (Cambridge: Harvard University Press, 1977).

Parr, Catherine, *The lamentacion of a sinner* (London, 1547).

Petrarch, Francesca, *Petrarch's Lyric Poems: The* Rime sparse *and Other Lyrics*, ed. and trans. Robert M. Durling (Cambridge: Harvard University Press, 1976).

———, *Petrarch's Canzoniere in the English Renaissance*, ed. Anthony Mortimer (Amsterdam: Rodopi, 2005).

Pole, Reginald, *Pole's Defense of the Unity of the Church*, trans. Joseph Dwyer (Westminster: Newman Press, 1965).

Proctor, John. *The historie of Wyattes rebellion* (London, 1554).

Puttenham, George, *The Art of English Poesy: A Critical Edition*, eds. Frank Whigham and Wayne A. Rebhorn (Ithaca: Cornell University Press, 2007).

———, *The Arte of English Poesie: A Facsimile Production*, ed. Edward Arber (Kent: Kent State University Press, 1970).

———, *The Arte of English Poesie*, eds. G.D. Willcock and Alice Walker (Cambridge: Cambridge University Press, 1936).

Record, Robert, *The Castle of Knowledge* (London, 1556).

Robinson, Clement, *A Handful of Pleasant Delights* (London, 1584).

Shakespeare, William, *Mr. VVilliam Shakespeares comedies, histories, & tragedies. Published according to the true originall copies* (London, 1623).

———, *The Complete Pelican Shakespeare*, eds. Stephen Orgel and A.R. Braunmuller, (New York: Penguin Books, 2002).

———, *The Complete Sonnets and Poems*, ed. Colin Burrow (Oxford: Oxford University Press, 2002).

———, *The Riverside Shakespeare*, ed. G. Blakemore Evans et al. (2nd ed., Boston: Houghton Mifflin, 1997).

Sidney, Philip, "An Apology for Poetry," in Katherine Duncan-Jones (ed.), *Sir Philip Sidney* (Oxford and New York: Oxford University Press, 1991).

———, *Sir Philip Sidney's An Apology for poetry and Astrophil and Stella: Texts and Contexts*, ed. Peter Herman (Glen Allen: College Publishing, 2001).

Spingarn, J., ed., *Criticial Essays of the Seventeenth Century* (3 vols., Bloomington: University of Indiana Press, 1957).

Strype, John, ed., *Ecclesiastical Memorials, relating chiefly to Religion and its Reformation, under the Reigns of King Henry VIII, King Edward VI, and Queen Mary the First* (London: Samuel Bagster, 1816).

Vaux, Laurence, *A Chatechism or Christian Doctrine* (Menston: Scolar Press, 1969).

———, *A Chatechism or Christian Doctrine* (London, 1568).

Virgil, *The Aeneid*, trans. Robert Fagles (London: Penguin, 2007).

Whitney, Geffrey, *Whitney's Choice of Emblemes*, ed. Henry Green (London: Lovell Reeve, 1866).

Wyatt, Thomas, *Collected Poems of Sir Thomas Wyatt*, eds. Kenneth Muir and Patricia Thomson (Liverpool: Liverpool University Press, 1969).

———, *The Complete Poems*, ed. Ronald A. Rebholz (Harmondsworth: Penguin, 1978).

———, *The Complete Poems*, ed. Ronald A. Rebholz (New Haven: Yale University Press, 1981).

———, *The Complete Works of Sir Thomas Wyatt, the elder*, ed. Jason Powell (Oxford: Oxford University Press, 2012).

Secondary Sources

Adnitt, William, *Thomas Churchyard 1520–1604* (Oswestry: Woodall and Venables, 1880).

Baldwin, T., *William Shakespeare's Petty School* (Urbana: University of Illinois Press, 1943).

Bates, Catherine, *Masculinity, Gender and Identity in the English Renaissance Lyric* (Cambridge: Cambridge University Press, 2007).

Beal, Peter, (ed.), *Index of English Literary Manuscripts, vol. I: 1450–1625, Part 2: Douglas–Wyatt* (London: R.R. Bowker, 1980).

Beecher, Donald, "John Frampton of Bristol, Trader and Translator," in Carmine Di Biase (ed.), *Travel and Translation in the Early Modern Period* (New York: Rodopi, 2006), pp. 102–22.

Bellamy, Elizabeth, "The Sixteenth Century," in Frank Magill (ed.), *Critical Survey of Poetry. Revised Edition* (8 vols.; Pasadena: Salem Press, 1992): vol. 8, 3800–816.

Betteridge, Tom, *Literature and Politics in the English Reformation* (Manchester: Manchester University Press, 2004).

Blackburn, Thomas, 'The Date and Evolution of Edmund Bolton's *Hypercritica*', *Studies in Philology*, 63.2 (1966): 196–202.

Blevins, Jacob, *Catullan Consciousness and the Early Modern Lyric in England: From Wyatt to Donne* (Burlington: Ashgate, 2004).

Booty, John, *The Book of Common Prayer 1559: The Elizabethan Prayer Book* (Charlottesville: The University Press of Virginia, 1976).

Bourdieu, Peter, *Outline of a Theory of Practice*, trans. Richard Nice (Cambridge: Cambridge University Press, 1977).

Boynton, Owen, 'The *Trouthe/Routhe* Rhyme in Chaucer's *Troilus and Criseyde*', *The Chaucer Review*, 45.2 (2010): 221–39.

Bradshaw, Christopher, 'David or Josiah? Old Testament Kings as Exemplars in Edwardian Religious Polemic', in Bruce Gordon (ed.), *Protestant History and Identity in Sixteenth-Century Europe* (2 vols., Aldershot: Scolar Press, 1996), vol. 2: pp. 76–90.

Byrne, M. St. Clare, and Gladys Scott Thomson, '"My Lord's Books': The Library of Francis, Second Earl of Bedford, in 1584", *The Review of English Studies*, 7.28 (1931): 385–405.

Byrom, H.J., "Richard Tottel—His Life and Works," *The Library*, 8 (1927–28): 199–232.

Cambers, Andrew, *Godly Reading*: *Print, Manuscript and Puritanism in England, 1580–1720* (Cambridge: Cambridge University Press, 2011).

Carlson, David, "The Henrician Courtier Writing in Manuscript and Print: Wyatt, Surrey, Bryan, and Others" in Kent Cartwright (ed.), *A Companion to Tudor Literature* (Chichester: Blackwell Publishing, 2010): 151–77.

Carley, James, P., 'Brigham, Nicholas (*d.* 1558)', *Oxford Dictionary of National Biography*, Oxford University Press, 2004; online edn, Jan 2008.

Cavallo, Guglielmo, and Roger Chartier (eds.), *A History of Reading in the West*, trans. Lydia Cochrane (Amherst: University of Massachusettes Press, 2003).

Chance, Jane, *Medieval Mythography*: *From Roman North Africa to the School of Chartres, A.D. 433–1177* (Gainesville: Florida University Press,1994).

Chesterton, G.K., "A Midsummer Night's Dream," *Good Words*, 45 (1904): 621–6.

Child, Harold, "The New English Poetry," *Cambridge History of English Literature*: *Renascence and Reformation*, ed. A. Ward (15 vols., New York: Cambridge University Press, 1932): vol 3: p. 177.

Chism, Christine, "Robin Hood: Thinking Globally, Acting Locally in Fifteenth-Century Ballads" in Emily Steiner and Candace Barrington (eds.), *The Letter of the Law; Legal Practice and Literary Production in Medieval England* (Ithaca: Cornell University Press, 2002), pp. 12–39.

Coiro, Anne Baynes, *Robert Herrick's "Hersperides" and the Epigram Book Tradition* (Baltimore: Johns Hopkins University Press, 1988).

Crawford, Charles, "Tottel's 'Miscellany,' Sir Antony St. Leger, and John Harington, the elder", *Notes and Queries*, 11.3 (1911): 423–4.

Cressy, David, *Literacy and the Social Order: Reading and Writing in Tudor and Stuart England* (Cambridge: Cambridge University Press, 1980).

Crewe, Jonathan, *Trials of Authorship: Anterior Forms and Poetic Reconstruction from Wyatt to Shakespeare* (Berkeley: University of California Press, 1990).

Cummings, Brian, "Reformed Literature and Literature Reformed," in David Wallace (ed.), *The Cambridge History of Medieval English Literature* (Cambridge: Cambridge University Press, 1999): 842–7.

Dane, Joseph, *Who is Buried in Chaucer's Tomb? Studies in the Reception of Chaucer's Book* (East Lansing: Michigan State University Press, 1998).

Davis, Bryan, "John Day," in James Bracken and Joel Silver (eds.), *The British Literary Book Trade, 1475–1700* (Detroit: Gale Research, 1996), pp. 78–93.

Dubrow, Heather, *Echoes of Desire: English Petrarchism and Its Counterdiscourses* (Ithaca: Cornell University Press, 1995).

Duffin, Ross, *Shakespeare's Songbook* (New York: Norton, 2004).

Duffy, Eamon, *Fires of Faith: Catholic England under Mary Tudor* (New Haven: Yale University Press, 2009).

———, *The Stripping of the Altars*: *Traditional Religion in England, 1400–1580* (New Haven: Yale University Press, 1992).

Edwards, A.S.G., "Manuscripts of the Verse of Henry Howard, Earl of Surrey," *Huntington Library Quarterly*, 167.2 (2004): 283–93.

Enssle, Neal, "Patterns of Godly Life: The Ideal Parish Minister in Sixteenth- and Seventeenth-Century English Thought," *Sixteenth Century Journal*, 18.1 (1997): 3–28.

Estrin, Barbara, "Becoming the Other/The Other Becoming in Wyatt's Poetry," *English Literary History*, 51.3 (1984): 431–45.

Fantham, Elaine, *Roman Literary Culture: From Cicero to Apuleius* (Baltimore: Johns Hopkins University Press, 1996).

Fein, Susana, and David Raybin (eds.), *Chaucer: Contemporary Approaches* (University Park: Pennsylvania State University Press, 2010).

Fineman, Joel, *Shakespeare's Perjured Eye: The Invention of Poetic Subjectivity in the Sonnets* (Berkeley: University of California Press, 1986).

Fleming, John, "A Book from Shakespeare's Library Discovered by William Van Lennep," *Shakespeare Quarterly*, 15.2 (1964): 25–7.

Foley, Stephen, *Sir Thomas Wyatt* (Boston: Twayne Publishers 1990).

Foster, Hal, *Compulsive Beauty* (Cambridge: The MIT Press, 1993).

Fraser, Russell, "Political Prophecy in *The Pilgrim's Tale*," *South Atlantic Quarterly*, 56 (1957): 67–78.

Fumerton, Patricia, "'Secret' Arts: Elizabethan Miniatures and Sonnets," in Stephen Greenblatt (ed.), *Representing the English Renaissance* (Berkeley: University of California Press, 1988).

Garrett, Martin (ed.), *Sidney: The Critical Heritage* (London: Routledge, 1996).

Giamatti, Bartlett, *The Earthly Paradise and the Renaissance Epic* (Princeton: Princeton University Press, 1966).

Gillespie, Alexandra, *Print Culture and the Medieval Author: Chaucer, Lydgate, and Their Books*, *1473–1557* (Oxford: Oxford University Press, 2006).

Gillespie, Stuart, *Shakespeare's Books: A Dictionary of Shakespeare's Sources* (London: Athlone, 2001).

Goldberg, Jonathan, "The Female Pen: Writing as a Woman," in Jeffrey Masten, Peter Stallybrass, and Nancy J. Vickers (eds.), *Language Machines: Technologies of Literary and Cultural Production* (New York: Routledge, 1997): 17–38.

———, *Sodometries: Renaissance Texts, Modern Sexualities* (Stanford: Stanford University Press, 1992).

Grabes, Herbert, "England or the Queen? Public Conflict of Opinion and National Identity under Mary Tudor," in *Writing the Early Modern English Nation: The Transformation of National Identity in Sixteenth- and Seventeenth-Century England* (Atlanta: Rodopi, 2001).

Grafton, Anthony, *Defenders of the Text: The Traditions of Scholarship in an Age of Science, 1450–1800* (Cambridge: Harvard University Press, 1991).

Green, Ian, *The Christian's ABC*: *Catechisms and Catechizing in England, c. 1530–1740* (Oxford: Clarendon Press, 1996).

Green, Richard Firth, *A Crisis of Truth: Literature and Law in Ricardian England* (Philadelphia: University of Pennsylvania Press, 2002).

Greenfeld, Liah, *Nationalism: Five Roads to Modernity* (Cambridge: Harvard University Press, 1992).

Greening, Anna, "Tottel, Richard (b. in or before 1528, d. 1593)," Oxford Dictionary of National Biography (Oxford, 2004); online ed., May 2009.

Greg, W.W., "Tottel's Miscellany," *The Library*, 5.18 (1904): 113–33.

Guy, John, *The Reign of Elizabeth I: Court and Culture in the Last Decade* (London: Cambridge University Press, 1995).

———, *Tudor England* (Oxford: Oxford University Press, 1988).

Guy-Bray, Stephen, "Embracing Troy: Surrey's *Aeneid*," in Alan Shepard and Stephen D. Powell (eds.), *Fantasies of Troy: Classical Tales and the Social Imaginary in Medieval and Early Modern Europe* (Toronto: Centre for Reformation and Renaissance Studies, 2004): 177–92.

Hale, David, "'The Erle of Surries Sonnets': Another Reference," *Notes and Queries*, 50.4 (2003): 394.

Halpern, Richard, *The Poetics of Primitive Accumulation: English Renaissance Culture and the Genealogy of Capital* (Ithaca: Cornell University Press, 1991).

Hamilton, A.C. (ed.), *The Spenser Encyclopedia* (Toronto: University of Toronto Press, 1990).

Hammond, Paul, "Sources for Shakespeare's Sonnets 87 and 129 in *Tottel's Miscellany* and Puttenham's *The Arte of English Poesie*," *Notes and Queries*, 50 (2003): 407–10.

Hamrick, Stephen, *The Catholic Imaginary and the Cults of Elizabeth, 1558–1582* (Aldershot: Ashgate, 2009).

———, "*Tottel's Miscellany* and the English Reformation," *Criticism*, 44.4 (2002): 329–61.

Hardison, Jr., O.B., *Prosody and Purpose in the English Renaissance* (Baltimore: Johns Hopkins University Press, 1989).

Hardman, Malcolm, *A Kingdom in Two Parishes*: *Lancashire Religious Writers and the English Monarchy, 1521–1689* (Cranbury: Associate University Presses˙ 1989).

Harvey, Elizabeth, *Ventriloquized Voices: Feminist Theory and English Renaissance Texts* (London: Routledge, 1992).

Heale, Elizabeth, "The Fruits of War: The Voice of the Soldier in Gascoigne, Rich, and Churchyard," *Early Modern Literary Studies*, 14.1 (2008): 5.139, http://purl.oclc.org/emls/14-1/article4.htm.

————, "'Desiring Women Writing': Female Voices and Courtly 'Balets' in Some Early Tudor Manuscript Albums," in Victoria E. Burke and Jonathan Gibson (eds.), *Early Modern Women's Manuscript Writing: Selected Papers from the Trinity/Trent Colloquium* (Aldershot: Ashgate Publishing, 2004).

————, *Wyatt, Surrey and Early Tudor Poetry* (London: Longman, 1998).

Helgerson, Richard, "Language Lessons: Linguistic Colonialism, Linguistic Postcolonialism, and the Early Modern English Nation," *The Yale Journal of Criticism*, 11.1 (1998): 289–99.

————, *Forms of Nationhood: The Elizabethan Writing of England* (Chicago: University of Chicago Press, 1992).

————, *The Elizabethan Prodigals* (Berkeley: University of California Press, 1976).

Herrick, C.A., "The Early New Englanders: What Did They Read?," *The Library*, 33.9 (1918): 1–17.

Hutson, Lorna, *The Usurer's Daughter: Male Friendship and Fictions of Women in Sixteenth-Century England* (London: Routledge, 1994).

Hutton, James, *The Greek Anthology in France and the Latin Writers of the Netherlands to the Year 1800* (Ithaca: Cornell University Press, 1946).

————, *The Greek Anthology in Italy to the Year 1800* (Ithaca: Cornell University Press, 1935).

Jajdelska, Elspeth, *Silent Reading and the Birth of the Narrator* (Toronto: University of Toronto Press, 2007).

Jeauneau, Édouard, *Translatio Studii: The Transmission of Learning. A Gilsonian Theme* (Toronto: Pontifical Institute of Mediaeval Studies, 1995).

Johns, Adrian, *The Nature of the Book: Print and Knowledge in the Making* (Chicago: University of Chicago Press, 1998).

Jones, Richard Foster, *The Triumph of the English Language* (Stanford: Stanford University Press, 1953).

Kalas, Rayna, *Frame, Glass, Verse: The Technology of Poetic Invention in the English Renaissance* (Ithaca: Cornell University Press, 2007).

Kallendorf, Craig, *The Other Virgil: Pessimistic Readings of the Aeneid in Early Modern Culture* (Oxford: Oxford University Press, 2007).

Kay, Dennis, "Wyatt and Chaucer: They Fle from Me," *Huntington Library Quarterly*, 47.3 (1984): 211–25.

Kennedy, William, *Authorizing Petrarch* (Ithaca: Cornell University Press, 1994).

————, *The Site of Petrarchism: Early Modern National Sentiment in Italy, France, and England* (Baltimore: Johns Hopkins UP 2003).

Kerrigan, John, *The Sonnets and A Lover's Complaint* (London: Penguin, 1986).

King, John, *English Reformation Literature: The Tudor Origins of the Protestant Tradition* (Princeton: Princeton University Press, 1982).

————, *Tudor Royal Iconography* (Princeton: Princeton University Press, 1989).

————, "The Account Book of a Marian Bookseller, 1553–4," *British Library Journal*, 13 (1987): 33–57.

King, Ros, "'Seeing the rhythm': An Interpretation of Sixteenth-Century Punctuation and Metrical Practice," in J. Bray, M. Handley, and A. Henry (eds.), *Marking the Text: The Presentation of Meaning on the Literary Page* (Aldershot: Scholar Press, 2000).

Kinney, Arthur, "Textual Signs in *The Merry Wives of Windsor*," *Yearbook of English Studies*, 23 (1993): 206–34.

Knott, Christopher, "Richard Tottel," in James K. Bracken and Joel Silver (eds.), *Dictionary of Literary Biography*, vol. 170, *The British Literary Book Trade 1475–1700* (Detroit: Gale Research, 1996): 308–9.

Lerer, Seth, "Literary Histories," in James Simpson and Brian Cummings (eds.), *Cultural Reformations, From Lollardy to the English Civil War* (Oxford: Oxford University Press, 2010): 75–91.

———, "Receptions: Medieval, Tudor, Modern," in Susanna Fein and David Raybin (eds.), *Chaucer: Contemporary Approaches* (University Park: Pennsylvania State University Press, 2010): 83–95.

———, *Children's Literature: A Reader's History from Aesop to Harry Potter* (Chicago: University of Chicago Press, 2008).

———, "Medieval English Literature and the Idea of the Anthology," *PMLA*, 118 (2003): 1251–67.

———, *Courtly Letters in the Age of Henry VIII: Literary Culture and the Arts of Deceit* (Cambridge: Cambridge University Press, 1997).

———, *Chaucer and His Readers: Imagining the Author in Late-Medieval England* (Princeton: Princeton University Press, 1993).

Leslie, Michael, and Timothy Raylor (eds.), *Culture and Cultivation in Early Modern England: Writing and the Land* (Leicester: Leicester University Press, 1992).

Levao, Ronald, "Sidney's Feigned Apology," *PMLA*, 94.2 (1979): 223–33.

Lewis, C.S., *English Literature in the Sixteenth Century Excluding Drama* (London: Oxford University Press, 1954).

Lines, Candace, "The Erotic Politics of Grief in Surrey's 'So Crewell Prison'," *Studies in English Literature, 1500–1900*, 46.1 (2006): 1–26.

Loach, Jennifer, "The Marian Establishment and the Printing Press," *English Historical Review*, 101 (1986): 135–48.

Loades, D.M., *Mary Tudor: A Life* (London: Blackwell, 1989).

———, *The Reign of Mary Tudor: Politics, Government and Religion in England, 1553–1558* (New York: Longman, 1974).

Love, Harold, *Scribal Publication in Seventeenth-Century England* (Oxford: Clarendon, 1993).

Lyne, Oliver, *Further Voices in Vergil's Aeneid* (Oxford: Oxford University Press, 1987).

Lyne, Raphael, "George Turbervile," *Oxford Dictionary of National Biography* (Oxford: Oxford University Press, 2004).

MacFaul, Tom, *Poetry and Paternity in Renaissance England: Sidney, Spenser, Shakespeare, Donne and Jonson* (Cambridge: Cambridge University Press, 2010).

———, *Male Friendship in Shakespeare and Contemporaries* (Cambridge: Cambridge University Press, 2007).

Manning, John, *The Emblem* (London: Reaktion Books, 2003).

Marcus, Leah, *Unediting the Renaissance: Shakespeare, Marlowe, Milton* (New York: Routledge, 1996).

Marotti, Arthur, *Manuscript, Print, and The English Renaissance Lyric* (Ithaca: Cornell University Press, 1995).

Marquis, Paul A., "Editing and Unediting: Richard Tottel's *Songs and Sonettes*," *The Book Collector*, 56.3 (2007): 353–75.

———, "Politics and Print: The Curious Revisions to Tottel's *Songes and Sonettes*," *Studies in Philology*, 97 (2000): 145–64.

———, "Recent Studies in Richard Tottel's *Songes and Sonettes*," *English Literary Renaissance*, 28 (1998): 299–313.

Martz, Louis, "Introduction," in Thomas More, *A Dialogue of Comfort against Tribulation*, ed. Louis Martz and Frank Manley (New Haven: Yale University Press, 1976).

Mason, Harold, *Humanism and Poetry in The Early Tudor Period* (London: Routledge, 1959).

May, Steven, "Popularizing Courtly Poetry: *Tottel's Miscellany* and its Progeny," in Mike Pincombe and Cathy Shrank (eds.), *Oxford Handbook of Tudor Literature, 1485–1603* (Oxford: Oxford University Press, 2009).

———, *Elizabethan Poetry: A Bibliography and First Line of English Verse, 1599–1603* (3 vols., London: Continuum, 2004).

———, *The Elizabethan Courtier Poets* (2nd ed., Asheville: North Carolina University Press, 1999).

Meyer-Lee, Robert, *Poets and Power from Chaucer to Wyatt* (Cambridge: Cambridge University Press, 2007).

Miller, Paul Allen, *Lyric Texts and Lyric Consciousness: The Birth of Genre from Archaic Greece to Augustan Rome* (London: Routledge, 1994).

Moss, Anne, *Printed Commonplace-Books and the Structuring of Renaissance Thought* (Oxford: Clarendon Press, 1996).

North, Marcy, *The Anonymous Renaissance: Cultures of Discretion in Tudor–Stuart England* (Chicago: University of Chicago Press, 2003).

Nuttall, A.D., *Shakespeare the Thinker* (New Haven: Yale University Press, 2007).

Odabashian, Barbara, "Thomas Wyatt and the Rhetoric of Change," in Mario Di Cesare (ed.), *Reconsidering the Renaissance: Papers from the Twenty-First Annual Conference* (Binghamton: State University of New York Press, 1992): pp. 287–300.

Padelford, F.M., "The Manuscript Poems by Henry Howard, Earl of Surrey," *Anglia*, 29 (1906): 273–337.

Panofsky, Erwin, *Idea: A Concept in Art Theory*, trans. Joseph Peake (New York: Harper, 1968).

Parker, William, "The Sonnets in *Tottel's Miscellany*," *PMLA*, 54.3 (1939): 669–77.

Paterson, Don, *Reading Shakespeare's Sonnets: A New Commentary* (London: Faber and Faber, 2010).

Patterson, Mary, *Domesticating the Reformation*: *Protestant Bestsellers, Private Devotion, and the Revolution of English Piety* (Cranbury: Associated University Presses, 2007).

Pearsall, Derek, "Chaucer's Tomb: The Politics of Reburial," *Medium Aevum*, 64.1 (1995): 51–73.

Peterson, Douglas, *The English Lyric from Wyatt to Donne*: *A History of the Plain and Eloquent Styles* (Princeton: Princeton University Press, 1967).

Prendergast, Thomas, *Chaucer's Dead Body: From Corpse to Corpus* (New York: Routledge, 2004).

Price, Leah, *The Anthology and the Rise of the Novel* (Cambridge: Cambridge University Press, 2000).

Pollard, Alfred, and G.R. Redgrave (eds.), *A Short-title Catalogue of Books Printed in England, Scotland, & Ireland and of English Books Printed Abroad, 1475–1640* (2nd ed., 3 vols., London: Bibliographical Society, 1976–1991).

Pomeroy, Elizabeth, *Elizabethan Miscellanies: Their Development and Conventions* (Berkeley: University of California Press, 1973).

Powell, Jason, "Thomas Wyatt and Francis Bryan: Plainness and Disimulation," in Mike Pincombe and Cathy Shrank (eds.), *The Oxford Handbook of Tudor Literature, 1485–1603* (Oxford: Oxford University Press, 2009), pp. 187–202.

Quint, David, *Epic and Empire: Politics and Generic Form from Virgil to Milton* (Princeton: Princeton University Press, 1993).

Rebholz, Ronald, "Love's Newfangleness: A Comparison of Greville and Wyatt," *Studies in the Literary Imagination*, 11:1 (1978): 17–30.

Reynolds, Matthew, *Godly Reformers and their Opponents in Early Modern England: Religion in Norwich 1563–1643* (Woodbridge: Boydell Press, 2005).

Ringler, Jr., William A., *Bibliography and Index of English Verse in Manuscript 1501–1558* (London: Mansell, 1992).

Rollins, Hyder Edward, "The Troilus-Cressida story from Chaucer to Shakespeare," *PMLA*, 32 (1917): 383–429.

Ryrie, Alec, "The Slow Death of a Tyrant: Learning to Live Without Henry VIII, 1547–1563," in Mark Rankin, Christopher Highley, and John King (eds.), *Henry VIII and his Afterlives: Literature, Politics, Art* (Cambridge: Cambridge University Press, 2009): 75–93.

Saenger, Paul, *Space Between Words*: *The Origins of Silent Reading* (Palo Alto: Stanford University Press, 2000).

Sarker, Sunil, *Shakespeare's Sonnets* (New Delhi: Atlantic, 2006).

Scott, David, "Wyatt's Worst Poem," *The Times Literary Supplement* (13 September 1963), p. 696.

Sessions, W.A., *Henry Howard*, *Earl of Surrey* (Boston: Twayne, 1986).

———, *Henry Howard, The Poet Earl of Surrey* (Oxford: Oxford University Press, 1999).

———, "Surrey's Wyatt: Autumn 1542 and the New Poet," in Peter Herman (ed.), *Rethinking the Henrician Era: Essays on Early Tudor Texts and Contexts* (Urbana: University of Illinois Press, 1994): pp. 168–92.

————, "'Enough Survives': The Earl of Surrey and European Court Culture," *History Today* (June 1991): 48–54.

————, "*Tottel's Miscellany* and the Metaphysical Poets," in Sidney Gottlieb (ed.), *Approaches to Teaching the Metaphysical Poets* (New York: Modern Language Association, 1990), pp. 48–53.

Seznec, Jean, *The Survival of the Pagan Gods: The Mythological Tradition and Its Place in Renaissance Humanism and Art*, trans. Barbara Sessions (New York: Bollingen, 1972).

Shakespeare, Joy, "Plague and Punishment," in Peter Lake and Maria Dowling (eds.), *Protestantism and the National Church in Sixteenth-Century England* (London: Routledge, 1987): 103–24.

Shrank, Cathy, *Writing the Nation in Reformation England 1530–1580* (Oxford: Oxford University Press, 2004).

Simpson, James, "Chaucer's Presence and Absence, 1400–1550," in Jill Mann and Piero Boitani (eds.), *The Cambridge Companion to Chaucer*, 2nd ed. (Cambridge: Cambridge University Press, 2004): 251–69.

————, "The Elegiac," in *The Oxford English Literary History, Volume 2, 1350–1547: Reform and Cultural Revolution* (Oxford: Oxford University Press, 2002).

Spearing, A.C., *Medieval to Renaissance in English Poetry* (Cambridge: Cambridge University Press, 1985).

Spiller, Michael, *The Development of the Sonnet: An Introduction* (London: Routledge, 1992).

Stallcup, Stephen, "With the Poynte of Remembrannce: Re-Viewing the Complaint in *Anelida and Arcite*," in Bonnie Wheeler (ed.), *Representations of the Feminine in the Middle Ages* (Dallas: Academia, 1993): pp. 43–67.

Stamatakis, Chris, *Sir Thomas Wyatt and the Rhetoric of Rewriting*: "*Turning the Word*" (Oxford: Oxford University Press, 2012).

Stark, Ryan, "Protestant Theology and Apocalyptic Rhetoric in Roger Ascham's *The Schoolmaster*," *Journal of the History of Ideas*, 69.4 (2008): 517–32.

Strohm, Paul, *Social Chaucer* (Cambridge: Harvard University Press, 1989).

Strong, Roy, *The Renaissance Garden in England* (London: Thames and Hudson, 1979).

Tigner, Amy, "*The Winter's Tale*: Gardens and the Marvels of Transformation," *English Literary Renaissance*, 36 (2006): 114–34.

Tilley, Morris Palmer, *A Dictionary of the Proverbs in England in the Sixteenth and Seventeenth Centuries : A Collection of the Proverbs found in English Literature and the Dictionaries of the Period* (Ann Arbor: University of Michigan Press, 1950).

Trigg, Stephanie, *Congenial Souls: Reading Chaucer from Medieval to Postmodern* (Minneapolis: University of Minnesota Press, 2002).

Trudeau-Clayton, Margaret, "What is my Nation? Language, Verse, and Politics in Tudor Translations of Virgil's *Aeneid*," in Mike Pincombe and Cathy Shrank (eds.), *Oxford Handbook of Tudor Literature, 1485–1603* (Oxford: Oxford University Press, 2009), pp. 389–403.

Wakelin, Daniel, "Stephen Hawes and Courtly Education," in Mike Pincombe and Cathy Shrank (eds.), *Oxford Handbook of Tudor Literature, 1485–1603* (Oxford: Oxford University Press, 2009), pp 53–68.Walker, Greg, *Writing Under Tyranny: English Literature and the Henrician Reformation* (Oxford: Oxford University Press, 2005).

Wall, Wendy, "Authorship and the Material Conditions of Writing," in Arthur F. Kinney (ed.), *The Cambridge Companion to English Literature 1500–1600* (Cambridge: Cambridge University Press, 2000): 64–89.

———, *The Imprint of Gender: Authorship and Publication in the English Renaissance* (Ithaca: Cornell University Press, 1993).

Waller, Gary, *English Poetry of the Sixteenth Century* (New York: Longman, 1986).

Warkintin, Germaine, "'Love's sweetest part, variety': Petrarch and the Curious Frame of the Renaissance Sonnet Sequence," *Renaissance & Reformation*, 11 (1975): 14–23.

Warner, J. Christopher, "'Sonnets en Anglois': A Hitherto Unknown Edition of Tottel's Miscellany (1559)," *Notes and Queries*, 58.2. (2011): 204–6.

Watkins, John, "Wrastling for this World: Wyatt and the Tudor Canonization of Chaucer," in Theresa Krier (ed.), *Refiguring Chaucer in the Renaissance* (Gainesville: University Press of Florida, 1998): 26–30.

Wenig, Scott, *Straightening the Altars: The Ecclesiastical Vision and Pastoral Achievements of the Progressive Bishops Under Elizabeth, 1559–1579* (New York: Peter Lang, 2000).

West, E.J., "On Master Slender," *College English*, 8.5 (1947): 228–30.

Westerweel, Bart, "On the European Dimension of European Emblem Production," in Alison Adams and Marleen van der Weij (eds.), *Emblems of the Low Countries: A Book Historical Perspective*, *Glasgow Emblem Studies*, vol. 8 (Glasgow: Glasgow University Press, 2003), pp. 1–16.

Wiggins, Alison, "What Did Renaissance Readers Write in Their Printed Copies of Chaucer?," *The Library: The Transactions of the Bibliographical Society*, 9 (2008): 3–36.

Williams, Deanne, *The French Fetish From Chaucer to Shakespeare* (Cambridge: Cambridge University Press, 2004).

Womack, Peter, "The Writing of Travel," in Michael Hattaway (ed.), *A Companion to English Renaissance Literature and Culture* (Malden: Blackwell, 2000), pp. 148–61.

Woudhuysen, H.R., *Sir Philip Sidney and the Circulation of Manuscripts, 1558–1640* (Oxford: Clarendon, 1996).

Wyatt, Michael, *The Italian Encounter with Tudor England: A Cultural Politics of Translation* (Cambridge: Cambridge University Press, 2005).

Zucker, Adam, *The Places of Wit in Early Modern English Comedy* (Cambridge: Cambridge University Press, 2011).

Zwicker, Steven, "Habits of Reading in Early Modern Literary Culture," in David Loewenstein and Janel Mueller (eds.), *The Cambridge History of Early Modern English Literature* (Cmbridge: Cambridge University Press, 2002), pp. 170–98.

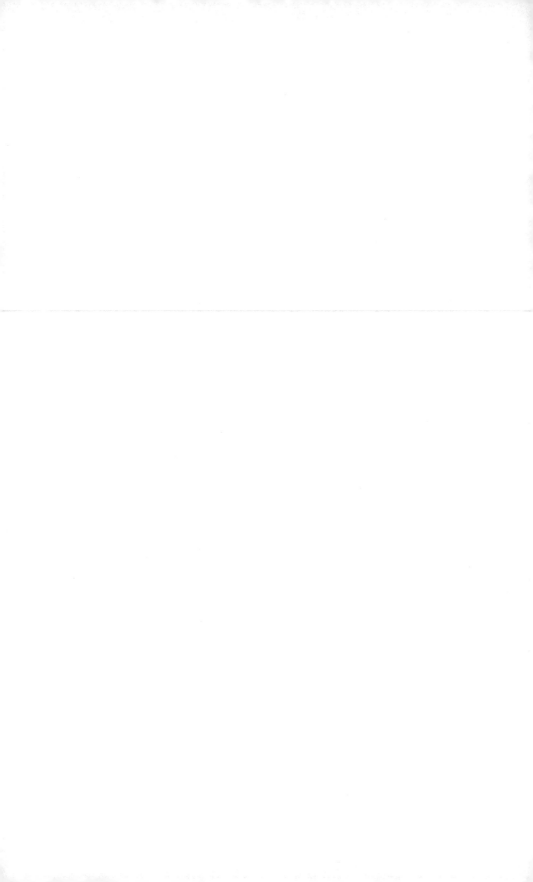

Index

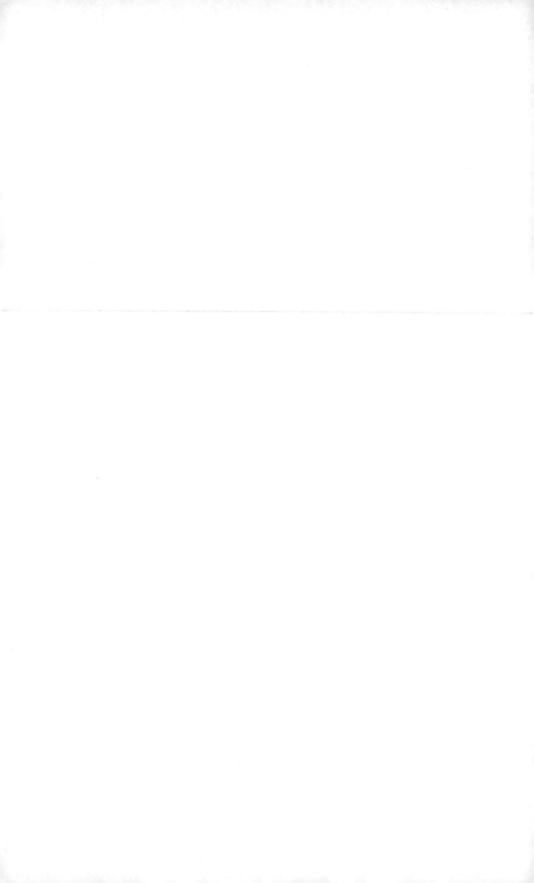